Esther 4:14

[signature]

Divine Providence

FIFTY LIFE LESSONS FROM THE BOOK OF ESTHER

Howard D. Wilcox M.D., M.P.H.

CROSSBOOKS
PUBLISHING

CrossBooks™
A Division of LifeWay
1663 Liberty Drive
Bloomington, IN 47403
www.crossbooks.com
Phone: 1-866-879-0502

Cover design by Matthew Skinner

First published by CrossBooks 11/16/2010

ISBN: 978-1-6150-7317-7 (sc)

Library of Congress Control Number: 2010935506

Printed in the United States of America

This book is printed on acid-free paper.

ACKNOWLEDGMENTS

Dallas Theological Seminary—Teach Truth, Love Well.

Dr. Ken Hanna—senior professor of Bible Exposition, Dallas Theological Seminary—you opened my eyes to methodical, critical Bible study.

R. B. Thieme, Jr.—previous pastor of Berachah Church, Houston, Texas, presently face-to-face with the Lord—words cannot express my gratitude for your years of study and teaching.

Robert Edgar—every believer needs an accountability partner—thanks for your friendship.

Mark Land— pastor of Beaumont Bible Church—my pastor, teacher, and friend. Your words are written in this book, both directly and indirectly.

Elders and body of Beaumont Bible Church—particularly for those of you who endured six months of Esther. You are a big part of this book.

JT, Nancy, and Linda—thanks for your friendship, wisdom and editing.

Howard R. and Irma Lou Wilcox—my father and mother, presently face-to-face with the Lord—you started me in the right direction and gave me opportunity and encouragement. I hope you get to see how God is blessing me now.

Laura, Martha, Emily, Nick—my four children, of whom I am very proud.

Sarah—my wife, best friend and soul mate—your words, patience and editing have made the difference in this book.

Contents

Chapter 1

INTRODUCTION

Esther is required reading during "BE 101: Bible Study Methods and Hermeneutics," a first-year course at Dallas Theological Seminary. When I took the class in the fall of 2007, the book was discussed as an example of an historical narrative. We spent only one week on it and did not do an in-depth analysis of the book. During the last class period of the semester, my professor, Dr. Ken Hanna, made the recommendation that each of us should periodically take one of the books of the Bible and do an in-depth study. In the summer of 2008, I decided to do just that with the book of Esther.

When I read Esther in my hermeneutics class, I thought it was a very simple story of God's deliverance. Once I began to study the book in detail, my opinion changed. Esther is much more than a simple story with a simple message. As a biblical narrative piece of literature, it is quite intricate. This book has it all: suspense, intrigue, mystery, sex, death, heroes, villains, multiple plots, and a happy ending. The setting is in the time period of the Persian Empire, toward the end of recorded Old Testament history. The characters are complex and exhibit personalities that are present in people today. In my opinion, Hollywood has never come up with a story line as intricate, powerful, and true-to-life as what is found in Esther. The thing that really grabs me is how events which occurred in 474 BC Persia can teach such wonderful life lessons for us today.

Sovereignty and Free Will

Sovereignty and free will are words that usually elicit a strong response. The coexistence of the two has been debated by theologians for years. The question is, "How can God design and implement a perfect plan that can not be altered by man and at the same time allow man to exercise personal volition?"

Sovereignty is the divine attribute which states God is "the supreme Being of the universe."[1] Supreme authority rests solely in God. "He is not subject to any power or law which could be conceived as superior to or other than Himself."[2]

> "Know therefore today, and take it to your heart, that the Lord, He is God in heaven above and on the earth below; there is no other" (Deuteronomy 4:39).

God has "absolute right to do all things according to his own good pleasure" (Daniel 4:25, 35; Romans 9:15–23; 1 Timothy 6:15; Revelation 4:11).[3] As supreme authority, He has perfect will and volition. He is in control of everything in heaven and on earth (1 Chronicles 29:11-14; Isaiah 45:5-12). His design for all of existence cannot be altered by any external source. Whatever He determines will be, is. Whatever He determines will not be, is not. Along with sovereignty, God has the attributes of perfect righteousness (Psalm 11:7, 97:6; Romans 10:3), justice (Deuteronomy 32:4; Romans 3:26), love (John 3:16; Romans 5:8; Ephesians 2:4-5), eternal life (Psalm 90:2, 102:27; Revelation 1:8), immutability (Malachi 3:6; Hebrews 13:8), veracity (John 14:6, 17:17), omniscience (Psalm 147:4-5; Proverbs 15:3; Hebrews 4:13), omnipotence (Isaiah 44:24; Colossians 1:16-17), and omnipresence (Deuteronomy 4:39; Psalm 139:8; Proverbs 15:3).

Free will is the ability to make conscious choices. God has designed higher beings with this privilege. He first gave volition to the angels, and then man. As human beings, we choose what we think, do, and say. While our environment often limits what we can do and say, we nevertheless have

---

1   Thieme, R. B. Jr. 1998. *The Integrity of God.* Houston: R. B. Thieme, Jr., Bible Ministries, 222.

2   Kohlenberger, John R. III. 1994. *NIV Naves Topical Bible.* Grand Rapids: Zondervan Publishing House, 962.

3   Easton, M. G. 1996. *Easton's Bible Dictionary.* Oak Harbor, WA: Logos Research Systems, Inc., 1897.

the ability to choose what we will think. Along with free will or volition, there are consequences of choice.

The most important issue regarding volition is choosing to be for God or against Him. Lucifer, and many fallen angels, used their volition and chose against God (Isaiah 14:12–14). The consequence of their choice was the lake of fire. Although God has pronounced his sentence, implementation of that eternal punishment will not occur until a future time.

> "Then He will also say to those on His left, 'Depart from Me, accursed ones, into the eternal fire which has been prepared for the devil and his angels'" (Matthew 25:41).

> "And the devil who deceived them was thrown into the lake of fire and brimstone, where the beast and the false prophet are also; and they will be tormented day and night forever and ever" (Revelation 20:10).

When Adam and Eve were created and placed in the garden, they were given everything necessary to sustain themselves in absolute happiness. The environment was perfect, there was plenty of food to eat, and there was no need to fear anything. Each evening they met with Jesus Christ (Genesis 3:8). What a wonderful period of existence this was.

Adam and Eve were also given free will to choose for or against God. This was done in the form of a command God gave them regarding not eating from the tree of the knowledge of good and evil.

> "The Lord God commanded the man, saying, 'From any tree of the garden you may eat freely; but from the tree of the knowledge of good and evil you shall not eat, for in the day that you eat from it you will surely die'" (Genesis 2:16–17).

As we know, Adam and Eve used their volition and chose against God.

> "When the woman saw that the tree was good for food, and that it was a delight to the eyes, and that the tree was desirable to make one wise, she took from its fruit and ate; and she gave also to her husband with her, and he ate. Then the eyes of both of them were opened, and they knew that they were naked; and they sewed fig leaves together and made themselves loin coverings" (Genesis 3:6–7).

The consequence of their choice was separation from God. Sin has had the result of separating Adam, Eve, and all of mankind from God. God, in His grace and mercy, however, has given man redemption through His son, Jesus Christ.

> "Being justified as a gift by His grace through the redemption which is in Christ Jesus" (Romans 3:24).

In eternity past, God knew both Satan and man would reject Him. God did not cause either to occur, nor did the occurrence of either disrupt God's perfect plan. God's sovereignty was not threatened or affected by the sins of Lucifer, Adam, Eve, or you and me.

What about the history of mankind since the fall? Has God's sovereignty remained constant throughout the thousands of years and the lives of billions of human beings? Is anything left to chance, or is there in fact a divine plan that supersedes our own volition?

God, in His absolute, perfect character, has blessed mankind with the most fabulous and unique condition of life in which we live: Divine sovereignty and human free will coexist together. It is, of course, beyond the capability of man to fully understand how God can allow both to occur simultaneously. To accept it, we have to simply have faith in what God reveals to us.

Omniscience is the divine attribute which states God is all-knowing. Everything, past, present and future, along with every possibility, is known by God. Nothing man thinks, does or says occurs without God having always known it beforehand (Job 28:20-28; 34:21-22; Psalm 139:1-6; Isaiah 46:9-10).

Foreknown is defined as "to have previous knowledge of, to know beforehand."[4] The Greek word for foreknowledge is προγινώσκω (proginosko) and is defined as "to know beforehand or in advance" as found in 2 Peter 3:17, or "to choose beforehand" as found in Acts 26:5; Romans 8:29, 11:2; 1 Peter 1:20.[5] God knows all things before they happen. In eternity past He knew every decision every person would ever make. His perfect plan took into account man's free will. As such, His plan is unaltered by man's volition or the decisions he makes.

---

4   Merriam-Webster, Inc. 2003. *Merriam-Webster's Collegiate Dictionary, Eleventh ed.* Springfield, Mass.: Merriam-Webster, Inc.

5   Bauer, W., F. W. Danker, W. F. Arndt, and F. W. Gingrich. 2000. *A Greek-English Lexicon, Third ed.* Chicago: The University of Chicago Press, 866.

To illustrate this principle, let's look at the issue of salvation. While it is true that countless books have been written on divine sovereignty and human free will in relation to salvation, I believe the Bible is clear in stating the following: salvation through faith in Jesus Christ is offered to every human being.

> "For God so loved the world, that He gave His only begotten Son, that whoever believes in Him shall not perish, but have eternal life" (John 3:16).

Everyone who believes is saved and has eternal life. God further states in both the Old Testament and New Testament that He wants everyone to believe and receive this gift.

> "He says, 'It is too small a thing that you should be my servant to raise up the tribes of Jacob and to restore the preserved ones of Israel; I will also make you a light of the nations so that My salvation may reach to the end of the earth'" (Isaiah 49:6).

> "For this is the will of My Father, that everyone who beholds the Son and believes in Him will have eternal life, and I Myself will raise him up on the last day" (John 6:40).

> "This is good and acceptable in the sight of God our Savior, who desires all men to be saved and to come to the knowledge of the truth" (1 Timothy 2:3–4).

> "The Lord is not slow about His promise, as some count slowness, but is patient toward you, not wishing for any to perish but for all to come to repentance" (2 Peter 3:9).

God knew in eternity past who would believe in His Son and who would reject Him (divine sovereignty).

> "And we know that God causes all things to work together for good to those who love God, to those who are called according to His purpose. For those whom He foreknew, He also predestined to become conformed to the image of His Son, so that He would be the firstborn among many brethren; and these whom He predestined, He also called; and these whom He called, He also justified; and these whom He justified, He also glorified" (Romans 8:28–30).

Each human being chooses whether to believe or not believe in Jesus Christ (free will). The consequence of believing or not believing is clearly stated:

> "He who believes in Him is not judged; he who does not believe has been judged already, because he has not believed in the name of the only begotten Son of God" (John 3:18).

In eternity past, God knew what He had planned for every human being. He desires all to believe in His Son and be saved. Furthermore, He has prepared specific works for all who believe.

> "For we are His workmanship, created in Christ Jesus for good works, which God prepared beforehand so that we would walk in them" (Ephesians 2:10).

While the Holy Spirit is required to present and make known the Gospel (and all Bible doctrine) to man, human volition chooses whether or not to respond to divine truth. A positive response to God results in salvation for the unbeliever and spiritual growth for the believer. So what happens if God has something planned for you, yet you refuse to follow His plan? Either you do not believe in Jesus Christ (for salvation), or you fail to do those things He has designed for you (works). You have free will to choose, yet God knew in eternity past what your decision will be. Your decision, whether yes or no to God, does not alter His plan.

This is a study of the book of Esther, and the Bible is our source of truth. In our study, we will see a potential dilemma of sovereignty versus free will. Does God control events, including the actions of man, with the result that His plan is executed as He has determined? Does man have free will to do as he pleases, with the result that God's plan may or may not work out as He has determined? Is there a middle road in which God's sovereignty allows man's free will to function, yet at the same time ensures that His plan is executed perfectly? In Esther 4, Mordecai makes a brilliant case for the coexistence of divine sovereignty and human free will when he presents Esther with the truth of what she must do. We will also see the presence of God's foreknowledge of the characters and events at a crucial time in Jewish history.

When we try to rationalize from a human viewpoint the coexistence of God's sovereignty and man's free will, we often become confused and frustrated. If we elevate our own ability at the expense of God's sovereignty, we are filled with pride. If we discount our volition and do not accept consequences for our decisions, we fail in our responsibility to live our lives in the way He wants us to live.

The title of this book is *Divine Providence: Fifty life lessons from the book of* Esther. Providence is defined as "God conceived as the power sustaining and guiding human destiny."[6] What is the relationship of providence to sovereignty and free will? Regarding Esther, divine providence is the sovereignty of God that sustains and guides the Jews in fifth century B.C Persia during a time when an attempt was made to exterminate them.

When we view the book of Esther from a big-picture perspective, we will clearly see God's sovereignty in the lives of men and the events of the time. When we view the book from each character's perspective, we will see the free-will decisions that person makes. Our challenge and privilege will be to correctly interpret the story from all vantage points.

Bible Heroes and Villains

Who are your favorite Bible heroes? What makes them unique? What is it about them you admire? Is it what they thought, what they did, or what they said? Is it something about their character or how they responded in difficult situations? Is it how they related to people or how they related to God? Think of the two or three most important things they accomplished. How were these people able to do what they did? What factors went into forming their characters and personalities? Were they *born* with the ability to do great things, were they *trained* to do great things, or did they *grow through failure* in order to learn to do great things? Were their accomplishments solely due to their own ability, through the help of others, or from God's grace and mercy? Finally, were these people used by God? If so, how were they used, and for what purpose? Was God glorified?

When you have answered these questions, take a minute and ask yourself the question, "What faults did these people have?" What did they think, do, or say that was either sinful or just simply wrong? When we answer this question honestly, we realize that even the greatest Bible heroes had faults, sinned, and failed God on occasion. They were much like you and me.

Now think of ominous Bible "bad guys" or villains. What makes them stand out? What is it about them you find repulsive? Is it what they thought, what they did, or what they said? Is it something about their character or how they reacted in difficult situations? Is it how they related

---

6   Ibid., Merriam-Webster, Inc.

to people or how they related to God (rejecting Him)? Think of the two or three most devious things they did that were wrong. How were these people able to do what they did? What were the factors that went into forming their characters and personalities? Were they *born* with the desire to do wrong things, were they *trained* to do wrong things, or did they *grow through failure* in order to learn to do wrong things? Were their failures due solely to their own inability, through the *help* of others, or did God in some way play a roll in their failure? Finally, were these people used by God? If so, how were they used, and for what purpose? Was God glorified?

When we boil things down, we have to ask, "Do Bible heroes sin and fail to follow God's plan at times?" and "Does God still use them for His plan?" The answer to both is yes. The next question we need to ask is, "What is the difference between Bible heroes who sin and Bible villains who sin?" Think about the answer to this as we go through the book of Esther. We will see good guys and bad guys (and good girls and bad girls) as well as successes and failures from each.

Show and Tell

One of my favorite activities as a young schoolboy was show and tell. Within reason, you could bring almost anything to school, show it, and tell about it. I once brought my father's war medals to school and felt very proud. The story that sticks in my mind, however, is when I brought an Estes rocket engine to school and fired it off in the classroom. For those who do not know, it is a four to five inch solid fuel rocket engine used to power twelve to eighteen inch rockets upwards of 1,000 feet in the air.

I had nailed an engine to a twelve inch two-by-four piece of wood and fired it off on the concrete driveway at home. Since the surface was rough, the two-by-four did not move when the engine was ignited. Any smoke generated quickly dissipated with the outside breeze. When I repeated the event inside the classroom at school, I placed the two-by-four on a slick desktop. As you can imagine, when the engine ignited, the two-by-four flew across the desktop and on to the floor. No one was hit or injured; however, there was no breeze to remove the smoke. The classroom quickly filled with smoke, and we evacuated outside. Of course, fire alarms went off, and fire trucks soon arrived. It was some time before I was allowed to bring anything else for show and tell.

When you think about it, this is what we all do when we fellowship with other believers. I am speaking of show and tell, not shooting off rocket engines in school. We share things, and we learn about God and how He is working in our lives. We all do this—or should. Some people have been trained to show and tell the Word (Bible college or seminary). But every one of us, at one time or another, does some showing and telling.

Our subject is, of course, God. Our primary resource is His Word. But it is also our personal relationship with Jesus Christ, our prayer life, what we learn from the adversities and blessings we experience, as well as the process we go through in our spiritual growth that are important to show and tell. Every believer has something to share.

The subject matter God gives us to show and tell is perfect. God's revelation to us is perfect. The Bible is perfect. The problem is that our interpretation of His revelation is imperfect. When we try to show and tell our imperfect interpretation, we often get in trouble. Human viewpoint obscures the truth of divine viewpoint. Sometimes we think we have a clear, stable, accurate understanding of God's Word, when in reality, our interpretation flies off the table, makes a lot of smoke, and empties the classroom. This is the dilemma we face. So we are accurate in our show and tell, we pray, study, and live as Bereans, taking everything back to the Word.

> "Now these were more noble-minded than those in Thessalonica, for they received the word with great eagerness, examining the Scriptures daily to see whether these things were so" (Acts 17:11).

This study will be a show and tell of the book of Esther. As with any show and tell, the greater the participation, the more fun and rewarding the experience.

Objectives

We have four objectives in our study of Esther.

1) Gain an in-depth understanding of the contextual relationships leading up to and including the events in Esther. Include historical background, grammatical context, cultural context, and literary form.

When studying any book of the Bible, you want to know not only what happens, but why it is happening. Context is critical in determining the *why*. When I taught this class at Beaumont Bible Church, I used the example of "blue roofs." For those not aware of the term, they refer to blue tarps used to cover holes in roofs. If someone from the Midwest read a story about blue roofs on houses in Beaumont, Texas, or they saw an aerial picture of the area showing houses with blue roofs, they would not understand unless they knew all about Rita and Ike (hurricanes that hit the area in 2005 and 2008). Being aware of the cause and effect of words such as pine trees, wind, Entergy, FEMA, insurance, and evacuation would be helpful in understanding the *what* and *why* behind "blue roofs."

The more we know about the context of Scripture, the better we understand what the writer is trying to tell us. The result is that our translation is more accurate. Bible encyclopedias are good sources for historical background. Many authors have written commentaries that help define the context. We will use some of these in our study. Do not let yourself be limited, however. Read as much as you can, and use as many reputable sources as you see fit.

Understanding context is absolutely necessary for accurate interpretation of the Bible. Words mean different things depending upon the context in which they are used. One of my daughters is in culinary school. When she prepares a meal and says "it is hot," it could mean the meal is spicy-hot, temperature-hot, or that it is the latest and most popular type of cuisine.

We want to answer the question, "How does Esther fit into Old Testament history, and what does it mean today?" We want to know everything that precedes, causes, and results in the events that occur in the book.

2) Gain an in-depth understanding of the narrative of Esther. Include God's purpose in presenting this book in the canon of Scripture as well as a paragraph-by-paragraph interpretation of the book.

These details are going to be the meat and potatoes of the book. While it is true that a paragraph-by-paragraph analysis may be tedious at times, it is necessary. Doing so will open up some wonderful treasures in the book. At times, we will look at the forest, at times the trees, and occasionally the leaves on the trees.

As we go through the book, we will discuss many facts. In this study, I have occasionally made suppositions based on high probability of occurrence. At times you may disagree with my conclusions. That is okay. If you disagree, be sure to support your opinion with Scripture or supporting research.

Two illustrations show the importance of this type of study. For engineers, reading a technical manual can be tedious; however, it is necessary if you want to operate a machine or understand a process. Details are important. For ladies who get love letters, you know how you read every word over and over. You not only read, you read in between what went into writing the words. Details are important.

3) Gain an initial understanding of the principles of hermeneutics. Include methods on how to methodically interpret Scripture, which will make future studies more profitable.

When reading the Bible, there is a natural tendency to interpret Scripture before actually studying it. When we do, we miss things God has put in His Word for us to learn. Learning how to study the Bible is almost as important as learning specific doctrines from the Bible. Although I am not a scholar of Chinese proverbs, Lao Tzu, the founder of Taoism, is credited with the following saying, which is relevant to our third objective, "Give a man a fish, and you feed him for a day. Teach a man to fish, and you feed him for a lifetime."[7] As we use proven hermeneutical techniques in our study, I hope we all become better fishermen and fisherwomen of the Word. Hopefully we will then be able to better follow the vocation our Lord Jesus Christ commands of us.

> "And Jesus said to them, 'Follow Me, and I will make you become fishers of men'" (Mark 1:17).

Be patient as we go through the mechanics. Remember, they are tools to help us understand the Bible. They are a means to an end, not the end in itself.

4) Gain an understanding of godly principles as they relate to Esther. Include contemporary illustrations for our lives.

If we do not learn new things from Scripture or reaffirm old doctrines and then apply this knowledge to our personal lives, we might as well limit our reading to self-help books written from the human viewpoint. God reveals Himself in Scripture, and He commands us to be transformed. Unbelievers become believers through personal belief in Jesus Christ (John 3:36). Believers learn *the mind of Christ* through the Word, *grow in knowledge,* and become *transformed.*

---

7   BrainQuote. http://www.brainyquote.com.

"For who has known the mind of the Lord, that He will instruct him? But we have the mind of Christ" (1 Corinthians 2:16).

"But grow in the grace and knowledge of our Lord and Savior Jesus Christ. To Him be the glory, both now and to the day of eternity. Amen" (2 Peter 3:18).

"And do not be conformed to this world, but be transformed by the renewing of your mind, so that you may prove what the will of God is, that which is good and acceptable and perfect" (Romans 12:2).

In 2 Peter 3:18, αὐξάνετε ("grow") is an imperative command Peter gives for all believers. The lexical form is αὐξάνω ("auzano"). As used in this verse, it means "to become greater, *grow, increase*."[8] In Romans 12:2, μεταμορφοῦσθε ("be transformed") is an imperative command Paul gives for all believers. The lexical form is μεταμορφόω ("metamorphoo"). As used in this verse, it means "to change inwardly in fundamental character or condition, *be changed, be transformed*."[9]

It is, of course, the Holy Spirit who teaches us; however, we must become aware of what the Word says before we can learn. Through our own volition, we choose whether or not to follow God's command and learn His Word.

In this book application of God's Word is presented in three categories: God in relation to man; man in relation to God, himself and others; and those in positions of authority or leadership. Whether during Old Testament times or present day history God is immutable in His sovereignty, righteousness, justice and love. Principles will be presented which reveal God's character toward mankind and nations. Biblical examples in the Old Testament will show relevance to how God deals with us today.

Materials

So, what do we need for our Bible study? The first thing is a good translation of the Bible—one that is as close to the original languages as possible. God revealed Old Testament Scripture to writers who wrote in Hebrew. He revealed New Testament Scripture to writers who wrote in Koine Greek.

8   Ibid., Bauer, 151 s.v. 2b.

9   Ibid., 639 s.v. 2.

When words are translated into English, the question arises, "Am I reading what God has truly revealed, or is the translation less than accurate?"

Dr. Ken Hanna, senior professor of Bible Exposition, Dallas Theological Seminary, and course professor of "BE 101: Bible Study Methods and Hermeneutics" defined this dilemma when he said, "Translators face a challenge, and at times a choice, between adhering to the original wording and meaning on the one hand and making the text understandable to a modern audience that lacks knowledge of the original languages and meaning. There is a natural tension between accuracy and readability. Translations are often called 'versions' because of the insertion of the translator's view or selection. The most commonly used 'translations' may be classified by the degree to which they translate the text literally (formal equivalent)."[10]

While I believe it is better to use a formal equivalent translation such as the NASB or a dynamic equivalent such as the NIV rather than a paraphrase such as the Living Bible when one is doing serious Bible study, I believe it is critical to use the Bible you are most comfortable reading. It is better to study the Bible with the Living Bible than to have a copy of the NASB and never open it. As you progress in your desire to know what God has revealed and your skills at Bible study increase, you are likely to want to change to a more literal translation.

A good biblical encyclopedia will be invaluable when it comes to looking up terms and historical events. Several were used for this study, and they will become apparent with the footnotes. For word studies, a dictionary, concordance, and lexicon are needed. Most of these resources are computer-based and many are Web-based.

Probably the second most important thing you will need after your Bible is dedicated time for study—and finally, a burning desire to know the truth. Be like the Bereans. Well, let's get started.

We will be studying Esther by means of the hermeneutic process. Terms and principles will be presented as each paragraph is discussed. Chapter Two gives an overview of hermeneutics. Chapter Three will present the context leading up to and including the time period of the events in the book. Chapter Four will begin with the first chapter in Esther. The study will be done paragraph by paragraph. The study template found in appendix A will be used for the first two paragraphs of Esther 1. After that, the study will progress verse by verse.

---

10   Hanna, Ken. 2007. BE101 class notes. Dallas Theological Seminary, 41.

Repetition

Many Bible verses and principles will be repeated throughout the study. There may be a tendency to skip over something you may have read before. I encourage you to look at things afresh each time they are presented. See how each verse fits into the discussion. Repetition is a necessary tool in Bible study. Let me give two examples—one in medicine and one in seminary.

When I was in the Air Force the available medications we could dispense were limited compared to civilian pharmacies. After separating from the military I was faced with a great number of newer medications available for use. In family practice we potentially write prescriptions for every drug available. In order to accurately prescribe each new medication long hours of study was required.

Seminary presents Biblical truth in two primary ways—exegesis and exposition, in which biblical text is studied and communicated from beginning to end, and theology, in which the meaning of biblical texts are structured around dominant themes of Scripture. Both are absolutely necessary for understanding God's Word. Repetition of God's Word presented in different ways is helpful. We will study the book of Esther primarily through the exegetical process. We will, however, also present Bible doctrine from a theological approach. Repetition and presentation of information from different perspectives will be used throughout the study.

Things to Remember

Study Objectives:

1. Gain an in-depth understanding of the contextual relationships leading up to and including the events in Esther. Include historical background, grammatical context, cultural context, and literary form.

2. Gain an in-depth understanding of the narrative of Esther. Include God's purpose in presenting this book in the canon of Scripture as well as a paragraph-by-paragraph interpretation of the book.

3. Gain an initial understanding of the principles of hermeneutics. Include methods on how to methodically interpret Scripture, which will make future studies more profitable.

4. Gain an understanding of godly principles as they relate to Esther. Include contemporary illustrations for our lives.

Chapter Two

HERMENEUTICS:
SCIENCE AND ART

Normal Bible study follows the *inductive* method, which "begins by observing facts of Scripture and pursues them to their logical conclusion or meaning."[1] The *deductive* method of Bible study "begins with a conclusion or meaning and proceeds to test it by examining the details or facts of Scripture."[2] During the majority of this study, we will use the inductive method.

Details

With the exceptions of Bible study and the practice of medicine, I generally do not like to read books or manuals that are detail-specific. It is simply the way my brain is wired. My wife says I have a visionary mentality rather than a detail one. I am blessed; she is detail-focused. Any electronic device we purchase with an instruction manual has to be installed by her, because she is the one who reads the manuals. I say these things so you will know that if a non-detail person like me can learn these concepts, so can you. The details presented in this chapter and Appendix B will help you study the Bible and understand God's Word more clearly.

In order to accurately read and interpret Scripture, attention to detail must be present at two levels. The obvious is that one must be aware of

---

1   Hanna, Ken. 2007. BE101 class notes, Dallas Theological Seminary, 3.

2   Ibid.

the details present *in* Scripture. The less obvious, but just as important, is that one must be aware of the details of *how* to study Scripture. This is discussed in the next few pages.

We will be studying Esther by means of the hermeneutic process. Roy B. Zuck, Senior Professor/Emeritus of the Bible Exposition Department at Dallas Theological Seminary, writes, "Hermeneutics is the science [principles] and art [task] by which the meaning of the biblical text is determined."[3] As a science, it requires the student to follow specific proven techniques. As an art, it requires the student to take the information learned and make a relevant application to everyday life.

The goal of hermeneutics is to understand Scripture in terms of truth and clarity. God reveals Himself to us in His Word. To understand Him through His Word, we must accurately and clearly understand what He says.

In many ways, studying the Bible through the hermeneutic process is similar to how medicine is practiced. As a science, medicine requires the knowledge of anatomy, physiology, biochemistry, pharmacology, and pathology, as well as other disciplines. History-taking, physical examination, and laboratory and radiology testing are objective investigative techniques that help the physician make a diagnosis. Treatment of the patient is based on proven science. Where does the art come in? Application of basic sciences, diagnostic tools, and treatment plans is individualized for each patient based on a multitude of factors. Every patient is different, and treatment must be specific for each person. There is an art to the practice of medicine as there is an art to Bible study.

Physician-patient communication is another area where there is relevance to Bible study. As a family physician, I know it is necessary to diagnose and treat the patient accurately; however, after twenty-five years of practice, I have found that much more is needed to complete the doctor-patient relationship. One-on-one communication is critical. Clearly conveying to the patient what is going on and what needs to be done, in a manner that can be understood, is almost as important as the diagnosis and treatment.

The Bible is the authority to diagnose and treat the disease of sin and how it has destroyed the relationships people have with God. God's Word further provides us with instruction on how we are to communicate the cure. Jesus personally communicated the Gospel to people while He was

---

3   Zuck, Roy B. 1991. *Basic Bible Interpretation.* Colorado Springs: Cook
     Communications Ministries, 19.

on earth. Before his ascension, He told the disciples what to communicate and to whom they were to communicate. Present-day believers are also responsible to follow this command:

> "Go therefore and make disciples of all the nations, baptizing them in the name of the Father and the Son and the Holy Spirit, teaching them to observe all that I commanded you; and lo, I am with you always, even to the end of the age" (Matthew 28:19–20).

With the understanding we are to communicate God's Word, let's begin with the hermeneutic process. Four basic mechanisms are required. They include observation, interpretation, correlation, and application. Although discussed independently, they are interrelated. There is progression from one to the next. Additional information is presented in Appendix B.

Observation

Observation is defined as "an act or instance of observing a custom, rule, or law, an act of recognizing and noting a fact or occurrence often involving measurement with instruments, a record or description so obtained, a judgment on or inference from what one has observed."[4] In relation to Scripture, Robert A. Traina, author of *Methodical Bible Study,* states it is "the means by which the data of a passage becomes part of the mentality of the student."[5]

The importance of observation in Bible study can not be overstated. It is *the* most important mechanic, and we will spend more time on it than the others. Accurately and completely becoming aware of everything written may seem a simple task, yet it is far from such. Observation requires discipline, concentration, patience, and repetition. Human nature is to assume, rather than observe. The result of incomplete observation is inaccurate interpretation, which leads to inaccurate application.

To emphasize this point, let me give you the same assignment Dr. Hanna, my Hermeneutics professor, gave us the first day of class. We were told to read Acts 1:8 and write down twenty-five observations from the verse alone. Try it. It is not as easy as it seems. When we turned in the assignment the next week, Dr. Hanna challenged us to write down twenty-five *different*

---

4   Merriam-Webster, Inc. 2003. *Merriam-Webster's Collegiate Dictionary, Eleventh ed.* Springfield, Mass.: Merriam-Webster, Inc.

5   Traina, Robert A. 1980. *Methodical Bible Study.* Grand Rapids: Zondervan, 32.

observations of the same verse. When reading Scripture, the key is to observe all *facts* present and at the same time exclude all *assumptions*.

There is a tendency to not observe everything that is written down, and there is a tendency to add personal opinion to what is written down. John tells us not to add or take away from Scripture.

> "I testify to everyone who hears the words of the prophecy of this book: if anyone adds to them, God will add to him the plagues which are written in this book; and if anyone takes away from the words of the book of this prophecy, God will take away his part from the tree of life and from the holy city, which are written in this book" (Revelation 22:18–19).

Both are mistakes and will negatively affect Bible study. Any error in observation will cause error in all the other areas of hermeneutics. It is much like entering data into a computer. If the data is inaccurate, the results will be flawed. Take time in the observation process.

In the observation process *terms*, *structure*, *literary form* and *atmosphere* or *context* are recorded. Appendix B has additional information on this, as well as a template to use in recording observations.

Interpretation

The second mechanism in the hermeneutic process is *interpretation*. Interpretation is defined as "the act or the result of interpreting: explanation."[6] "Interpretation asks the question, 'What does it mean?'"[7] The following is an overview of some of the issues that define interpretation. With the exception of specific citations, they come directly from class notes prepared by Dr. Ken Hanna.

Biblical interpretation begins with understanding the foundation of the original languages. Accurate translation is required. As mentioned in the first chapter, a formal equivalent or literal translation, such as the New American Standard Bible, is recommended. At Dallas Theological Seminary, we are taught the Bible is given by inspiration of God and thus is inerrant.

> "All Scripture is inspired by God and profitable for teaching, for reproof, for correction, for training in righteousness" (2 Timothy 3:16).

---

6   Ibid., Merriam-Webster, Inc.

7   Ibid., Zuck, 10.

Inspired is defined as "outstanding or brilliant in a way or to a degree suggestive of divine inspiration"[8] The Greek word θεόπνευστος (theopneustos) is found only once in the New Testament and is translated as "inspired by God."[9]

In addition to divine inspiration and inerrancy, Scripture is sufficient, meaning God's revelation in his Word is complete in what He has determined we are to have from Him at this time. All Scripture makes up the canon, meaning the Bible is "a rule of beliefs and behaviors for all of God's people at all times."[10] Finally, all Scripture is authoritative, meaning the Bible carries the full weight of God's self-disclosure and thus requires "acknowledgement of His truth and obedience to His will."[11]

Correct application of hermeneutic principles is the key to accurate interpretation of Scripture. Using all the tools discussed in observation in a systematic manner will facilitate understanding God's Word.

We will begin with the paragraph. "The paragraph is the basic unit of study. Word studies, grammatical diagramming, and analysis are the principal tools used."[12] This portion of our study will be reflected in our second objective, "gain an in-depth understanding of the narrative of Esther. Include God's purpose in presenting this book in the canon of Scripture as well as a paragraph-by-paragraph interpretation of the book."

Following the completion of the paragraph analysis, the Biblical or literary context is studied. "Contextual research and examination of the literary genre are primary in this step."[13] In completing the process of Biblical interpretation, extra-Biblical sources such as "archeology, comparative literature, history, manners, and customs"[14] are researched.

If you are confused on how to interpret Scripture, be patient. Sometimes the best way to understand something new is to see it as it unfolds. As we observe and record information we will also interpret. As we do so, you will become proficient with this mechanism.

---

8   Ibid., Merriam-Webster, Inc

9   Bauer, W., F. W. Danker, W. F. Arndt, and F. W. Gingrich. 2000. *A Greek-English Lexicon, Third ed.* Chicago: The University of Chicago Press, 450.

10   Packer, James, I. 1980 . *Inerrancy.* Grand Rapids, Michigan: Zondervan, 199.

11   Ibid., 207.

12   Ibid., Hanna, 43.

13   Ibid.

14   Ibid.

Correlation

The third mechanism in the hermeneutic process is *correlation*. Correlation is defined as "the state or relation of being correlated *specif:* a relation existing between phenomena or things or between mathematical or statistical variables which tend to vary, be associated, or occur together in a way not expected on the basis of chance alone."[15] In the following paragraph, Dr. Hanna so perfectly defines correlation as it relates to hermeneutics.

> "In hermeneutics, correlation is the art of relating the Bible as a whole to life as a whole. It necessarily follows the steps of observation and interpretation and is the basis of the fourth and final step, application. Though often neglected in the pulpit, correlation is indispensable to the servant of God who desires to 'walk in the truth' and to teach and preach the Word faithfully and fruitfully. Correlation is the bridge between interpretation and application, between the 'then' and the 'now.' It is also the bridge between Bible study and public preaching and teaching."[16]

The hallmark of correlation is the identification and presentation of principles. A principle is defined as "an outstanding and abiding truth that is not limited to a moment in time."[17] The development of principles requires "the familiarity of the text and its context and the ability to think with the whole text and context in mind."[18] Step-by-step procedures to identify principles include: "ask the questions, 'who, what, where, when, why, and how;' record all the truths identified, whether great or small; combine the truths by subject; concentrate on major truths; and finally, reword major truths into three to five simple sentences in the principle format."[19]

Often a passage will have a primary, overriding principle. "The theme is the outstanding and abiding truth of the passage [principle] stated in a succinct, simple sentence. It is the timeless principle that rises above all others in the passage and unites them into one statement."[20]

---

15   Ibid., Merriam-Webster, Inc.

16   Ibid., Hanna, 94.

17   Ibid.

18   Ibid.

19   Ibid., 96.

20   Ibid.

Application

The fourth mechanism in the hermeneutic process is *application*. Application is defined as "an act of putting to use, a use to which something is put."[21] In relation to hermeneutics, Dr. Hanna states, "Truth not lived is truth not learned."[22] In a more graphic statement, Dr. Hendricks says, "Observation plus interpretation without application equals abortion."[23] The Bible is explicit in our command to apply the truths of the Word.

> "This book of the law shall not depart from your mouth, but you shall meditate on it day and night, so that you may be careful to do according to all that is written in it" (Joshua 1:8).

> "All Scripture is inspired by God and profitable for teaching, for reproof, for correction, for training in righteousness; so that the man of God may be adequate, equipped for every good work" (2 Timothy 3:16–17).

The goal in application is "to make the facts of Scripture meaningful to everyday life [relevance], to foster living as well as learning God's truth [realization], and to issue an appeal for commitment to the truth not just consideration [response]."[24] Zuck gives nine guidelines on how to apply the Bible to one's life:[25]

1. Build application on interpretation.

2. Determine what was expected of the original audience.

3. Base application on elements present-day readers share with the original audience.

4. Recognize how God's working varies in different ages.

5. Determine what is normative for today.

6. See the principle inherent in the text.

---

21   Ibid., Merriam-Webster, Inc.

22   Ibid., Hanna, 98.

23   Ibid., Hendricks, 290.

24   Ibid., Hanna, 99.

25   Ibid., Zuck, 282-292.

7. Think of the principle as an implication (or extrapolation) of the text, and as a bridge to application.

8. Write out specific action-responses.

9. Rely on the Holy Spirit.

In this study of Esther, I have combined the two mechanisms, correlation and application, and presented the findings as principles of life or life lessons. The purpose is to give a simple statement that relates what the Scripture says with direct application which will help us in our daily lives.

How to Study

So now that we understand the mechanisms (or at least know the terminology), how do we use these tools to study Scripture? We will do three things in our study: observe and analyze content, research context, and synthesize the content and context. These three processes will be done first with the paragraph and then with the book of Esther. This process comes from *Living by the Book* by Dr. Howard Hendricks and Dr. William Hendricks and class notes prepared by Dr. Ken Hanna. If there is any discipline in which practice is required to become proficient, methodical Bible study is such.

Hermeneutics is awkward when first attempted. Do not get discouraged, and do not let uncertainty inhibit your study. Use this section as a guideline, and persevere. When there is confusion regarding interpretation, correlation, application always go back to methodical observation. As stated before, additional information on this process is found in Appendix B.

Things to Remember

Hermeneutics—"the science [principles] and art [task] by which the meaning of the biblical text is determined."[26]

Four mechanisms of the hermeneutic process—observation, interpretation, correlation, and application.

Observe terms, structure, literary form, and atmosphere or context.

Interpretation follows observation.

---

26   Ibid., Zuck, 19.

Correlation and application combine for principles or life lessons.

Study by content analysis, then context research, and finally content and context synthesis.

Paragraph templates will be used.

Chapter Three

CONTEXT:
THE ROAD TO ESTHER

The first objective of our study is to "gain an in-depth understanding of the contextual relationships leading up to and including the events in the book of Esther. Include historical background, grammatical context, cultural context, and literary form." Let's start with some biblical and historical facts.

Facts of Esther[1]

Test your general knowledge of Esther with the following questions. The book of Esther is one of five books called the *megillah,* or the "scroll" by Jewish readers because of its immense popularity. What are the other four? Song of Solomon, Ruth, Lamentations, and Ecclesiastes. It is one of two Old Testament books named for a woman. What is the other one? Ruth. It is one of several books that are not quoted in the New Testament. It is one of two Old Testament books that do not mention God. What is the other? Song of Solomon. It is interesting that in writing about the events during the time period of Esther, the first century historian, Josephus, uses the name God in his *Antiquities of the Jews,* Book XI, chapter 6, "Concerning Esther and Mordecai and Haman; and how in the reign of Artaxerxes the whole nation of the Jews was in danger of perishing."[2] It is one of two that deals

---

1   Huey, F. B. Jr. 1988. *The Expositor's Bible Commentary.* Grand Rapids: Zondervan Publishing House, Volume 4, 776.

2   Antiquities of the Jews. http://www.earlyjewishwritings.com/text/josephus/ant11. html.

specifically with the persecution of the Hebrew people. What is the other? Exodus. Esther contains the account of the origin of the Feast of Purim, one of two festivals adopted by the postexilic Jewish community not found in the Mosaic Law. What is the other? Hanukkah. The events of the book are set in Susa during the reign of Xerxes or Ahasuerus, king of Persia (486–465 BC), whose empire reached from India to Ethiopia. Esther is the only Old Testament book in which the entire narrative takes place in Persia.

Historical context of Esther

Who is the author of Esther? He or she is not identified. God does not tell us. In Esther 9:20 it says, "Then Mordecai recorded these events." This could possibly mean Mordecai wrote some or all of Esther. Speaking of one's self in the third person is a literary style also found in Esther 1:15, with the king speaking of himself as king Ahasuerus. If Mordecai is indeed the author it might also explain why the name of God is not found in the book. "The absence of God's name in the Book of Esther may be due to the fact that the author intended the book to become part of the official Persian court record. The use of God's name might have prevented that from happening."[3]

Studying the book tells us several things about the author and suggests he had firsthand knowledge of the events in the story. He gives detailed descriptions of the furnishings in the palace, describes the events of royal banquets, and discusses the application of Persian law. "His intimate knowledge of Persian life and customs argues for his Persian domicile; the nationalism that permeates the story, knowledge of the feast of Purim, makes it almost certain that he was Jewish."[4]

Is there any significance to the fact that we do not know the name of the author? It is possible that by deemphasizing the author, the message of divine providence is more apparent. If we knew the author, his or her personal history may have become a distraction.

When does the story of Esther occur? It occurs during the time period of the reign of King Ahasuerus, 485–465 BC. When was the book written? Two principal periods are usually proposed as the most likely date. "They are an early date, 450–300 BC, and a late date, 175–100 BC"[5] I believe the

---

3   Elwell, Walter A. and Barry J. Beitzel. 1988. *Baker Encyclopedia of the Bible.* Grand Rapids: Baker Book House, 722.

4   Harrelson, Walter. 1964. *Interpreting the Old Testament.* New York: Holt, Rinehart and Winston, Inc., 449.

5   Ibid., Volume 4, 778.

earlier date is more accurate. Historical and structural changes occurred in Persia after the events in Esther which would more likely be known to an earlier writer. We will see those events as we go through the story.

Jews in 485 BC Persia had distinct characteristics that separated them from their ancestors before. In order to understand the people, as well as the relationships and responses between Jews and non-Jews and between Jews and God, we need to understand the historical events of the time. The more we know about *who, what, where, when, why,* and *how,* the better we will be able to interpret the events in the book. The question is, "How far back should we go?"

When I taught this book at Beaumont Bible Church, I asked the question, "When was the high point of Old Testament Jewish history?" I presented the idea that it was somewhere between the end of David's reign and the first half of Solomon's. God was showing favor on His chosen people. This is where we will begin our study.

```
          ----David (1010–970 BC)----
                              ----Solomon (970–930 BC)----

   1025           1000           975           950           925
```

Solomon

Solomon was the third king over Israel and the second son of David and Bathsheba. He reigned some forty years, 970–930 BC. When God asked Solomon what it was he wanted, Solomon asked for "an understanding heart" (1 Kings 3:9). He was given wisdom and found favor in God's eyes for most of his reign. God allowed him to build the temple, and the country prospered.

Solomon's spiritual relationship with God deteriorated when he began to marry women from different countries. He was swayed by different pagan beliefs, and he turned away from God.

> "Did not Solomon king of Israel sin regarding these things? Yet among the many nations there was no king like him, and he was loved by his God, and God made him king over all Israel; nevertheless the foreign women caused even him to sin" (Nehemiah 13:26).

How could Solomon, who had such wisdom, turn away from God? Before answering this, we need to see a few more examples of Israel's failure to trust. For now, I will just say that this should be a lesson for all of us. When God shows us favor and we are blessed by Him, we should be on guard against those things that would turn us away from Him.

What did God think when Solomon and the Israelites sinned? What does God think when you and I sin? What does God think about any sin? To answer these questions, we need to first ask, "What is sin?" R. B. Thieme, Jr. gives an excellent synopsis of sin in his book, *Slave Market of Sin.* "Man is born into this world with three strikes against him: Adam's original sin is imputed at birth, man inherits the nature to sin, and man commits personal sins .... Personal sin is disobedience to God and His expressed will—any mental, verbal, or overt activity contrary to the character and standards of God .... The Bible defines personal sin by means of several synonyms: falling short (Romans 3:23), transgressions—rebellion against or overstepping the Law (Psalm 51:1), acting unfaithfully—self-will over God's will (Joshua 22:20), trespasses (Ephesians 2:1), lawlessness and rebellion—failure in relation to the Mosaic Law (1 Timothy 1:9–10), unbelief—the only unpardonable sin (John 8:24, 16:9)."[6]

Sin may be an act of commission or omission. Doing what God tells us not to do or not doing what God tells us to do are both sins. James explicitly states that not doing what God wills for us is sin:

> "Therefore, to one who knows the right thing to do and does not do it, to him it is sin" (James 4:17).

God's perspective and response is the same. God hates sin. From Adam's first sin in the garden to our present day, God deals harshly with sin.

> "Therefore, just as through one man sin entered into the world, and death through sin, and so death spread to all men, because all sinned" (Romans 5:12).

> "For the wages of sin is death, but the free gift of God is eternal life in Christ Jesus our Lord" (Romans 6:23).

Thankfully, God has shown grace and mercy on us by providing a solution to the penalty of sin.

---

6   Thieme, R. B. Jr. 1994. Slave Market of Sin Houston: R. B. Thieme, Jr., Bible Ministries, 10-11.

"But God demonstrates His own love toward us, in that while we were yet sinners, Christ died for us" (Romans 5:8).

When God gave the Ten Commandments to the Israelites, He knew they would not keep all of them all of the time. He knew they would sin. Breaking any one of the commandments was sin and required an offering from the high priest for atonement. God emphasized His anger towards sin when the first two commandments were violated.

> "I am the Lord your God, who brought you out of the land of Egypt, out of the house of slavery. You shall have no other gods before Me. You shall not make for yourself an idol, or any likeness of what is in heaven above or on the earth beneath or in the water under the earth. You shall not worship them or serve them; for I, the Lord your God, am a jealous God, visiting the iniquity of the fathers on the children, on the third and the fourth generations of those who hate Me, but showing loving kindness to thousands, to those who love Me and keep My commandments" (Exodus 20:2–6).

This is the sin the Israelites committed which resulted in the most discipline against them. It is the sin they committed over and over again. Note in Exodus 20:6 God's response when His commandments are kept. When God says He is jealous, He is stating an *anthropopathism,* giving a human characteristic to Himself so that we can understand His nature.

What did Solomon do (commission) he was not supposed to do, and what did he not do (omission) he was supposed to do?

> "Solomon did what was evil in the sight of the Lord, and did not follow the Lord fully, as David his father had done" (1 Kings 11:6).

What was God's response to Solomon's sin?

> "So the Lord said to Solomon, 'Because you have done this, and you have not kept My covenant and My statutes, which I have commanded you, I will surely tear the kingdom from you, and will give it to your servant … I will tear it out of the hand of your son … I will give one tribe to your son for the sake of My servant David and for the sake of Jerusalem which I have chosen" (1 Kings 11:11–13).

"He said to Jeroboam, 'Take for yourself ten pieces; for thus says the Lord, the God of Israel, "Behold, I will tear the kingdom out of the hand of Solomon and give you ten tribes" … because they have forsaken Me, and have worshiped Ashtoreth the goddess of the Sidonians, Chemosh the god of Moab, and Milcom the god of the sons of Ammon; and they have not walked in My ways, doing what is right in My sight and observing My statutes and My ordinances, as his father David did …. Thus I will afflict the descendants of David for this, but not always'" (1 Kings 11:31–39).

Both Solomon and the people had turned from God. As a result, God punished the entire nation. Who was more responsible for the sin and the punishment, Solomon or the people? I think Solomon has to bear most of the responsibility. He was king and had absolute authority over the people. He not only allowed evil to occur, he proposed it. It is time for our first principle.

Principle 1: When a leader sins and rejects God's authority, all those under the leader's authority are affected.

A leader is anyone who has responsibility or authority over others. Good leaders act responsibly in their duties for those under them. Poor leaders act irresponsibly. When a leader sins and rejects God's authority, bad things happen to the leader and those he or she oversees. Suffering is not limited to the leader alone. Regarding the history of Israel, the Jews will suffer under this principle for hundreds of years. The failure of both kings and the people to follow God leads to discipline.

Can you think of when and where the Israelites failed in this principle years before? Look back 500 years when Moses led the Exodus. In Numbers 13, God told Moses He was giving the land of Canaan to the Israelites.

"Then the Lord spoke to Moses saying, 'Send out for yourself men so that they may spy out the land of Canaan, which I am going to give to the sons of Israel; you shall send a man from each of their fathers' tribes, every one a leader among them'" (Numbers 13:1–2).

Twelve men, each representing a tribe, were given the responsibility and authority to obey God. As commanded, they gathered the information from Canaan and reported back to Moses and the entire congregation. At this meeting, two of the spies, Caleb and Joshua, follow God's authority by showing trust and obedience to Him. They knew God would lead them to victory.

"Then Caleb quieted the people before Moses and said, 'We should by all means go up and take possession of it, for we will surely overcome it'" (Numbers 13:30).

"Joshua the son of Nun and Caleb the son of Jephunneh, of those who had spied out the land, tore their clothes; and they spoke to all the congregation of the sons of Israel, saying, 'The land which we passed through to spy out is an exceedingly good land. If the Lord is pleased with us, then He will bring us into this land and give it to us, a land which flows with milk and honey. Only do not rebel against the Lord; and do not fear the people of the land, for they will be our prey. Their protection has been removed from them, and the Lord is with us; do not fear them'" (Numbers 14:6-9).

The other ten spies rejected God's authority through their expression of fear.

"But the men who had gone up with him said, 'We are not able to go up against the people, for they are too strong for us.' So they gave out to the sons of Israel a bad report of the land which they had spied out, saying, 'The land through which we have gone, in spying it out, is a land that devours its inhabitants; and all the people whom we saw in it are men of great size. There also we saw the Nephilim (the sons of Anak are part of the Nephilim); and we became like grasshoppers in our own sight, and so we were in their sight.'" (Numbers 13:31–33).

As a result, the Israelites wondered in the desert forty years. Of the twelve spies, only Caleb and Joshua were allowed to enter the Promised Land (Numbers 14:30). Remember this illustration as we will see this event in two other principles later in the book (Principles 25 and 43).

This principle is true in every organization, whether it be in school, business, government, or church. When leadership fails in integrity, honor, truthfulness, selflessness, righteousness, and justice and turns away from the principles which create and maintain freedom, opportunity, and motivation for individual and group achievement, the organization suffers.

What does the New Testament say about this? God gives believers spiritual gifts and the opportunity to use those gifts to serve the body and to do His will. In fact, God has prepared specific works for every believer they are to accomplish.

"For we are His workmanship, created in Christ Jesus for good works, which God prepared beforehand so that we would walk in them" (Ephesians 2:10).

Προητοίμασεν (prepared) is a third-person singular, aorist, active indicative verb. The lexical form is *προετοιμάζω* (proetoimazo), meaning "to prepare beforehand."[7] In eternity past, God prepared those things He wanted you and I to do as believers. *Περιπατήσωμεν* (walk) is a first-person plural, aorist, active subjunctive verb. The lexical form is *περιπατέω* (peripateo), meaning "to conduct one's life, comport oneself, behave, live."[8] In our daily lives, we are to make use of the opportunities we have to do those things God prepared for us beforehand. How does this relate to leadership and to Principle 1?

Failure to walk in those things God has prepared for us is sin and negatively affects the body—both the local church body and the body of Christ. At the beginning of an elder retreat in May 2008, my pastor, Mark Land, read:

"Obey your leaders and submit to them, for they keep watch over your souls as those who will give an account. Let them do this with joy and not with grief, for this would be unprofitable for you" (Hebrews 13:17).

---

7   Bauer, W., F. W. Danker, W. F. Arndt, and F. W. Gingrich. 2000. *A Greek-English Lexicon, Third ed.* Chicago: The University of Chicago Press, 869.

8   Ibid., 903 s.v. 2aδ.

Talk about a sobering verse. At that moment, I realized I would stand before the Father and give an account of my actions as an elder at Beaumont Bible Church. As a leader, what I do and do not do affects the body of believers for whom I am responsible. Two other things stand out in this verse. Elders are required not only to do their work, but they are required to do it with joy—and if they do not do their work with joy, it will be unprofitable for the church body, meaning the body will suffer.

Now I know some of you are thinking, "I am not a king, and I am not an elder, so I can skate on this." Think again. Hebrews 13:17 is similar to the upper room discourse in John 14–17, which was written for disciples, but is relevant for all believers. This verse may have been written to pastors and elders; however, it applies to every believer. Whether or not you have a recognized position at your church, you have a responsibility to that body. Whether or not you are a member of a local church, you have a responsibility in the body of Christ. Sin and rejection of God's authority will have effects similar to those Solomon and the Israelites experienced.

Personal application of this principle begins with understanding God has given all of us spiritual gifts (Romans 11:29, 12:6–8; 1 Corinthians 12:4–11, 28–30; Ephesians 4:7–11; 1 Peter 4:10–11). Every believer is a leader and has authority over those things God has given them. Failure in the use of your gift will affect the body, and you will be accountable to God. Sin of omission can be just as destructive as sin of commission. Whatever your spiritual gift, whatever your position in the body, you are accountable to God for how you apply and to whom you apply the gifts God has given you. Whether you are a Sunday school teacher, a boss, a supervisor at work, a husband, a wife, a father, or a mother, this principle relates to you. If you sin and reject God's authority, you and those around you will suffer.

At this point I would like to clarify the "good works" Paul discusses in Ephesians 2:10. These are not human deeds done in the flesh, they are not legalistic activities done to earn the favor of God, on earth or in heaven, and they have absolutely nothing to do with salvation, either obtaining it or maintaining it. One has only to look at the two previous verses, Ephesians 2:8-9, to see that God's grace is the sole source of salvation. Good works are those things designed by God for believers which are accomplished by means of the filling of the Holy Spirit. Being consistently filled with the Holy Spirit and learning and applying Bible doctrine in your daily life are the foundation of good works. Good works done through the filling of the Holy Spirit will result in rewards in heaven while those done in the flesh will be burned up (1 Corinthians 3:10-15).

Principle 1 is seen on a national level as well. When our government leaders fail to follow God's plan, choose to reject His ways, and turn away from divine principles of conduct, our nation suffers. Leaders should strive for honor, morality, and integrity and should follow the Constitution, which they are sworn to uphold. God will not prosper our nation as long as we defy Him.

What does this principle specifically have to do with Esther? We are getting ahead of ourselves; however, it is important to see that what we are talking about now has direct application to our study. We will see that God gave Esther many gifts. Physically, she was very beautiful. Her character and personality were such that she gained the trust and acceptance of almost everyone she met. She was extremely capable. With all she was given, God prepared her to do His will at a specific time. He gave her responsibility over the entire Jewish race when they were on the verge of extermination. In Esther 4, she is placed in a situation where she must use what God gave her in order to save her people. She has to choose whether or not to submit to God's authority and follow His plan for her.

The same issue exists for you and me. Do we or do we not follow, on a daily basis, what God has planned for us? The results of our decisions may not be as historically significant as Esther's; however, they are just as important in our relationship with God. Who among us, when we are face-to-face with Him in heaven (1 Corinthians 13:12; 2 Corinthians 5:8), does not want to hear our Lord say, "Well done, good and faithful servant. You were faithful with a few things, I will put you in charge of many things; enter into the joy of your master" (Matthew 25:21, 23)?

The question arises, "What does God do when people sin and reject Him?" How does God discipline individuals and nations? Let's see what He did in the Old Testament with the Israelites. First, God raised up adversaries against His people.

"Then the Lord raised up an adversary to Solomon, Hadad the Edomite; he was of the royal line in Edom" (1 Kings 11:14).

"God also raised up another adversary to him, Rezon the son of Eliada, who had fled from his Lord Hadadezer king of Zobah" (1 Kings 11:23).

This is a fascinating concept. God raised up enemies *of* His chosen people to *discipline* His chosen people. I would like to ask you two questions: Have you ever wondered why unbelievers are allowed to cause harm to and hurt believers, and have you ever wondered why unbelievers are successful in worldly matters at the expense of believers? Habakkuk asked this same question regarding the Jews when God allowed the Babylonians to invade Judah.

Your eyes are too pure to approve evil, and You cannot look on wickedness with favor. Why do You look with favor On those who deal treacherously? Why are You silent when the wicked swallow up Those more righteous than they? (Habakkuk 1:13)

On the surface, it doesn't seem fair. This brings us to our next Principle.

Principle 2: God uses unbelievers and believers who are out of fellowship to discipline believers who are in sin and are rejecting Him.

This does not mean that every time something bad happens to you or someone hurts you, it is because you are living in sin and being disciplined. Bad things will happen to you, even when you are in fellowship with God, have an active prayer life, and are growing "in the grace and knowledge of our Lord and Savior Jesus Christ" (2 Peter 3:18). God does allow suffering for the purpose of blessing. Also, remember that Satan is the ruler of this world. You will have adversities and will be tested. This principle does mean that God will not tolerate one of His children, His chosen people, and (I believe) our nation living outside His perfect plan. He loves us so much, He will use discipline to get us back in line. Look again in Hebrews.

"And you have forgotten that word of encouragement that addresses you as sons: 'My son, do not make light of the Lord's discipline, and do not lose heart when He rebukes you, because the Lord disciplines those He loves, and He punishes everyone He accepts as a son.'" (Hebrews 12:5–6).

This principle is true on a national level, as well. The nation of Israel was disciplined because of personal and national sin. God used unbelieving nations to provide the discipline.

As we proceed in the history of Israel and as we go through the book of Esther, ask yourself these questions: How does this principle relate to the United States of America, and is our nation under discipline because of sin and rejection of God? Are the political, economic, and military adversities we face the result of divine discipline? Is God using other nations to punish us? Is there a point at which He will no longer allow us to recover?

How did Israel respond to God's mandate? What can we learn from Israel's response? Let's go back to the Old Testament.

Nation Divided

---Northern Kingdom (931–722 BC)-- **X** Assyrian captivity

----Southern Kingdom (931–586 BC)--- Babylonian captivity **X**

950	850	750	650	550

God divided the nation of Israel into northern and southern kingdoms in 931 BC. The Northern kingdom, Israel, or Samaria, was composed of ten tribes and was ruled by kings who were generally wicked. The Southern kingdom, or Judah, was ruled by some kings who were good and by some kings who were wicked.

Some general facts concerning the kingdoms: At various times, God allowed pagan nations to invade, kill, or capture portions of the northern and southern kingdoms because of their disobedience. In His fairness, God provided prophets to warn the people to stop their sin and to return to Him. Elijah, Elisha, Jonah, Amos, Joel, Hosea, Isaiah, Micah, Jeremiah, Ezekiel, and Obadiah are specifically identified. The people were fairly warned to stop their evil ways and to return to God. The northern and southern kingdoms fought each other for many years, 931–841 BC.[9] Later, the kingdoms learned to work together to some extent.

When the kings and the people followed God, the kingdom was blessed. King Asa, in the south for most of his reign, and King Hezekiah are examples. When the kings—and the people—turned from Yahweh, God disciplined the kingdoms. King Asa in the south in his later reign and most of the northern kings, including Ahab and Jezebel, are examples. This scenario is played out over and over until the nation is driven into exile.

When I was reading the history of Israel from Solomon to the exile, I had to ask myself, "Why did the people continue to reject God?" Historically, they had great leaders who trusted God, and as a result, the nation was blessed. Moses had led the people out of bondage, David had slain Goliath, and Solomon had built the temple. God directed all of these people and their successes. They also had historic examples of what happened when they disobeyed God. In most cases, they were first warned by the prophets, and then they were disciplined when they continued in disobedience. When a child puts his or her hand over a stove and gets burned, he or she learns not do it again. Why did the Israelites not learn to stop worshiping idols and to worship only God?

9   Easley, K. H. 2003. *The Illustrated Guide to Biblical History* Nashville, Tenn.: Holman Bible Publishers, 75.

Principle 3: Man's sinful nature leads him to disobey and reject God.

We, as church-age believers, often do no better than the ninth-century BC Israelites. Before we criticize God's chosen people for not following His specific instructions, we should look at ourselves and see what He has given us. We have knowledge of the complete life, death, and resurrection of Jesus Christ, which they did not have; we have the complete canon of Scripture, which they did not have; we are indwelt by the Holy Spirit, which most of them were not; and we are being sanctified daily—at least, we should be. Yet we sin, disobey, and reject God. Why? Paul writes of this conflict and its result.

"For I know that nothing good dwells in me, that is, in my flesh; for the willing is present in me, but the doing of the good is not. For the good that I want, I do not do, but I practice the very evil that I do not want. But if I am doing the very thing I do not want, I am no longer the one doing it, but sin which dwells in me" (Romans 7:18–20).

Paul writes in Romans 5:12 that sin entered the world through Adam, and everyone is guilty of sin. John writes in 1 John 1:8, 10 that if anyone believes they do not sin, they are deceiving themselves and calling God a liar. So what is it that leads us to continue sinning? Paul uses the terms "sin" in Romans 7:13, "flesh" in Galatians 5:16, and "old man" in Ephesians 4:22 to describe the force or nature inside every human being that tempts one to sin.

Does this mean man is not responsible when he sins? Does this mean we can put the blame on someone or something else? Of course not. We are responsible for what we think, do, and say. We cannot put the blame for our failures onto others. We also cannot put the blame on God, as the Bible is very specific in telling us that He does not let us be tempted beyond what we can resist.

"No temptation has overtaken you but such as is common to man; and God is faithful, who will not allow you to be tempted beyond what you are able, but with the temptation will provide the way of escape also, so that you will be able to endure it" (1 Corinthians 10:13).

In addition, when we are tempted, we should also remember that it is not God who tempts us.

"Let no one say when he is tempted, 'I am being tempted by God;' for God cannot be tempted by evil, and He Himself does not tempt anyone. But each one is tempted when he is carried away and enticed by his own lust. Then when lust has conceived, it gives birth to sin; and when sin is accomplished, it brings forth death" (James 1:13–15).

All sin separates man from God. It is God's desire to restore broken relationships when man sins. Jesus Christ redeemed us from the penalty of sin through His work on the cross. God provided a mechanism for the Old Testament Israelites to be restored when they sinned.

"Seek the Lord while He may be found; call upon Him while He is near. Let the wicked forsake his way and the unrighteous man his thoughts; and let him return to the Lord, and He will have compassion on him, and to our God, for He will abundantly pardon" (Isaiah 55:6–7).

For the nation of Israel, the following led to restoration:

"And My people who are called by My name humble themselves and pray and seek My face and turn from their wicked ways, then I will hear from heaven, will forgive their sin and will heal their land" (2 Chronicles 7:14).

He provides a mechanism for us, as church-age believers, to be restored when we sin.

"If we confess our sins, He is faithful and righteous to forgive us our sins and to cleanse us from all unrighteousness" (1 John 1:9).

So after the discipline, did the northern and southern kingdoms change their ways? Did they learn to stop worshipping idols, and did they begin to worship God?

No way! So what does God do next? He ups the ante. God uses the Assyrians, the world's superpower at that time, to discipline the Israelites, beginning first with the northern kingdom.

What do we know of the Assyrians? They have been described as an "ancient empire considered the symbol of terror and tyranny in the Near East for more than three centuries."[10] They were known for extreme cruelty. It is no wonder Jonah resisted when God commanded him to go to Nineveh, an Assyrian city. Israel's fall to Assyria in 722 BC and the reason why is recorded in 2 Kings.

Assyria Empire - **X** - captures Northern Kingdom - 722 BC

Fall of Ninevah to Babylonians - 612 BC - **X**

800	700	600

"Then the king of Assyria invaded the whole land and went up to Samaria and besieged it three years. In the ninth year of Hoshea, the king of Assyria captured Samaria and carried Israel away into exile to Assyria, and settled them in Halah and Habor, on the river of Gozan, and in the cities of the Medes. Now this came about because the sons of Israel had sinned against the Lord their God ... they had feared other gods and walked in the customs of the nations whom the Lord had driven out before the sons of Israel .... The sons of Israel did things secretly which were not right against the Lord their God .... They set for themselves sacred pillars and Asherim on every high hill and under every green tree, and there they burned incense on all the high places as the nations did which the Lord had carried away to exile before them; and they did evil things provoking the Lord. They served idols, concerning which the Lord had said to them, 'You shall not do this thing'" (2 Kings 17:5–12).

---

10   Ibid., Elwell, 219.

Reading further, we see that in spite of the behavior of the Israelites, God warns Israel and Judah before their discipline.

> "Yet the Lord warned Israel and Judah through all His prophets and every seer, saying, 'Turn from your evil ways and keep My commandments, My statutes according to all the law which I commanded your fathers, and which I sent to you through My servants the prophets.' However, they did not listen, but stiffened their neck like their fathers, who did not believe in the Lord their God. They rejected His statutes and His covenant which He made with their fathers and His warnings with which He warned them .... They forsook all the commandments of the Lord their God and made for themselves molten images, even two calves, and made an Asherah and worshiped all the host of heaven and served Baal. Then they made their sons and their daughters pass through the fire, and practiced divination and enchantments, and sold themselves to do evil in the sight of the Lord, provoking Him. So the Lord was very angry with Israel and removed them from His sight; none was left except the tribe of Judah. Also Judah did not keep the commandments of the Lord their God, but walked in the customs which Israel had introduced. The Lord rejected all the descendants of Israel and afflicted them and gave them into the hand of plunderers, until He had cast them out of His sight .... So Israel was carried away into exile from their own land to Assyria until this day" (2 Kings 17:13–23).

God gave them chance after chance to return to Him, but they did not listen. This behavior goes on for 300 years. Even after the northern kingdom fell, the southern kingdom did not repent and turn back to God. Judah deteriorated and met with disasters from 722–586 BC. The bright spot was King Hezekiah, and the dark spot was King Manasseh, Hezekiah's son.

The Assyrians continued to plague Judah. Sennacherib, whose name means "sin has replaced brothers,"[11] was the Assyrian king from 705–681 BC. He had plans to capture Jerusalem; however, God intervened. Hezekiah, who was the king of the southern kingdom at the time, was faithful to God and turned to Him. God provided military deliverance to the Israelites. Specifically, God ordered the killing of the Assyrians.

---

11   Ibid., 1924.

The events are recorded in 2 Kings 18–19, 2 Chronicles 32, and Isaiah 36–37.

> "Then it happened that night that the angel of the Lord went out and struck 185,000 in the camp of the Assyrians; and when men rose early in the morning, behold, all of them were dead. So Sennacherib king of Assyria departed and returned home, and lived at Nineveh" (2 Kings 19:35–36).

Let's stop a minute and consider what has happened. Israel had been captured, and Judah has been unrepentant. Scripture tells us that Hezekiah:

> "He did right in the sight of the Lord, according to all that his father David had done. He removed the high places and broke down the sacred pillars and cut down the Asherah. He also broke in pieces the bronze serpent that Moses had made, for until those days the sons of Israel burned incense to it; and it was called Nehushtan. He trusted in the Lord, the God of Israel; so that after him there was none like him among all the kings of Judah, nor among those who were before him. For he clung to the Lord; he did not depart from following Him, but kept His commandments, which the Lord had commanded Moses" (2 Kings 18:3–6).

What was God's response? The angel of the Lord killed 185,000 of the Assyrian enemy. The angel of the Lord may be referring to Jesus Christ Himself (Exodus 3:2, Judges 2:1) or to an angel sent by Him. Either way, God showed mercy and grace on Judah by destroying the Assyrian army.

Do you find it difficult to accept that God kills people? He removes people from the face of the earth when His divine will requires such action. There is a tendency to sometimes focus on God's love at the expense of His righteousness and justice. Many believers often have difficulty accepting that God expresses His wrath against evil.

God's justice and righteousness do not violate His divine love. His justice and righteousness operate or function perfectly within His divine will and plan. His decisions to save Hezekiah and Judah and to slaughter Sennacherib's army were the result of His perfect love, righteousness, and justice.

Principle 4: God's righteousness and justice work in perfect union with His love, and the three together are in harmony with His divine will and plan.

God is absolute righteousness. Everything about Him is perfect and right (Deuteronomy 32:4; Psalm 11:7, 97:6, 119:137; John 17:25; Romans 1:17, 10:3; 1 John 2:29). God is absolute justice. Everything about Him is fair and just (Job 37:23; Ecclesiastes 12:14; Psalm 50:6, 89:14; Romans 3:26; Hebrews 10:30–31). God is absolute love. As a noun, God *is* perfect love (1 John 4:7–8). As a verb, God *loves* perfectly (John 3:16). Since these three attributes are present in God in a perfect state, all three must function together. If God is perfect—and He is—what makes up God and what comes from Him must also be perfect.

God is not a pacifist, and He is not politically correct as defined by humans. He may allow human sin, cruelty, and atrocities to occur for a certain period. There are times, however, when He wipes such persons, nations, and behavior off the face of the earth. When He does so, it does not violate His perfect character. Sometimes God directly causes the death and destruction, and sometimes He allows Satan and his demons to do the destruction. God unleashes His wrath at His pleasure (Exodus 32:9-10; Romans 1:18, 2:5; Revelation 6:16-17).

With what we have just learned about how God dealt with Sennacherib and the Assyrians, I would like to revisit Principle 2, "God uses unbelievers and believers who are out of fellowship to provide discipline to believers who are in sin and who are rejecting Him." In the book of Revelation, John speaks of an event which is truly horrific.

"And the four angels, who had been prepared for the hour and day and month and year, were released, so that they would kill a third of mankind. The number of the armies of the horsemen was two hundred million; I heard the number of them. And this is how I saw in the vision the horses and those who sat on them: the riders had breastplates the color of fire and of hyacinth and of brimstone; and the heads of the horses are like the heads of lions; and out of their mouths proceed fire and smoke and brimstone. A third of mankind was killed by these three plagues, by the fire and the smoke and the brimstone which proceeded out of their mouths" (Revelation 9:15–18).

It is my opinion that John is speaking of demons who are unleashed for the purpose of killing one third of humanity. It is unbelievers who are being killed, and this is being done under the will of God. Here, God does use evil to accomplish His purpose. We read further and see that these end-time unbelievers did not repent of their ways.

"The rest of mankind, who were not killed by these plagues, did not repent of the works of their hands, so as not to worship demons, and the idols of gold and of silver and of brass and of stone and of wood, which can neither see nor hear nor walk; and they did not repent of their murders nor of their sorceries nor of their immorality nor of their thefts" (Revelation 9:20–21).

God warns both His people and those who reject Him. He judges people and nations. The book of Nahum addresses this issue. "Theologically, Nahum stands as an eloquent testimony to the particularity of God's justice and salvation. To the suffering remnant, there was little question that God would and did punish his own covenant people; but whether he was equally able and willing to impart justice to the powerful heathen nations surrounding Israel was untested. Among those nations, none had dominated world affairs in the second millennium BC as had imperial Assyria. Arrogant, self-sufficient, cruel, and assertive, the Assyrians had dominated every small nation in the region at one time or another from the days of the first Tiglath-pileser (1115-1076) onward." [12] The question of whether God punishes His enemies is answered:

---

12   Armerding, Carl E. 1984. *The Expositor's Bible Commentary.* Grand Rapids: Zondervan Publishing House, Volume 7, 456.

"A jealous and avenging God is the Lord; The Lord is avenging and wrathful. The Lord takes vengeance on His adversaries, and He reserves wrath for His enemies. The Lord is slow to anger and great in power, and the Lord will by no means leave the guilty unpunished. In whirlwind and storm is His way, and clouds are the dust beneath His feet" (Nahum 1:2–3).

"Nineveh's day would come to an end; no power on earth can long endure when it sets itself against the Lord and his anointed in Zion."[13] Psalm 2 describes the fate of nations who do not "worship the Lord with reverence" (Psalm 2:11). We will see this principle at the end of Esther.

Principle 5: God uses nations to punish His chosen people, and then He judges those nations.

It is clear—when we look at the history of the Egyptians, the Assyrians, the Babylonians, and the Persians, we see God's hand directing the history of nations. I think we sometimes forget this is true today as well. It is sometimes difficult to see the work of God in the history of nations in 2010. We do not have present-day prophets as they did in the Old Testament, and it is hard to see things until after they occur. We do need to remember, however, that Jesus Christ controls history.

"For by Him all things were created, both in the heavens and on earth, visible and invisible, whether thrones or dominions or rulers or authorities— all things have been created through Him and for Him. He is before all things, and in Him all things hold together" (Colossians 1:16–17).

Two questions arise from principle 5. First, is it fair that God uses nations to punish His chosen people, and then judges those nations? Second, does God make people (and nations) sin to serve His purpose and then punish them?

Let's answer the second question first. God does not make people or nations sin. Individual sinful nature, volitional choice, sin in the world, and Satan result in immoral decay and human degeneracy. The result is that people and nations sin. Paul describes this process in Romans 1. My comments are in bold.

---

13   Ibid.

"For the wrath of God is revealed from heaven against all ungodliness and unrighteousness of men who suppress the truth in unrighteousness, because that which is known about God is evident within them; for God made it evident to them. For since the creation of the world His invisible attributes, His eternal power and divine nature, have been clearly seen, being understood through what has been made, so that they are without excuse. [**God has been revealed to every human being; no one has a legitimate excuse for saying they do not know God.**]

For even though they knew God, they did not honor Him as God or give thanks, but they became futile in their speculations, and their foolish heart was darkened. [**Those who reject God do so through their own volition.**]

Professing to be wise, they became fools, and exchanged the glory of the incorruptible God for an image in the form of corruptible man and of birds and four-footed animals and crawling creatures. [**Degenerate people reject God.**]

Therefore God gave them over in the lusts of their hearts to impurity, so that their bodies would be dishonored among them. For they exchanged the truth of God for a lie, and worshiped and served the creature rather than the Creator, who is blessed forever. Amen. For this reason God gave them over to degrading passions; for their women exchanged the natural function for that which is unnatural, and in the same way also the men abandoned the natural function of the woman and burned in their desire toward one another, men with men committing indecent acts and receiving in their own persons the due penalty of their error. And just as they did not see fit to acknowledge God any longer, God gave them over to a depraved mind, to do those things which are not proper, [**When people reject God and turn away from Him, at a certain point God turns them over to their depraved minds.**]

being filled with all unrighteousness, wickedness, greed, evil; full of envy, murder, strife, deceit, malice; they are gossips, slanderers, haters of God, insolent, arrogant, boastful, inventors of evil, disobedient to parents, without understanding, untrustworthy, unloving, unmerciful; [**Left to their depraved minds, people live in degeneracy, and are capable of all forms of sin.**]

and although they know the ordinance of God, that those who practice such things are worthy of death, they not only do the same, but also give hearty approval to those who practice them [**The degenerate know they will be punished, but live in degeneracy anyway.**]" (Romans 1:18–32).

Individually, a person can degenerate to total depravity. Nations can do the same. Without God, humans and nations will do the things the Assyrians did. God uses those people and nations with those behaviors, but does not make them do the things they do. God disciplines His people to get them back in line. This sometimes requires the use of cruel people and nations. He also eventually punishes those people and nations who are doing evil to His chosen people. In answering the first question above, the bottom line is that God is justified in punishing degenerate people and nations.

After seeing what God had done to save Judah, including giving Hezekiah another fifteen years to live, do you think his son, Manasseh, learned to obey and follow? Just as many kings before him, Manasseh rejected God. The same pattern is repeated.

A succession of father-son southern kings follows: Ahaz rules for sixteen years and is generally wicked; Hezekiah, his son, rules for twenty-nine years and is generally righteous; Manasseh, his son, rules for forty-four years and is generally wicked; Amon, his son, rules for two years and is generally wicked; Josiah, his son, rules for thirty-one years and is generally righteous.[14]

Do you notice anything in the above paragraph? Did family relationships determine a king's decision to follow or reject God? Is there

---

14   Ibid., Easley, 104-114.

a relationship between whether a father followed God and his son followed God? There does not seem to be. In studying kings from David to the Exile, we have all four possible father-son relationships: father obeys, son obeys (Solomon, son of David); father obeys, son does not obey (Manasseh, son of Hezekiah); father does not obey, son obeys (Hezekiah, son of Ahaz); father does not obey, son does not obey (Amon, son of Manasseh).

> **Principle 6: Your spiritual life and your relationship with God are determined by *your* decision to trust and obey God, not by your parents.**
>
> When I first presented this principle at Beaumont Bible Church, I was correctly challenged with the issue of parental responsibility. How we are reared and how we rear our children does make a difference. It is critical to bring children up knowing God and show them how to have a relationship with our Lord Jesus Christ.
>
> Is there a contradiction between Principle 6 above and Principle 1, "When a leader sins and rejects God's authority, all those under the leader's authority are affected"? Parents are leaders, and if they fail in parenting, will it affect their children? The answer is, of course; yes, it will.
>
> When parents fail in their responsibility of parenting, children suffer. Child neglect, abuse, and indifference can devastate a child for a lifetime. Physical, mental, emotional, and spiritual abuse of a child can affect his or her ability to have relationships as an adult, both with people and with God. The Bible is clear on the responsibility of parents in regards to children.
>
> "Train up a child in the way he should go, even when he is old he will not depart from it" (Proverbs 22:6).
>
> "Fathers, do not provoke your children to anger, but bring them up in the discipline and instruction of the Lord" (Ephesians 6:4).

Does this mean the two principles contradict each other? I do not think so. When people become adults they are responsible for their own decisions and their own relationship with God. Every person has volition. No one can base their spiritual life on who their parents were and what they did or did not do. We have no excuse for not trusting and obeying God, even if our family life growing up was not based on trusting and obeying God.

I believe God is just, and everyone is presented with the knowledge of saving grace. Everyone has an opportunity to believe or not believe. It may seem like some people have a greater opportunity than others to know God. Growing up in a family or a church where there is love and God is revered as the ultimate authority will positively influence children toward belief.

Contrast this with the child who is abused, grows up with hate in his or her heart, and does not trust anyone. This type of environment may negatively influence one to believe. In these situations, I believe God can repair the damage done by people and the environment and present Himself to that person in such a way that His saving grace is desirable and receivable. God will provide a fair opportunity for the abused and mistreated to accept Him. Does that person respond to God when He provides a solution to the pains of life, or does that person reject God because of the pains of life? I think it goes back to free will, personal choice, or volition. As an adult who is able to make decisions, he or she has to be responsible to accept or reject God and must accept the consequence.

While God is just, life is not equal—and certainly does not seem fair. We may spend much of eternity learning how God was truly fair to every human being. Remember, it is God's desire that everyone is saved.

"This is good and acceptable in the sight of God our Savior, who desires all men to be saved and to come to the knowledge of the truth" (1 Timothy 2:3–4).

> "He came as a witness, to testify about the Light, so that all might believe through him" (John 1:7).
>
> As such, I believe God is fair in offering salvation to everyone. Furthermore, I believe God is fair in His offer to provide opportunities and solutions to everyone's problems.

Exile

X 605 BC—First captives taken to Babylon
First exiles returned to Jerusalem 536 BC X

X 586 BC—Destruction of Solomon's temple
Dedication of the second temple 516 BC X

625	600	575	550	525	500

Sennacherib died in 681 BC, and the Assyrian empire deteriorated over the next several years. The Neo-Babylonian Empire came to power with the emergence of prince Nabopolassar. The Assyrian empire was defeated, Ninevah was captured in 612 BC, and Egypt was defeated in 605 BC. The empire lasted from 626–539 BC and fell to Persia in 539 BC.[15]

Babylon played a significant role in the history of the Jews. Nabopolassar's son, Nebuchadnezzar, reigned from 604–562 BC. He invaded Judah four times: 605 BC, 597 BC, 587–586 BC, and 582 BC. The first invasion is recorded in Daniel 1:1–2. The second invasion is recorded in 2 Kings 24:10–16. During the third invasion, the temple, palace, and important buildings were destroyed, and many Israelites were taken away as captives to Babylon. This was the beginning of the Exile. The fourth invasion is recorded in Jeremiah 52:30. "The total number of captives taken in all the deportations from Judah probably did not exceed a total of 70,000 men, women, and children."[16]

What did God want the Jews to do when they were taken into captivity? God was very clear as to what He wanted them to do and not to do, and He

---

15   Ibid., Elwell, 247-248.

16   Ibid., 733-734.

provided the prophet Jeremiah to tell them. They were to go to Babylon as captives. Jeremiah gives an interesting analogy in explaining to the people what they were to do and how God would deal with them based on how they responded.

> "One basket had very good figs, like first-ripe figs, and the other basket had very bad figs which could not be eaten due to rottenness …. Then the word of the Lord came to me, saying, 'Thus says the Lord God of Israel, "Like these good figs, so I will regard as good the captives of Judah, whom I have sent out of this place into the land of the Chaldeans. For I will set My eyes on them for good, and I will bring them again to this land; and I will build them up and not overthrow them, and I will plant them and not pluck them up. I will give them a heart to know Me, for I am the Lord; and they will be My people, and I will be their God, for they will return to Me with their whole heart"''" (Jeremiah 24:2–7).

There is discipline here; yet God is telling the Israelites He will bless them. They were going to come out of their captivity with a better relationship with God. Not everyone went to Babylon as God commanded, however. During this time, many Jews in Judah chose to flee to Egypt. God was very clear; this violated His plan. Jeremiah records His response.

> "Nevertheless hear the word of the Lord, all Judah who are living in the land of Egypt, 'Behold, I have sworn by My great name,' says the Lord, 'never shall My name be invoked again by the mouth of any man of Judah in all the land of Egypt, saying, "As the Lord God lives." Behold, I am watching over them for harm and not for good, and all the men of Judah who are in the land of Egypt will meet their end by the sword and by famine until they are completely gone'" (Jeremiah 44:26–27).

What can we learn from the Jews being sent into exile?

Principle 7: God blesses through adversity. He uses hardship for believers to improve their relationship with Him. Obedience to God is required for blessing. Obedience to God's discipline results in blessing for the believer.

Think of times you have been in difficult situations. Maybe you were responsible; maybe you were not. Maybe the adversity went on for years. During this time period, did you or did you not trust and obey God? When you think about it, you really have only two choices when things are going bad. Trust and obey God—or do not trust, and disobey.

When in adversity, our natural tendency is to whine, complain, run away, or ask God to remove the problem. Even Paul struggled when faced with adversity.

"Because of the surpassing greatness of the revelations, for this reason, to keep me from exalting myself, there was given me a thorn in the flesh, a messenger of Satan to torment me—to keep me from exalting myself! Concerning this I implored the Lord three times that it might leave me. And He has said to me, 'My grace is sufficient for you, for power is perfected in weakness.' Most gladly, therefore, I will rather boast about my weaknesses, so that the power of Christ may dwell in me. Therefore I am well content with weaknesses, with insults, with distresses, with persecutions, with difficulties, for Christ's sake; for when I am weak, then I am strong" (2 Corinthians 12:7–10).

Paul learned that God provided him with adversity so he would keep his eyes on Him. When he relied on God in his weakness, Paul was strong because of God's power, not his own. Everyone has faced some form of adversity in his or her life. When it is your turn, do you whine, complain, make excuses, and curse God—or do you thank Him and look to see what He is teaching you?

The solution to adversity is, of course, to confess sin if one is in sin, and then to trust and obey God. There is blessing for the individual and glory for God.

What happens when there is no trust or obedience?

"But like the bad figs which cannot be eaten due to rottenness—indeed, thus says the Lord—so I will abandon Zedekiah king of Judah and his officials, and the remnant of Jerusalem who remain in this land and the ones who dwell in the land of Egypt. I will make them a terror and an evil for all the kingdoms of the earth, as a reproach and a proverb, a taunt and a curse in all places where I will scatter them. I will send the sword, the famine and the pestilence upon them until they are destroyed from the land which I gave to them and their forefathers" (Jeremiah 24:8–10).

To sum things up, the Jews disobeyed and were sent into exile. Some of the Jews accepted the discipline and went to Babylon. Some of the Jews disobeyed God's command and fled to Egypt. God further punished them. What happens to us when we resist God and disobey Him when He is disciplining us?

Principle 8: Disobedience to God in times of discipline leads to further discipline.

Have you ever tried to escape from God's discipline, either through mental, emotional sin or physical, overt sin? It is very easy to do. When you are under the pressure of discipline, it is easy to justify almost any thought or action. But it does not work. It just makes things worse. I do not know what your sin patterns are, but I do know that if you let the stress of discipline overwhelm you, your resistance to temptation is lowered. It is a mistake to say, "Well, I might as well try to escape from the situation, because things could not get any worse than they are." Believe me, things can and will get worse if you resist God's discipline. Face it—all of us are going to screw up some time or another. When God disciplines us, we have two choices. If we trust and obey Him, we will come out ahead. If we reject Him, things will get worse.

God has a plan for every church-age believer. When we get out of line, He disciplines us. He continues the discipline until we get back in line. If we never get in line, He may end our life and bring us to heaven. Yes, divine discipline can result in believers losing their life on earth and being sent to heaven (Acts 5:1–11; 1 Corinthians 11:27–32; James 5:19–20; Revelation 2:18–29).

Once again, God allowed enemies of Israel to punish His chosen people, and then judged those nations.

> "This whole land will be a desolation and a horror, and these nations will serve the king of Babylon seventy years. 'Then it will be when seventy years are completed I will punish the king of Babylon and that nation,' declares the Lord, 'for their iniquity, and the land of the Chaldeans; and I will make it an everlasting desolation'" (Jeremiah 25:11–12).

X Jehoahaz 609 BC—3 months
X Jehoiakim 609–598 BC

X Jehoiachin 598–597 BC—100 days
X ----Zedekiah 597–586 BC ----

610	600	590	580

Let's take a quick look at the last four kings of Judah.[17] Each was not acting as a true king, but rather as a vassal of a greater empire—either Egypt or Babylon. Jehoahaz, or Shallum, was a son of Josiah, king for only three months and taken prisoner by Pharaoh Neco. He was followed by another son of Josiah, named Jehoiakim, or Eliakim. Initially subject to Neco, Jehoiakim became a vassal to Babylon when Nebuchadnezzar defeated the Egyptian army in 605 BC. He reigned from 609 to 598 BC and persecuted Jeremiah during his time in power. During his reign, Daniel was carried off to Babylon (606 BC).

Jehoiachin, or Coniah, was the second to last king. He was the son of Jehoiakim and ruled for only 100 days, December 598 BC until March 597 BC During his reign, Jerusalem was besieged, and Ezekiel was taken away as captive. Zedekiah, or Mattaniah, was the last king. He was the son of Josiah and reigned from 597 to 586 BC. His visitation to Babylon is recorded in Jeremiah 51:59. His rebellion against Babylon resulted in Nebuchadnezzar's third invasion of Jerusalem.

Let's take a minute and talk about Jeremiah. Born around 657 BC, he prophesied during the time period of Judah's last five kings. He called on the Jews to believe God, obey the laws of Babylon, and reject false hopes in Egypt. He prophesied that there would be seventy years of exile. Two ways

---

17   Ibid., Easley, 117-120.

can be used to calculate the time in exile: years between the time the first captives went to Babylon and the time the first exiles returned, 605–536 BC; or time between the destruction of Solomon's temple and the dedication of the second temple, 586–516 BC.[18]

Jeremiah gave explicit instructions to the Jews going into exile. They are recorded in Jeremiah 29. Excerpts from this chapter include:

> "Thus says the Lord of hosts, the God of Israel, to all the exiles whom I have sent into exile from Jerusalem to Babylon, 'Build houses and live in them; and plant gardens and eat their produce. Take wives and become the fathers of sons and daughters, and take wives for your sons and give your daughters to husbands, that they may bear sons and daughters; and multiply there and do not decrease. Seek the welfare of the city where I have sent you into exile, and pray to the Lord on its behalf; for in its welfare you will have welfare'" (Jeremiah 29:4–7).

The Jews are to make their homes in Babylon, they are to become a part of society, and they are to flourish. And what does God promise He will do?

> "For thus says the Lord, 'When seventy years have been completed for Babylon, I will visit you and fulfill My good word to you, to bring you back to this place. For I know the plans that I have for you,' declares the Lord, 'plans for welfare and not for calamity to give you a future and a hope. Then you will call upon Me and come and pray to Me, and I will listen to you. You will seek Me and find Me when you search for Me with all your heart. I will be found by you,' declares the Lord, 'and I will restore your fortunes and will gather you from all the nations and from all the places where I have driven you,' declares the Lord, 'and I will bring you back to the place from where I sent you into exile'" (Jeremiah 29:10–14).

Is this good or what? God had a plan for them and was letting them know He would keep His promise. So what was the purpose of the exile? Why did God put His chosen people under the authority of the Babylonians? Several reasons explain both why God required the Jews to be exiled and the benefit resulting from their discipline.

---

18   Ibid., 118.

Discipline

The Jews were put into exile because God was disciplining His people for their years of disobedience. God had given clear instructions to the Israelites—they were not to worship idols. As we have seen, the people did not listen. They disobeyed and worshiped idols. For over 300 years, God provided various forms of discipline when the people disobeyed. Ultimately, God disciplined the Jews with exile.

Education of His people

God's purpose in disciplining His people was not simply to punish. It was to educate and orient the people so they would understand God's sovereignty. When God told them to do something or to not do something, they needed to obey. Some people learn easily when they are presented with the truth. Some people do not learn easily. For the Israelites, the problem was that the people refused to learn at all. Through the exile, most would eventually learn.

Weeding out of those who reject God

There were those who still refused to learn. Their fate was destruction. We saw what happened to the Jews who fled to Egypt instead of going to Babylon.

Sanctification for those who obeyed and followed God

There was spiritual growth for those Jews who trusted and obeyed God during their captivity in Babylon. When they returned to Jerusalem after seventy years, they had a renewed and stronger relationship with God. This relationship was present both individually and for the nation.

Refinement of the Jewish people

As they focused on God, they stopped many of their sinful ways. Certainly, there was a turning away from idols and a turning toward God.

Preservation of God's chosen people who were on the verge of disappearing

At the time of the Exile, the Jews were unable to defend themselves against the world powers of the day. If God had not protected them with exile, they could easily have been destroyed.

Spreading of the message of God

Jewish beliefs and knowledge of God were spread around the world during the Exile. We will see a direct application of this in Persia during our study.

Jews had to learn to trust God and be faithful

They did not learn this when they were a nation. When God delivered them from previous enemies, they quickly turned away from Him. It took time in exile for the people to learn to trust and be faithful to God, both in times of prosperity and adversity.

A relationship was built between God and His people

God showed grace and mercy to a very ungrateful group of people. He wanted the people to know Him. It took the Exile for the Jews to see that it was God who was sustaining them.

The Jews learned to hope in the Lord. They learned that their focus in life was God, not themselves. They learned humility toward God and to follow His authority. In a similar way, when we disobey God, we are often disciplined. When we are suffering, it may even seem like we have been put in exile. Hopefully, we learn the things the Jews learned.

Principle 9: God puts us on the sideline so we will learn to follow His game plan.

For the athletes who are reading this, I would like to ask, "Did you ever screw up in a game, and did the coach pull you out and make you sit on the bench?" I played college football at Hastings College in Nebraska, and it happened to me a couple times. I played safety, and I remember missing a tackle in a game and being pulled. Another time, I was fooled into thinking the quarterback handed the ball to the running back. I came up to make the tackle and let the receiver get behind me. It was a pass, and the result was a touchdown for the offense. The coach pulled me.

When you are on the sideline, what is the one thing you want to do? You want to get back in the game and prove yourself. You can't, because the coach has other ideas. His reasoning may be that he thinks you need a rest, he may be giving you time to think of how you messed up and how you can do better, he may have one of the other coaches give you some instruction while you sit on the bench, he may be giving someone else time to play, or he simply may not trust you to do what he wants you to do. You want to get back in, but you have to follow the coach's authority.

I like sports movies that teach principles. The movie *Hoosiers* is one of my favorites, and it does a very good job of defining the principle of following authority. There is a scene in one of the early basketball games. The small town of Hickory only has seven players on the team. One player fouls out and is on the bench. One player rejects the coach's authority and disobeys his instructions to pass the ball before shooting. The coach pulls him from the game. Another player then fouls out. To the amazement of everyone, the coach decides to play with four players instead of letting the player who had defied him go back in the game and play. They lose the game, of course; however, the end result is that all the players learn to respect and follow the coach's game plan. They become a team instead of a bunch of individuals. They end up winning the state championship.

Being in exile was kind of like being on the sideline. The people had not followed God's game plan. The only way they would ever learn to do what God wanted them to do was to sit on the bench and wait on God.

The issue is not that we are taken out of the game. The issue is how we respond. Some people get worked up because they are not in the game all the time. This, of course, is the wrong attitude. Everybody gets put on the sideline from time to time. The reasons vary. It may be discipline for wrongdoing, or it may just be that God wants to teach us something and bless us. Ultimately, it is for God's glory and His perfect plan. If we react with anger, pouting, arrogance, or we try to escape from where God has us, we will be there for a long time—maybe indefinitely—or possibly, we will be kicked off the team. If we respond with humility, honest self-analysis, and respect toward God, He will put us back in the game at the exact right time—for Him and us.

One final thing you need to remember when you are taken out of the game is that you are in good company. Many biblical heroes spent time on the bench. Moses spent forty years on the sideline after he fled Pharaoh and settled in the land of Midian (Exodus 2:15). His forty years in the land helped prepare him to lead the Israelites out of Egypt. Paul spent two or three years in Arabia after his conversion. He would not have been able to do the work he did if he had not received God's teaching during this time period.

So God tells the Jews in exile to build houses, have families, and be prosperous. They are to worship Him. He has made it clear that He will take care of them. He has a plan for them. And what is God doing during this time? He is working. Oh, how He is working.

Persia

```
-----------Babylonian Empire ------X King Cyrus captures Babylon in 539 BC
                                 X Persian Empire -----------------------------------------
```

| 575 | 550 | 525 | 500 |

The Persians entered the scene when King Cyrus captured Babylon in 539–538 BC. He was an innovator, a great warrior, and a great builder. Those he captured in war were treated in a very unique way. Rather than enslaving them, he was generous and benevolent. Captives were incorporated into the empire. King Cyrus was more of a liberator than a conqueror. God certainly used him in fulfilling His promise to return the people to Jerusalem.[19] In treating captives this way, Cyrus increased the military security of Persia. The Jews who returned to Judea provided a buffer between Egypt and Persia. The remarkable things he did in returning the people to Jerusalem are recorded in Ezra.

> "Now in the first year of Cyrus king of Persia, in order to fulfill the word of the Lord by the mouth of Jeremiah, the Lord stirred up the spirit of Cyrus king of Persia, so that he sent a proclamation throughout all his kingdom, and also put it in writing, saying: 'Thus says Cyrus king of Persia, "The Lord, the God of heaven, has given me all the kingdoms of the earth and He has appointed me to build Him a house in Jerusalem, which is in Judah. Whoever there is among you of all His people, may his God be with him! Let him go up to Jerusalem which is in Judah and rebuild the house of the Lord, the God of Israel; He is the God who is in Jerusalem. Every survivor, at whatever place he may live, let the men of that place support him with silver and gold, with goods and cattle, together with a freewill offering for the house of God which is in Jerusalem'" (Ezra 1:1–4).

This is simply incredible. God used Cyrus, the king of Persia, to forward His plan regarding His chosen people. This is proof to me that He can use anybody, anywhere, anytime. I do have to ask the question,

---

19   Achtemeier, Paul J. 1984. *Harper's Bible Dictionary*. San Francisco: Harper & Row, S. 200.

however—would the Jews have been sent back to Jerusalem had they not followed Jeremiah's command in Jeremiah 29? What happened to those who disobeyed and went to Egypt?

One might ask why all of the Jews did not return to Jerusalem. "They should have done so, for Isaiah and Jeremiah had urged the yet-to-be-exiled nation to come out of Babylon (Isaiah 48:20; Jeremiah 50:8, 51:6) after seventy years (Jeremiah 29:10) and return to the place where the Lord could bless them under the covenantal promises (Deuteronomy 28)."[20] The reasons for this are not specifically stated in the Bible or secular recordings.

Cyrus **X** 559–530 BC
    Cambyses **X** 530–522 BC
        Darius I **X** 521–486 BC
            Ahasuerus/Xerxes **X** 485–465 BC

575	550	525	500	475	450

Following Cyrus, Cambyses II ruled from 530 to 522 BC. Darius I the Great then became king and ruled from 521–486 BC. As a military leader, he expanded the borders of Persia. He also attempted two invasions of Greece. "The first expedition was destroyed by a storm in the Aegean Sea; the second was defeated by the Athenians in the famous Battle of Marathon in 490 BC."[21] He was an administrator and a builder. "His greatest architectural accomplishment was the founding of Persepolis, a new royal city to replace the emperor's residence at Pasargadae."[22] The importance of these events to our study of Esther is that Darius' son, Ahasuerus, appears to make an attempt to reproduce his father's architectural successes while avenging his father's military defeats. Ahasuerus, also known as Xerxes, became king of Persia in 486 BC.

---

20   Walvoord, John F. and Roy B. Zuck. 1983. *The Bible Knowledge Commentary.* Wheaton, IL: Victor Books, S. 1:699.

21   Ibid., Elwell, 578.

22   Ibid.

X Battle of Marathon—490 BC
      Battle of Thermoplyae—August, 480 BC **X**
        Battle of Salamis—September, 480 BC **X**

490	485	480	475

The Persian-Greek wars have importance in the story of Esther. They lasted from 492 to 449 BC. In the Battle of Marathon, the Greeks defeated the Persians (under King Darius) in 490 BC. This is when Pheideppides ran twenty-five miles from Marathon to Athens to announce the defeat of the Persians and then died of exhaustion.

When Ahasuerus became king four years later, he planned a military campaign to invade Greece. Esther 1:1–4 occurs during the preparation for the invasion. During the invasion, Ahasuerus exhibits irrational behavior. "Xerxes' preparations included digging a canal near Athos and having a bridge built over the Hellespont by Phoenician and Egyptian engineers. When a storm destroyed the bridge, Xerxes ordered the engineers' heads cut off and the waters of the Hellespont given 300 lashes."[23]

In the Battle of Thermopylae, Persia, under King Ahasuerus, defeated the Greeks—specifically, the Spartans, led by King Leonidas—in 480 BC. Although they lost, the sacrifice of the 300 Spartans rallied the Greeks, and the battle has become immortalized.

Following this battle, the Persians marched on Athens in 480 BC. Athenians had already evacuated the city as Greek military leaders were preparing to meet the Persians at Salamis. Ahasuerus burned Athens to the ground in a fit of rage, and then immediately regretted it. "Later that year, the Persian fleet suffered a disastrous defeat at Salamis, and Xerxes ordered the execution of the Phoenician admiral; after this, both the Phoenician and Egyptian fleets deserted him."[24] These impulsive acts in war are examples of the king's irrational behavior seen throughout the book of Esther.

In 480 BC, Themistocles led the Greek navy in a battle with the Persian navy. He lured them into the narrow strait at Salamis and destroyed the Persians in the naval battle known as the Battle of Salamis. This was the

---

23   Bromiley, Geoffrey W. 2002. *The International Standard Bible Encyclopedia, Revised.* Wm. B. Eerdmans, S. 4:1161.

24   Ibid.

turning point in the Persian-Greek Wars. Following this defeat, Ahasuerus went back to Persia.

Remember this defeat when we get to Esther 2. We will want to ask two questions. First, "How do you think Ahasuerus felt when he went home to Persia after being defeated at Salamis?" And second, "How do you think everyone back home felt when they had to interact with Ahasuerus?"

Literary Form

Esther is an historical narrative. Characters, plots, and setting are masterfully presented. "Its principal characters are skillfully portrayed with a minimum of words. Their clear delineation can be compared to Shakespearean characters: Haman, the consummate villain; Esther, the beautiful and courageous heroine; Mordecai, the shrewd advisor; and Xerxes, the sensual and indifferent king."[25]

The plot is simple in its basic premise, yet detailed in the many events that occur during the presentation and resolution of the conflicts. In this way, the plot further emphasizes our second objective, "gain an in-depth understanding of the narrative of Esther. Include God's purpose in presenting this book in the canon of Scripture as well as a paragraph-by-paragraph interpretation of the book." The mechanics behind God's providence are beyond the capability of man's ability to understand. God's intricate plots are known only to Him. It is only after the fact that we are able to understand what God has done. In Chapter 14, we will try to record all of the events that were required to occur (God-directed) in order for the Jews to avoid annihilation. The plot of Esther provides a glimpse of God as the absolute, real-life, master story-writer.

Anti-Semitism

Approximately 1,500 years before the time of Esther God made the following promise to Abram:

> "Now the Lord said to Abram, 'Go forth from your country, and from your relatives and from your father's house, to the land which I will show you; and I will make you a great nation, and I will bless you, and make your name great; and so you shall be a blessing; and I will bless those who bless you, and the one who curses you I will curse'" (Genesis 12:1–3).

---

25   Ibid., Huey, Volume 4, 781.

By saying He would curse those who cursed Abram, God was making it clear that there would be animosity toward His chosen people. From Old Testament times to our present day, history has proven this to be true. Individuals and nations have tried to destroy God's chosen people. Paul Tan, author of *Encyclopedia of 7700 Illustrations,* writes, "The greatest persecution in the history of the world may be pinpointed as that of the Jews."[26]

The history of the Israelites from the Exodus to the Exile is filled with both offensive and defensive military struggles against oppressors. On many occasions, God commanded the Israelites to destroy their enemies. At times they obeyed, and at times they did not. On other occasions, the Israelites defended themselves against pagan attacks. The Amalekites, the Assyrians, the Syrians, the Phoenicians, and the Philistines were nations who were antagonistic toward the Jews and attempted to destroy them.[27]

As to the source and reason for anti-Semitism, one needs to look to the source of sin in the world. Thieme writes, "The annals of history have proved conclusively that anti-Semitism is a masterstroke of evil genius. The author and sponsor is that phenomenal prehistoric supercreature, Lucifer, who was renamed 'Satan' in his fallen state. Anti-Semitism is one of the primary weapons used in his attempts to usurp the plan of God."[28]

The book of Esther presents one of the most insidious plots designed to thwart God's perfect plan. One has to believe the author of this plot was Satan himself. As we go through the book, we will see how an attempt is made to wipe the Jewish race off the face of the earth as well as to negate Messianic prophesies, with the result of preventing the birth of Jesus Christ. These prophesies include Jesus, who was to be the seed of Abraham (Genesis 12:3; 18:18), of the tribe of Judah (Genesis 49:10), of the seed of Jacob (Numbers 24:17, 19), and of the seed of David (Psalm 132:11; Jeremiah 23:5, 33:15; Isaiah 11:10).

---

26 Tan, Paul Lee. 1996. *Encyclopedia of 7700 Illustrations: A Treasury of Illustrations, Anecdotes, Facts and Quotations for Pastors, Teachers and Christian Workers.* Garland, TX: Bible Communications, 1979.

27 Thieme, R. B. Jr. 2003. *Anti-Semitism.* Houston: R. B. Thieme, Jr., Bible Ministries, 18-30.

28 Ibid., 85.

Points to remember

1. God told the Israelites to have no other gods before Him.

2. The Israelites repeatedly disobeyed God and worshipped idols.

3. God disciplined the Israelites with increasing levels of punishment.

4. Continued disobedience resulted in exile.

5. Obedience during the exile resulted in deliverance and a renewed relationship with God.

6. Jews after the exile were more committed to following God and were more unified in their relationship with Him.

7. Figures in human history are present throughout Scripture.

8. Historical events in Scripture are often recorded in secular writings.

9. Anti-Semitism is Satanic and was prevalent in the Old Testament.

Principles

1. When a leader sins and rejects God's authority, all those under the leader's authority are affected.

2. God uses unbelievers and believers who are out of fellowship to discipline believers who are in sin and are rejecting Him.

3. Man's sinful nature leads him to disobey and reject God.

4. God's righteousness and justice work in perfect union with His love, and the three together are in harmony with His divine will and plan.

5. God uses nations to punish His chosen people, and then He judges those nations.

6. Your spiritual life and your relationship with God are determined by *your* decision to trust and obey God, not by your parents.

7. God blesses through adversity. He uses hardship for believers to improve their relationship with Him. Obedience to God is required for blessing. Obedience to God's discipline results in blessing for the believer.

8. Disobedience to God in times of discipline leads to further discipline.

9. God puts us on the sideline so we will learn to follow His game plan.

Chapter Four

ESTHER 1:
BANQUETS AND A DISMISSAL

It is time to start the paragraph analysis. Paragraphs are defined per the New American Standard Bible translation. For the first two paragraphs in chapter one, verses 1–4 and 5–9, we will use the template from chapter two. Beginning with Esther 1:10, we will proceed with the study verse-by-verse.

Official banquets

"Now it took place in the days of Ahasuerus, the Ahasuerus who reigned from India to Ethiopia over 127 provinces, in those days as King Ahasuerus sat on his royal throne which was at the citadel in Susa, in the third year of his reign he gave a banquet for all his princes and attendants, the army officers of Persia and Media, the nobles and the princes of his provinces being in his presence. And he displayed the riches of his royal glory and the splendor of his great majesty for many days, 180 days" (Esther 1:1–4).

Terms, Words, Phrases

Observe and record words, terms, or phrases that stand out. These may be things you do not know much about or things you want to study more closely. There is no right or wrong. These are things you observe and want to study further.

Non-routine _____

Key _____

Main nouns _____

Verbs _____

Repetition _____

This is what I put down:

Non-routine—royal throne, citadel in Susa, third year of reign, princes and attendants, army officers (Persia and Media), nobles and princes (of his provinces), riches of royal glory, splendor of majesty, 180 days

Key—banquet

Main nouns—Ahasuerus, India to Ethiopia, 127 provinces

Verbs—displayed

Repetition—reign(ed)

It seems like I recorded almost every word in the paragraph. At the beginning of a book, it can be normal to do this. Everything you are seeing is new. As the story progresses, you end up writing down fewer words, because you have seen many of them before, and you know what they mean. As we study this paragraph, most of these will come up and will be discussed. Instead of defining each of them now, we will wait until we get to the *who, what, when, where, why,* and *how* under the detail analysis section.

Structure

Structure is everything that binds or holds the words, terms, and phrases into a literary unit.

Connectors _____

Structural Progression _____

Literary Laws _____

This is what I put down:

Connectors—"*Now, in* those days, *in* the third year" (temporal or time connectors).

These words focus on the time of events in relation to either the year or date in history or to other events.

Progression—Esther is an historical narrative. There is an *historical progression,* which emphasizes the "what" of the story; *biographical progression,* which emphasizes the "who;" and *chronological progression,* which emphasizes the "when." In Esther, there is definitely a lot of "what" that goes on.

Literary Laws—For this paragraph, I found introduction to the narrative, generalization and particularization, and interchange (chiasm).

Content Analysis

Content analysis is studying the paragraph as a whole unit.

Compare/contrast _____

Paragraph progression _____

Relationship of connectors _____

There are several things to record under this heading. This is what I put down:

Compare/contrast—Nothing specific for this paragraph alone. We will, however, see comparison and contrast between the first and second paragraphs.

Paragraph progression—In introducing the setting, the author uses generalization and particularization to present the *who, what,* and *when.* Regarding time, or *when,* the author progresses from the general, "days of Ahasuerus;" to the more specific, "in those days;" and finally to the exact, "third year of reign." Regarding people, or *who,* the author reverses the progression from those living closest and most well-known to the king, "all his princes and attendants;" to those living further away with a formal military relationship, "army officers of Persia and Media;" and finally to those living furthest away with a more stately relationship, "nobles and princes of his provinces." Regarding administrative control, or *what,* this progression also identifies those Ahasuerus most directly controlled to those he least directly controlled.

Why is progression important? Here it shows that the author reveals order and clarity to what he is writing and his attention to detail. When he gives details, it means the details are needed to understand the story, and we should be aware of them. When details are not present, they do not need to be known. When there is order and clarity of *who, what, when* and *where,* it is easier to understand the *why* and *how.* Here it will help us answer the question, "Why was Ahasuerus having this banquet?" We will see there were actually many banquets.

Relationship of Connectors—What is important about the relationship of connectors, and how are they used in this paragraph? Words of connection move the reader from one idea to another.

When you pick up a book and begin reading, how important is the opening sentence? You want something that immediately connects you to the story. Esther begins with the words, "Now it took place in the days of Ahasuerus." The Hebrew word for *now* is "hayah" (haw-yaw), which means "to exist, i.e., be or become, come to pass".[1] *Hayah* is the first word in what other Old Testament books? There are seven of them. They are Joshua, Judges, Ruth, 1 Samuel, 2 Samuel, Ezekiel, and Jonah.

Have you ever known someone who could tell a story really well—someone who made you hang on to every spoken word? The opening phrase, "now it took place in the days of Ahasuerus," makes me think the writer had this ability.

---

1   Unless otherwise stated, all Hebrew translations are from Biblesoft's *New Exhaustive Strong's Numbers and Concordance with Expanded Greek-Hebrew Dictionary.* 1994, 2003. Biblesoft, Inc. and International Bible Translators, Inc.

Everyone who heard the telling of Esther knew about the exile, Persian rule, hardships, anti-Semitism, and deliverance. Here they were going to get a firsthand account of those people God used in their deliverance. This story was very personal to every Jew who heard it.

I have a deep respect for all those who fought in World War II. Since my early childhood, I have been fascinated with movies and stories of men and women who served in all branches of the military during this time period. The phenomenal acts of heroism during D-Day have always captured my interest. I can just imagine how I would feel if I heard Dick Winters from Stephen Ambrose's book *Band of Brothers* say, "Now it took place on 6 June 1944 in the days Easy Company jumped into Normandy." You are captivated from that moment on, and you want to hear every word spoken. I think the Jews were completely captivated when the story of Esther was told.

Detail analysis

This is where we observe and record answers to the following six questions:

Who _____

What _____

Where _____

When _____

Why _____

How _____

This is what I put down:

Who—King Ahasuerus, princes and attendants, army officers of Persia and Media, nobles and princes of his provinces.

What—A six-month banquet.

Where—Citadel (palace) in Susa (Nehemiah 1:1).

When—Third year of the reign of Ahasuerus, 483 BC.

> **Why**—Why is Ahasuerus having a banquet? This is critical. Why does Ahasuerus display "the riches of his royal glory and the splendor of his great majesty"?
>
> **How**—How did Ahasuerus do this?

Before we go further, we should acknowledge that Herodotus, who lived from around 490 to 431 BC, wrote of historical events during the time period of Esther. At times, we will mention his work in relation to the context of the story. We have already seen that Josephus has written about Esther. We will reference additional information from him as we go through the story.

Who

Let's start with King Ahasuerus. "The Hebrew word used throughout the book is *ahasweros* ("Ahasuerus") which is considered a variant of Xerxes's name. Xerxes is the Greek form of the Persian *Khshayarsha*."[2] The name "Xerxes" is found in many quotations used in this book. Footnotes are presented. I will use the name "Ahasuerus" when speaking of the king.

What do we need to know about him? He was king of Persia for twenty-one years, 485 to 465 BC. He is mentioned in Ezra 4:6 and Daniel 9:1. He is the son of Darius I, 520–486 BC and is the grandson of Cyrus the Great, 550–530 BC. "Xerxes was designated heir-apparent by his father and served as satrap of Babylon from 498 BC to his accession in 486."[3]

He was very different from his grandfather and father. Where Cyrus was generous and benevolent and Darius was an effective administrator and builder, "Xerxes lacked the toleration and sensitivity of Cyrus and the foresight of Darius."[4] He was impulsive and tended to listen to bad advice. Remember what we said in the historical context—how he burned Athens after the battle of Thermopylae? At times, he was selfish, uncaring, whiny, petty, and foolish. He had an irrational temper and occasionally exhibited fits of rage. Examples are found in Esther 1:12 and 7:10.

Although he tried to live up to the legacies of his father and grandfather, he could not. We will see the above characteristics throughout the book of

2   Huey, F. B. Jr. 1988. *The Expositor's Bible Commentary.* Grand Rapids: Zondervan Publishing House, Volume 4, 797.

3   Bromiley, Geoffrey W. 2002. *The International Standard Bible Encyclopedia, Revised,* S. 4:1161.

4   Ibid.

Esther. Like his father, he left an army defeated in the field and came home. Darius left the battle of Marathon to go home. Ahasuerus left the battle of Salamis to go home.

Despite his personality flaws, Ahasuerus is king, and he has great power. We will see he sometimes has difficulty making decisions without input from others, yet he is not afraid to issue edicts or laws that negatively affect the lives of everyone in the empire.

The Persian Empire was huge. It consisted of 127 provinces from India to Ethiopia (Esther 8:9). India would be present-day western Pakistan, and Ethiopia would include present-day southern Egypt to northern Ethiopia. The Hebrew word for *provinces* is "mediynah" (med-ee-naw'), which means a "jurisdiction; by implication, a district (as ruled by a judge); generally, a region."

Although all people were technically under Persian rule, there were different nationalities with different languages throughout the provinces. In some ways, the king had absolute authority over everyone in the Empire; yet with such a large landmass and a diverse population, it was difficult for the king to keep track of everything going on. We will see this was particularly true for Ahasuerus, who was often more interested in personal interests than national concerns.

Ahasuerus invited his princes and attendants. These were people in his palace or close by in Susa. He may well have known everyone by name. This would be like the President inviting everyone from the US Senate and House of Representatives in Washington, DC.

He invited the army officers of Persia and Media. These were the military leaders in the Empire. He specifically identifies army officers from Media, which had been defeated by Persia in 550 BC, yet had retained a prominent position in the Persian empire. To invite these people means Ahasuerus was planning something big. This would be like the President inviting all the military leaders—not only from the Pentagon, but also from every military base in the world under the control of the Department of Defense.

He invited the nobles and the princes of his provinces. These were all the local authorities in the Persian Empire. This is like the President inviting every governor of every state as well as mayors of big cities in the United States. Ahasuerus has brought all of the military and state officials to Susa.

What

Ahasuerus is inviting his guests to a series of banquets that lasted for a total of 180 days. When it says, "and he displayed the riches of his royal glory and the splendor of his great majesty for many days, 180 days," does it mean everyone sat around for six months, drank, and partied? I do not think so. I think these banquets were more like State dinners with a strong emphasis on political, administrative, and military planning. It would be like the president inviting dignitaries to the White House. All of the people invited were under the authority of Ahasuerus; however, some lived very far away. I think the military people would have had meetings at the "Persian Pentagon," and the political people would have discussed administrative issues with Ahasuerus's staff. I think these were working banquets. The reason *why* is coming up.

Where

These events take place at the citadel in Susa, which was the winter place of residence. Other palaces were located in Persepolis, Babylon, and Ecbatana. Susa is named in Nehemiah 1:1. On a sidelight, the son of Ahasuerus, Artaxerxes, wrote that the citadel in Susa was destroyed by fire. What does this mean? Remember our question, "When was Esther written?" "An author from a later period probably would not have known about the palace, so it can be inferred that the author of this book was someone who was close to the events chronologically."[5]

When

The paragraph occurs during the third year of Ahasuerus' reign, 483 BC. Since Ahasuerus was born in 520 BC, we can assume he is thirty-seven years old at the beginning of the story. He is certainly old enough to be responsible for his actions. We will keep track of time as we study the book. In the context, we covered a lot of years, and a lot of events had to occur in order to set up the main conflicts that the book discusses. We will see as we get closer to the climax of the story, time will shift to months, days, and hours instead of years.

X 486 BC—Ahasuerus becomes king

X 483 BC—story begins

490	485	480

---

5   Walvoord, John F. and Roy B. Zuck. 1983. *The Bible Knowledge Commentary.* Wheaton, IL: Victor Books, S. 1:702.

Why

Why is Ahasuerus having banquets? This is critical. Remember, the Greeks defeated the Persians at the Battle of Marathon in 490 BC. Darius was king of Persia at the time. This defeat and the idea that he had to avenge his father's military failure was a primary motivation for Ahasuerus in his early reign. From the moment he became king, he believed he had to fight and defeat the Greeks. In 483 BC, he was preparing to invade Greece. He did so in 481 BC. "According to Herodotus, it took Xerxes four years to get ready for the invasion he launched in 481."[6]

Ahasuerus knew the campaign he was planning was going to be costly in money, lives, and time. Logistically, it was going to be a monumental task to invade Greece. If you look at how the Persians crossed the Bospherus strait and built a pontoon bridge connecting Asia and Europe, you will see what it took in those days to prosecute a war. It took six months to dig a canal across the Isthmus of Athos.

Ahasuerus was giving a series of banquets or state dinners with military, political, and administrative emphasis. He was gathering support from all 127 provinces in order to prepare for war. He included the Carthaginian navy in the invasion, and I imagine they were invited to the banquets as well.

Why does it say Ahasuerus "displayed the riches of his royal glory and the splendor"? If you go to the bank to borrow money, it is helpful to show you have assets to back up your loan request. Ahasuerus was trying to impress everyone because he wanted their assistance to go to war. It takes money and wealth to wage a war, and people are more likely to support the effort if there are ample resources backing them. Wealth gives confidence in victory and encourages everyone to participate.

As we know, the invasion was unsuccessful. We will see how this fits into our story. After his defeat, Ahasuerus returns to Persia with the idea of building things—much like his father, Darius.

How

How did Ahasuerus do the things he did? He was in absolute power. When he said he wanted to have a banquet for 180 days and prepare to go to war, the wheels moved.

---

6   Ibid.

Interpretation

Ahasuerus reigned over the Persian Empire, which included land from India to Ethiopia. During the early part of his reign, he was most interested in preparing a military campaign against Greece. In order to do this, he had to garner support from political and military leaders in the country. In the third year of his reign, he wined and dined all those who were necessary to help him wage war. For six months, he discussed military strategy, logistics, and administrative requirements. To bolster his perceived capability, he displayed his immense wealth.

Theme

The theme is the central thought of the paragraph.

Theme Statement _____

This is what I put down:

Theme Statement

Ahasuerus gives banquets; obtains military and political support for war.

What do you think about the above observations for paragraph one? Were you amazed at the amount of information available in these few verses? It may be more than you normally find when studying a passage. If the above exercise seemed tedious, don't be discouraged. As we do this next paragraph it will seem easier.

Celebration banquets

"When these days were completed, the king gave a banquet lasting seven days for all the people who were present at the citadel in Susa, from the greatest to the least, in the court of the garden of the king's palace. There were hangings of fine white and violet linen held by cords of fine purple linen on silver rings and marble columns, and couches of gold and silver on a mosaic pavement of porphyry, marble, mother-of-pearl and precious stones. Drinks were served in golden vessels of various kinds, and the royal wine was plentiful according to the king's bounty.

The drinking was done according to the law, there was no compulsion, for so the king had given orders to each official of his household that he should do according to the desires of each person. Queen Vashti also gave a banquet for the women in the palace which belonged to King Ahasuerus" (Esther 1:5–9).

Words, Terms, Phrases

Non-routine—citadel in Susa, court of the garden of the king's palace, white and violet linen, purple linen, silver rings, marble columns, couches of gold and silver, porphyry, marble, mother-of-pearl, precious stones, golden vessels, royal wine, king's bounty, according to the law.

Key—banquet.

Main nouns—king, Queen Vashti, women in the palace.

Verbs—king had *given orders.*

Repetition—banquet.

Structure

Connectors—*When* these days were completed (temporal connector), Queen Vashti *also* gave (logical connector of comparison) …

Structural progression—Same as first paragraph. There are historical, biographical, and chronological progressions.

Content Analysis

Compare/contrast:

There are things we can compare and contrast in this paragraph as well as with the first paragraph. Banquets are mentioned both in the first and second paragraphs. Let's begin by comparing the king's two banquets (present in the first and second paragraphs) and then the two banquets in the second paragraph (the one given by the king and the one given by the queen).

1:1–4	1:5–9
WHO (Is attending)	**WHO (Is attending)**
His princes and attendants, the army officers of Persia and Media, the nobles and the princes of his provinces being in his presence *Select group (larger number)*	People who were present at the citadel in Susa, greatest to the least *Everybody (smaller number)*
WHAT	**WHAT**
Displayed the riches of his royal glory and the splendor of his great majesty *Showing off (See Why)*	Objects of wealth identified specifically in great detail *Showing off (See Why)*
WHERE	**WHERE**
The citadel in Susa (stronghold, fortress) *Formal atmosphere*	In the court of the garden of the king's palace *Informal Atmosphere*
WHEN	**WHEN**
180 days	Seven days
WHY	**WHY**
Purpose—prepare for war Gain support	Purpose—celebrate Thank people

Two banquets in second paragraph:

King's banquet	Queen Vashti's banquet
All the people	*The women*
A lot is said	Not much is said
Great detail	No detail
Royal wine	No mention of wine
In the garden of the king's palace	In the palace which belonged to king Ahasuerus
King has wealth	Nothing identified as belonging to queen
King has authority and power	No authority or power identified with queen

We can see what the authority structure is in the kingdom. Everything belongs to the king. The king has absolute authority over people and property. Although this was a normal, accepted right of being the king, in the following paragraphs, we will see devastating results when the king misuses his authority.

Relationship of Connectors

"*When* these days were completed"—Separates the official, military, and political banquet that was going on for 180 days from what appears to be a celebration banquet.

"Queen Vashti *also* gave"—A comparison is made between the two banquets—the one the king gave and the one the queen gave.

Detail Analysis

Who

"People at the citadel in Susa, greatest to the least"—I think the king wants to include everybody in his immediate administration, no matter what their position, status, or wealth. Both royalty and commoners were invited. It is possible that Mordecai, who we will meet later, was invited to this banquet.

Queen Vashti—we meet the queen. Other than the Bible, there is no recorded history of Ahasuerus having a queen named Vashti. It is recorded that he did have a queen named Amestris, only in the sense she was the mother of Artaxerxes, the son of Ahasuerus who became ruler after his assassination. Herodotus describes Amestris by giving an account of what she did in her later life. "I am informed that Amestris, the wife of Xerxes, when she had grown old, made return for her own life to the god who is said to be beneath the earth by burying twice seven children of Persians who were men of renown."[7] This descriptive act reveals a definite cruelty in Amestris.

The fact that nothing is recorded of Vashti does not mean she did not exist. It is possible that Vashti and Amestris are one in the same. If this is true, it may shed light on what happens to her at the end of this chapter.

What

The king and queen are having separate banquets. This was not unusual for Persian culture. According to the Greek author and philosopher Plutarch of Chaeronea, "Persian custom dictated that the kings would ordinarily eat with their legitimate wives, but when they wanted to 'riot and drink,' they would send their wives away and call in their concubines."[8]

The king now has the support he needs to go to war. The 180-day banquet was successful. It is now time to celebrate and thank the people of Susa. This is not too different from what goes on today. After a successful political campaign, the winning side usually celebrates its victory.

The king is rich and likes to show off his wealth. The sentence, "there were hangings of fine white and violet linen held by cords of fine purple linen on silver rings and marble columns, and couches of gold and silver on a mosaic pavement of porphyry, marble, mother-of-pearl and precious stones"

---

7   Histories. http://artflx.uchicago.edu/perseus-cgi/citequery3.pl?

8   Elwell, Walter A. and Philip Wesley Comfort. 2001. *Tyndale Bible Dictionary.* Wheaton, Ill.: Tyndale House Publishers, S. 1284.

indicates royalty, power, and wealth. Later in the book, we see additional references to royal wealth (Esther 8:15).

The detail given here suggests the author had firsthand knowledge of the settings and the occasion. Possibly he or she was an eyewitness. It may even have been Mordecai.

The king likes to drink, and he likes to share his good wine. He does not make anyone drink, but rather says, "he should do according to the desires of each person."

The statement, "according to the law" in Esther 1:8 is interesting. The Hebrew word for *law* is "dath" (dawth), which means "a royal edict or statute." Why does the author bring up the law at this point in the story? He or she may be preparing us for future events. Questions about who makes the law, who follows the law, how the law is changed, and what happens when the law is broken will come up several times in the story.

Can you see the problem arising? A bunch of guys, who have worked very hard for six months and have successfully put together support for a military campaign, sit around and drink wine for seven days. One happens to be king of the empire, is occasionally irrational, and listens to bad advice. Trouble is on the horizon.

Where

The banquet takes place "in the court of the garden of the king's palace." This location suggests a more informal atmosphere than the previous six-month banquet which was held "at the citadel in Susa."

When

The banquet occurred during the third year of the reign of Ahasuerus, 483 BC. It was after the 180-day banquet, when the work had been done.

X 486 BC—Ahasuerus becomes king
X 483 BC—story begins

483 BC—after 180-day banquets X

490   485   480

Why

Everyone had worked hard for six months, and the King wanted to celebrate.

How

Ahasuerus just did it. He was king. As we shall see, Ahasuerus listened to bad advice. There were probably those around him who wanted to have a big party as well.

Although there was nothing wrong with having a party and celebrating six months of hard work, the decision of the king and other leaders to drink for seven days was not a good idea.

Interpretation

After working hard for six months putting together a military and logistical plan to invade Greece, Ahasuerus throws a party for "all the people who were present at the citadel in Susa." This appears to be a celebration. The wealth and generosity of Ahasuerus is clearly seen. Guests are free to drink wine, but are not required to do so. While the king and his guests drank wine, queen Vashti and the women had their own banquet in the palace, which belonged to Ahasuerus.

Theme Statement

King gives banquet, shows wealth and thanks supporters.

From here on, each paragraph will be presented verse-by-verse, rather than using the template. It may still be beneficial to use the template when you do the study yourself, however. Observations will be recorded, and interpretations will be presented with the verses. When the template is needed to address something specific, it will be used.

A drunken command

> "On the seventh day, when the heart of the king was merry with wine, he commanded Mehuman, Biztha, Harbona, Bigtha, Abagtha, Zethar and Carkas, the seven eunuchs who served in

the presence of King Ahasuerus, to bring Queen Vashti before the king with her royal crown in order to display her beauty to the people and the princes, for she was beautiful. But Queen Vashti refused to come at the king's command delivered by the eunuchs. Then the king became very angry and his wrath burned within him" (Esther 1:10–12).

Where

Court of the garden of the king's palace.

When

483 BC, third year of the reign of King Ahasuerus.

After seven days of drinking.

> "On the seventh day ..." (Esther 1:10)

A temporal connector is used, identifying a specific moment in time. It tells us they have been drinking for seven days. Would the party have gone on longer than seven days if the king had not summoned the queen? I think it might have.

> "when the heart of the king was merry with wine ..." (Esther 1:10)

"Merry with wine" is a figure of speech, a euphemism for "the king was drunk."

> "he commanded Mehuman, Biztha, Harbona, Bigtha, Abagtha, Zethar and Carkas, the seven eunuchs who served in the presence of King Ahasuerus ..." (Esther 1:10)

Hebrew words: Eunuch cariyc (saw-reece'); or caric (saw-reece'); from an unused root meaning "to castrate." A eunuch is a male who was castrated.

When the king gives a command, people obey—and things happen. Here he gives a command to seven specific eunuchs. It is possible they are the same eunuchs in Esther 6:14. Eunuchs were important in the operation of the palace duties. They were generally trusted, because it was thought they would be less likely to challenge the king in two areas.

First, they would not be a threat to the king's wives or the women in his harem. Second, they would be less likely to be a threat to overthrow the king. Eunuchs play a significant role in the plot development in Esther, both directly and indirectly. Esther develops a good relationship with one of the eunuchs; Mordecai is honored because of his discovery that two eunuchs were trying to assassinate the king; and one of the above eunuchs, Harbona, later plays a role in the death of Haman. Eunuchs are also found elsewhere in the Bible.

> "And some of your sons who will issue from you, whom you will beget, will be taken away, and they will become officials [eunuchs] in the palace of the king of Babylon" (Isaiah 39:7).

God placed Jewish eunuchs in the Babylonian palace. It is possible He also placed them in the Persian palace. We will meet a very important eunuch in Esther 2. It is very likely God placed him in the palace for a specific purpose:

> "to bring Queen Vashti before the king with her royal crown
> in order to display her beauty to the people and the princes,
> for she was beautiful" (Esther 1:11).

The king did not just want to see his wife, Vashti. He wanted to see the queen "with her royal crown, in order to display her beauty to the people and the princes, for she was beautiful." I know it is early in the story; however, this verse generates controversy, and there are issues to discuss. Ask yourself the following: Does the king have the right to order the queen to come before him to "display her beauty to the people and the princes"? Does the king have the right to order the queen to come before him—but is he making a mistake in doing so? Is the king simply behaving like a drunken pig?

What was the king's motive in summoning the queen? What does it mean when it says "to display her beauty to the people and the princes, for she was beautiful"? Does it mean the king's intentions were immoral, possibly having Vashti expose herself? Commentaries have been written suggesting Vashti was to appear naked. "Some Jewish sources interpreted the order to mean that she was to appear nude, except for her crown."[9]

---

9   Ibid., Huey, Volume 4. 800.

I find no evidence to suggest the king planned for the queen to do anything immoral. It is my opinion, the king simply wanted to display the queen's beauty (clothed) so people would think highly of him. In Esther 1:4, he "displayed the riches of his royal glory and the splendor of his great majesty" to all those who attended the six-month banquets. I think the king looked at the queen as a possession and simply wanted to impress his guests.

Even if the king had no intention of showing off Vashti in an immoral fashion, was he commanding her to do something against Persian law, just by coming into the presence of the other guests? Josephus writes in *Antiquities of the Jews* that Persian laws "forbid the wives to be seen by strangers."[10] He does not state if this includes being fully clothed as well as being naked. If such an action was against Persian law, it is unlikely the king had the authority to command the queen to violate the law. It should be noted that the events Josephus writes about occurred 500 years earlier. His source for the knowledge of the events is not known. His recordings are very similar to what is written in the Bible, which does not mention the king's command as a violation of Persian law.

In the next paragraph, we will discuss how the king and his advisors manipulate Persian law. On the surface, they appear to want to follow the law as it is written. In reality, they create new laws to serve their needs. I think in the situation with Vashti, the king was possibly commanding her to do something that likely violated Persian law—or at least, was very objectionable to custom. Whether or not he knew exactly what he was doing is not known. Remember, he was drunk.

I do think it was unlikely the king was commanding the queen to do something immoral in front of his guests. It would have been extremely out of custom for that time period. In addition, the king has worked very hard for six months, gathering support for his military campaign. To display the queen in an immoral manner in front of his guests would diminish his reputation and could possibly affect the support he needed to wage war. In the next paragraph, we will see the king's wise men express a concern that if Vashti is not punished for refusing to come before the king when summoned, women throughout Persia will not show respect to their husbands. If this were truly the case, I think women would certainly not show respect to their husbands if the queen was required to be displayed inappropriately. I wonder how many times in the past Ahasuerus had a party, became drunk, and summoned Vashti?

---

10   Antiquities of the Jews. http://www.earlyjewishwritings.com/text/josephus/ant11. html.

So did the king have the right to summon the queen? If in fact Persian laws forbid women to be seen by strangers, even if fully clothed, the king did not have the right to summon the queen. If it were not against Persian law, and if the king did not have any immoral intentions for the queen, then it is my opinion he did have the right, because he was the king and could order people to do things.

The next question is, "Did the king make the right decision in summoning his wife in this manner?" For all the men reading this, when was the last time you "summoned" your wife, in this way or any way? The king was absolutely wrong in getting drunk and then summoning the queen to come to his party and show off her beauty. Husbands should not show off their wives as possessions, should not get drunk and summon their wives, and should not be inconsiderate in forcing their wives to appear in public. We will see this is a recurring problem for the king as the story develops. He is self-centered and makes bad decisions.

I want to take a minute and talk about the issue of making bad decisions. I do not want to pick on Ahasuerus too often; however, he is such a good example of someone who makes poor decisions. Many principles of personal character and conduct will be developed from the king's mistakes. The truth is that you and I often exhibit some of the same characteristics present in the king. Here he is definitely drunk, impaired, and is making decisions that are wrong.

Principle 10: Making decisions when you are not in fellowship with God often leads to actions that are not in line with His plan.

As a believer, hopefully you do not participate in seven-day drunken parties. But I guarantee you that everyone reading this book sins in some way. The reality is, when you sin, you are not in fellowship with God. When you are not in fellowship, your thoughts are not godly, and you cannot think clearly. Your decisions will likely be wrong, and they may not be in line with His plan. Sin may be lascivious or legalistic in nature, and one's expression may be mental, verbal, or overt. When you sin and are out of fellowship, you are incapable of making good decisions.

Recall a time you have been angry or hurt. What were your thoughts? Did you act on them? After the issue was resolved were your thoughts different from those you had when you were angry or hurt? Did you have to apologize for any wrong behavior?

For whatever reason, when you get out of line from God's viewpoint, you do not make good decisions. The result of making bad decisions leads to our next principle.

Principle 11: Mental sins lead to bad decisions, which often result in destructive behavior.

The temptation to sin begins in the mind. As explained above, the result may lead to mental, verbal, or overt expression of sin. Remember, God does not tempt anyone to sin (James 1:13–15).

This principle is seen many times in the book of Esther, and I believe all of us have fallen into this trap. Destructive events, which occur from bad decisions, are usually not sudden, spur-of-the-moment events. They are usually the result of many wrong decisions; each by itself appearing insignificant and harmless, yet when combined, put you in a position to commit a sin that may have catastrophic results. Furthermore, the expression of sin usually begins with the mental decision to turn away from God. Verbal and overt sins follow afterwards.

Let me illustrate. Assume point A represents being in fellowship with God, and point Z represents committing a sin that results in a destructive event. A person generally does not go directly from point A to point Z. A believer in fellowship who is walking daily with our Lord Jesus Christ is not expected to one day wake up, hate his neighbor, become a drunk, and have an affair.

The process of going from point A to point Z usually requires the person to go from A to B, from B to C, from C to D, and so on. Point B is usually a mental sin and may simply be turning your eyes away from God and looking for a human viewpoint rather than a divine viewpoint for answers. Point C may be letting yourself get into a situation where you are easily tempted. The process continues until you get to point Y. At this point, there is usually verbal or overt sin. From there, it is very easy to go to point Z—in fact, you can't wait to get to Z! You can even justify to yourself why you should go to Z.

At each letter, there is a decision. Each of us has volition and can choose to look to God for His solution—or we can look at what the world says. When we look to God and deal with the situation through biblical doctrine and the filling of the Holy Spirit, we immediately go back to point A. When we deal with the situation through the human viewpoint, we go to the next letter.

A	B (mental)	C (mental)	D (mental)
	Volition	**Volition**	**Volition**
Right—	Cover in love (or)	Forgive (or)	Forgive (or)
Wrong—	Take offense	Become angry	Justify anger

E (overt)	F (overt)	... on to Z
Volition	**Volition**	
Act lovingly (or)	Temptation (no)	
Malign	Temptation (yes)	

I believe the seeds of our sin patterns are planted at birth with the sin nature that resides in each of us. Certainly there are environmental influences which develop these patterns and lower the threshold of resistance to temptation. If your area of weakness falls under the category of lasciviousness, you may be inclined towards drunkenness, drug use, sexual sins, or violence. If your area of weakness falls under the category of legalism, you may be inclined towards jealousy, pride, gossip, or slander. All are sin in God's eyes.

When you are in fellowship with God and are growing in the "grace and knowledge of our Lord and Savior Jesus Christ" (2 Peter 3:18), you are unlikely to go down the pathway of lascivious degeneracy. What if you lose your job, your wife is unkind to you, or your neighbor's tree falls on your house? If your mental response to any of these events is anger, fear, or self-pity, you have sinned. You have gone from A to B or B to C. In looking away from God and toward a human viewpoint, you have lowered the threshold for other sin. You might justify to yourself that it is okay to surf the internet and look at things that excite you. They may not be pornography by man's definition, yet they turn your mind to ungodly thoughts. You can quickly get to point Y and then Z. Once you go down this path, there is little resistance to thinking, doing, or saying whatever makes you feel good physically. Marriages have been destroyed through sinful progression such as this.

It is easy to point a finger at those who are guilty of lascivious types of sins. It is important to be aware of the sins of legalism as well. Pride, jealousy, lust, hate, guilt, gossip, and bitterness can be just as devastating. Ladies, let's say you hear that one of your girlfriends is having marital problems. Do you go to God with this knowledge, asking Him what you should do, or do you pick up the phone and call another friend and gossip? If you gossip and malign, you have sinned. You may be contributing to the destruction of someone's marriage.

We all have to face the fact we are sinners and are tempted to sin. The best way to prevent spending time at point Z is *not* trying to prevent going from point Y to point Z. It is staying in fellowship and trying to prevent going from point A to point B.

"And do not get drunk with wine, for that is dissipation, but be filled with the Spirit" (Ephesians 5:18).

Do not make decisions when you are in a position of spiritual weakness or impairment. When you have gone from A to B, do not make decisions that continue the process to Y. Confess your sin and get back to A, and then make those decisions.

How does this principle relate to Esther? In the next paragraph, we will see Ahasuerus make a horrible decision that is very destructive. The seeds for that decision are being planted in this paragraph. Ahasuerus should not get drunk and hang out with certain people who have influence on him. It does not take much for him to make bad decisions.

"But Queen Vashti refused to come at the king's command delivered by the eunuchs" (Esther 1:12).

The connector of contrast *but* tells us something is changing and how it is changing. If you ever thought connecting words were not important, think about the importance of this *but*. This is one of the most important words in the book. Here, it is one of the reasons the rest of the book is written. If this *but* was not present, the events in the rest of the book may have turned out much differently. Think about it.

Why do you think Vashti refused to come when summoned by the king? The story is not clear on her reason not to go when she was called. According to Josephus, she did so "out of regards to the laws of the Persians."[11]

Did the queen have a right to refuse the king, and was she right in her refusal to go to the king? I have read and heard commentaries that state her refusal was morally a right thing to do. It is my opinion that if she was being commanded to do something illegal or immoral, she had a right to refuse the order. If it was not illegal or immoral, she did not have a right to refuse the

---

11   Antiquities of the Jews. http://www.earlyjewishwritings.com/text/josephus/ant11. html.

king, even if she did not want to go. The king was her legitimate authority, both by marriage and by the fact he was king. By refusing the king, Vashti did place herself in great danger. To not go to the king when summoned was very risky. A little later, we will see where it is risky going to the king when *not* summoned. Knowing what was to happen, would it have been better for Vashti to go to the king, even if such action was illegal or immoral? You decide.

So what was the king's response? He got mad. Why? He was used to getting his way, and now he was not. Everyone around him saw that he was not getting his way. The queen had just said no to him in front of all his subjects. Being drunk certainly had a negative effect on his emotional response. When it says "wrath burned within him," it means the king was pretty angry.

As we close this paragraph, think about Principle 11, "mental sins lead to bad decisions, which result in destructive behavior." The king has made a bad decision in getting drunk and summoning the queen, but no real harm has occurred. Trouble is on the horizon, however. The next paragraph will reveal the wrath of the king.

Theme Statement

Ahasuerus becomes drunk and summons Vashti, who refuses to appear.

For whatever reason, Vashti refused the king's summons. Whether you think she was morally right and honorable in doing so or simply foolish, her decision angered the king.

Law of convenience

"Then the king said to the wise men who understood the times—for it was the custom of the king so to speak before all who knew law and justice and were close to him: Carshena, Shethar, Admatha, Tarshish, Meres, Marsena and Memucan, the seven princes of Persia and Media who had access to the king's presence and sat in the first place in the kingdom— 'According to law, what is to be done with Queen Vashti, because she did not obey the command of King Ahasuerus delivered by the eunuchs?' In the presence of the king and the princes, Memucan said, 'Queen Vashti has wronged not only the king but also all the princes and all the peoples who are in all the provinces of King Ahasuerus. For the queen's conduct will become known to all the women causing them to look with contempt on their husbands by saying, "King Ahasuerus commanded Queen Vashti to be brought in to his presence, but she did not come." This day the ladies of Persia and Media who have heard of the queen's conduct will speak in the same way to all the king's princes, and there will be plenty of contempt and anger. If it pleases the king, let a royal edict be issued by him and let it be written in the laws of Persia and Media so that it cannot be repealed, that Vashti may no longer come into the presence of King Ahasuerus, and let the king give her royal position to another who is more worthy than she. When the king's edict which he will make is heard throughout all his kingdom, great as it is, then all women will give honor to their husbands, great and small.'" (Esther 1:13–20).

Where

Court of the garden of the king's palace, possibly in the palace

When

483 BC, third year of the reign of King Xerxes.

After seven days of drinking, the King's demand and the Queen's refusal:

> "Then the king said to the wise men who understood the times—for it was the custom of the king so to speak before all who knew law and justice" (Esther 1:13).

Then is a temporal connector from the previous paragraph. Remember, the king had a party and became drunk. He commanded the eunuchs to bring the queen, who refused. The king became angry, and his "wrath burned within him." Now the king is going to consult the wise men who understood the times.

Who were "the wise men," and what does "understood the times" mean? These were people who knew how things were supposed to work in Persia regarding law, protocol, customs, administrative procedures, etc. They were available to the king at all times. As we will see, the king was available to them as well. "Like their Babylonian counterparts, these wise men were astrologers and magicians who gave counsel according to their reading of celestial phenomena."[12] These men functioned much like a combination of the Chief of Staff, personal advisors to the President, Cabinet to the President, US Attorney General, and Supreme Court.

Why did the king consult "the wise men"? Notice the definite article *the* is used instead of the indefinite *a*. This was a very specific group of important people who were advising the king. This is the first of many examples where Ahasuerus reveals his inability to make decisions on his own. He repeatedly seeks advice from others before he acts—and in most cases, he receives wrong advice.

This verse does not say anything about this group having the responsibility of making policy for the kingdom; yet as we will see, that is exactly what they end up doing. Look at the phrase "law and justice." It sounds like they want to follow the law because it is the right thing. We are going to see something quite different in a minute.

> "… and were close to him: Carshena, Shethar, Admatha, Tarshish, Meres, Marsena and Memucan, the seven princes of Persia and Media who had access to the king's presence and sat in the first place in the kingdom" (Esther 1:14).

So now we get the names of "the wise men who understood the times." I get the feeling these princes came from different parts of the kingdom. They should know the law throughout the land as well as how people from different parts of the kingdom would respond to laws and edicts made by the king. With the recommendation they make to the king, it seems they had spent too much time in his presence and too little time with the people who lived in the kingdom.

As we go through this section, I am reminded of our present-day governmental leaders. Do they follow established law based on constitutional principles, or do they make new laws to enable and justify their goals? Do they put the citizens first, or do they put special interests or personal needs first? Do they speak the truth, or do they spin facts? Do they understand the reality of daily life for people throughout the country, or have they been so corrupted by power and influence in the inner circles of the elite that they are not aware of the harm they do? It is quite amazing to see the similarities between leadership in 480 BC Persia and present-day America.

---

12 Ibid., Huey, Volume 4. 801.

What do "close to him," "access to the king's presence," and "sat in the first place in the kingdom" mean? Physically, they were close to the king, meaning they could be in his presence. They were also close to the king, meaning they could influence him as well as prevent others from having influence. They likely could communicate with the king at any time. We will see later if when others went to the king without being summoned they could be put to death. There was probably no routine access to the king without going through these people. They may have also functioned as a corporate chief of staff. It certainly appears they had tremendous power. It is not stated whether or not they had been drinking for seven days as well.

> "According to law, what is to be done with Queen Vashti, because she did not obey the command of King Ahasuerus delivered by the eunuchs?" (Esther 1:15)

I think this is a fair question. Disobeying a command from the king was serious. It does not say much for a close relationship between Ahasuerus and Vashti; however, it does give additional insight into the king's priorities. Protocol, appearance, and the king's authority are more important than relationships. We will see this later in the book when Esther comments to Mordecai that she has not seen the king in thirty days and was afraid to ask to see him (Esther 4:11). If protocol is not followed and it upsets the king, one is in serious trouble.

How does the king address himself? He is being very formal. He addresses himself in the third person, as King Ahasuerus. Memucan appears to be the spokesman for the wise men. He speaks to the king with the other princes present.

> "In the presence of the king and the princes, Memucan said, 'Queen Vashti has wronged not only the king but also all the princes and all the peoples who are in all the provinces of King Ahasuerus'" (Esther 1:16).

What is wrong with this response? Memucan does not answer the king's question. Instead of answering what the law says should be done to the queen for a specific act of disobedience, Memucan inflames the issue with distortion, conjecture, and emotion. He begins to spin the facts. No longer are they dealing with a simple, factual event; they have conjured up a situation where they are now facing a national issue with catastrophic consequences. He is saying that every person in the kingdom has been wronged by Vashti. Right away, I get a distrust of the king's advisors.

Ahasuerus needs factual information to make a decision, not emotional spin to distract him from the issue. A question for you and me today is, "How do we respond when discussing issues that are important?"

Principle 12: Respond with truth, honesty, and integrity in your relationships.

Be truthful, honest, and show integrity in everything you do. Seems easy enough, right? This is hard to do all the time. It means putting aside personal agendas when you should help others. When you are responsible to others, it means thinking of their needs and putting them above yours. When you are in an organization and are asked to provide information to superiors, it means not communicating with false intentions.

This principle is very important in all organizations, including families, churches, schools, businesses, the military, and the government. Whether one is advising superiors who need information to determine policy, educating everyone in an organization, or functioning as a government representative, one's thoughts, actions, and words should reflect truth, honesty, and integrity. When truth, honesty, and integrity are not present in leadership, there is no confidence in the ability of those in authority to lead. A result is deterioration of the morale of those in the organization.

The failure of governmental leaders to follow this principle has had devastating results in our country. Approval ratings for congressional leaders is at an all-time low. We all should pray that our leaders and those who advise them understand and practice this principle.

Why is Memucan making these accusations? What are his motives? He goes on:

> "For the queen's conduct will become known to all the women causing them to look with contempt on their husbands by

saying, 'King Ahasuerus commanded Queen Vashti to be brought in to his presence, but she did not come.' This day the ladies of Persia and Media who have heard of the queen's conduct will speak in the same way to all the king's princes, and there will be plenty of contempt and anger" (Esther 1:17–18).

He continues to paint a picture of national upheaval. The advisors are saying the women of Persia and Media will not show respect to the men because of Vashti's refusal to go to the king when she was summoned. They are worried about female disrespect and marital discord.

Does Memucan really think women will not obey their husbands because Vashti did not go to the king's banquet, or does he simply want to spin a story so the king will get rid of the queen? I believe he knows what he wants to do with the queen. He wants to get rid of her. Memucan is leading the king down a path of which he may or may not be aware. With an advisors like these, the king did not need enemies. When Memucan had completed spinning the charges, he tells the king what to do in the next verse.

"If it pleases the king, let a royal edict be issued by him and let it be written in the laws of Persia and Media so that it cannot be repealed, that Vashti may no longer come into the presence of King Ahasuerus, and let the king give her royal position to another who is more worthy than she" (Esther 1:19).

Look for the words "if it pleases the king" throughout the book. It is used a total of seven times (Esther 1:19; 3:9; 5:4, 8; 7:3; 8:5; and 9:13). What does this phrase sound like? On the surface, it sounds okay—like the speaker wants to know if their suggestion meets with the king's approval. Reading between the lines and putting things in context, however, it often sounds like false praise. Here, Memucan has spun a tale, has the king believing him, and has just offered a solution to which he knows the king does not have the character to object. He wants the king to make a law and gives this false praise to get it.

Memucan never answers the king's question, "according to law …" It is not mentioned if there was in fact a law governing what the queen had done. He comes up with the result he wants, which is to have the queen removed, and then proposes to write a law that gives him the authority to do it. What about the new law? It is to be written in the laws of Persia and Media so it cannot be repealed. This is a serious breach of policy and a misuse of authority. Does the king see it? If he does, he does nothing to object.

What does the new law say? Vashti can no longer come into the presence of the king. The king will give her position to someone more worthy. It does not say that Vashti was to be executed. In Esther 4, we see that the king may execute a person if he or she goes to the king when not summoned.

A couple things regarding this whole process seem strange to me. First, in a culture where the king has supreme authority over life and death and men generally have authority over women, we find the wise men of the country worrying about how women will react to the queen's action. If you can kick the queen out of the palace and order every virgin in the kingdom to be enslaved in the palace (which we will see in the next chapter), why are they worried about what women think and might do? Memucan's analysis and solution in the context of the Persian Empire do not make sense.

Second, on the surface, Memucan gives the appearance of wanting to follow the law, yet he quickly spins the accusations so that the desire to eject the queen, rather than fact, is the deciding factor. In a country where laws are openly discussed, it appears there is a greater interest in creating new laws for personal expediency rather than following old laws which have been tried and tested. Memucan rationalizes a solution in order to justify the result he wants, which is to dismiss the queen.

What is it Memucan and the wise men wanted? Did they want to dismiss the queen so they could control their women? Did they use the excuse of controlling their women so they could have the queen dismissed? One thing we know is that Ahasuerus, who was the supreme authority in Persia, relies on others for advice and ends up being swayed in important decisions. This is something we see throughout the book. We will also see that when a law in Persia is made, it cannot be repealed. A different law must be written to solve the problems the first law creates.

What does this event say about leadership and law-making in Persia? What does it say about our government in the United States today?

Principle 13: When governmental leadership puts self-interest before law and freedom, there is national decay.

When there is an attempt to appease special interest groups at the expense of changing law that protects freedom, there is national decline. Changing law for personal gain is reprehensible. Here I define *law* as "the legal and moral standards by which an organization or nation is founded, by which it has sustained itself, and by which it is governed, with equal application to all."

There is tremendous application of Principles 12 and 13 in America today. We live in a country with the most incredible freedoms ever known to man. No period of history for any nation has ever offered such opportunities. Our freedom is based on principles written in the Constitution. It has been preserved by the millions of Americans who have fought in battles to protect these precious principles.

Our country has been blessed with great leadership in our short history; statesmen who have held to the principles of personal freedom, responsibility, and limited government control, with minimal intrusion into the lives of citizens.

When the government attempts to change the direction of the country by enacting laws which violate the fair and equal application of the law or enact laws to restrict freedom to pursue opportunity, there is national decay. Defining an issue, spinning the facts, transferring the focus onto a different issue, emotionalizing the situation, demonizing those who work hard and are successful, creating class or group envy or anger, and passing laws for the purpose of increasing governmental power are present-day realities in Washington, DC. Our country was founded on the principles of maximum personal freedom and opportunity, with the government's responsibility being to protect those principles. When laws are enacted which impair personal freedom and opportunity, the nation suffers. Our executive, legislative, and judicial branches of government should take notice of events in Persia and the results of leadership gone amuck.

Let's go back to the events in our story. If this new law is not enacted, will the women of Persia revolt as Memucan states? If the new law is enacted, will the women of Persia respect their men more? I think the answer is no in both cases. We have all heard the phrase, "Don't drink and drive." Here it is: "Don't drink and make national decisions." For us, it is "Don't be impaired with sin (or be out of fellowship with God) and make decisions."

Although not stated, the wise men may have simply wanted to get rid of Vashti. If Vashti was Queen Amestris, they might have feared her and wanted her removed from the palace. Remember, Amestris was a very cruel queen.

Regardless of the reason, the wise men saw an opportunity to control the king and took advantage of it. After seven days of drinking and the king's hurt pride, I think the wise men knew they could lead Ahasuerus to do whatever they wanted. With the king's state of mind, the case that Memucan presented, and the fact that all the princes were watching, the king did not have much choice. He did not want to look foolish in front of them.

One possible reason they wanted the king to issue the edict is that they did not want the king to lose face. He had just completed putting together a massive national plan to invade Greece, and it would not do him any good if he could not control his own queen.

> "When the king's edict which he will make is heard throughout all his kingdom, great as it is, then all women will give honor to their husbands, great and small" (Esther 1:20).

Phrases like "king's edict," "all his kingdom," and "great as it is" are nothing more than false praise. Can false praise and emotion affect your ability to make good decisions? It did with Ahasuerus.

Principle 14: Listening to false praise can lead to ungodly decisions.

We have already discussed not making decisions when you are not in fellowship with God. Here we see that when people are telling you things you want to hear—rather than the truth—you can easily be swayed into poor decisions. The root cause of this problem is pride. Pride is a vicious mental attitude and a sin. It can take a seemingly upright, moral, selfless individual and change him or her into the most self-righteous, self-centered, egotistical person imaginable. It can also destroy the lives of those who succumb to its lure.

The author of this sin was no other than Lucifer himself. Once the most beautiful angel in heaven, Lucifer was filled with pride when he wanted to be like the most high God (Isaiah 14:12–14). Instead of accepting his position, he wanted to usurp the authority of God.

This is a temptation many people have difficulty resisting. Everybody likes to be esteemed by others. If someone flatters you and says good things about you, it is easy to lose objectivity about yourself. It is a sad reality that many young girls fall victim to predators who lie with false praise and promise, when in reality their motive is only for personal pleasure. Entire lives can be ruined by believing false praise.

The solution to not falling victim to false praise is to stay grounded in the Word of God and to always stay on guard for this temptation. When presented with external praise that seems out of character, discuss things with a trusted friend before you act. Do not inflate yourself with internal praise that is false or beyond objective acknowledgment. Remember what Jesus said to the Pharisees:

> "For everyone who exalts himself will be humbled, and he who humbles himself will be exalted" (Luke 14:11).

James tells us the benefit of being humble as opposed to being proud:

> "But He gives a greater grace. Therefore it says, 'God is opposed to the proud, but gives grace to the humble." Submit therefore to God. Resist the devil and he will flee from you. Draw near to God and He will draw near to you. Cleanse your hands, you sinners; and purify your hearts, you double-minded. Be miserable and mourn and weep; let your laughter be turned into mourning and your joy to gloom. Humble yourselves in the presence of the Lord, and He will exalt you" (James 4:6–10).

When Memucan says "if it pleases the king" in Esther 1:19, he is really saying, "we have already made the decision of what to do, why don't you just put your kingly stamp on things, make it a law, and we can move on to something else." In Esther 1:20, Memucan seals the deal with more false praise—"throughout all his kingdom, great as it is."

Did the wise men respect the king? I don't think they have much respect for the king at this point. They probably fear him, but they do not respect him. It would have been great if the king had stood up to the wise men and said, "No." After this edict is passed, do you think the women will really give honor to their husbands?

Theme Statement

Wise men exaggerate queen's disobedience and recommend her dismissal.

How much time is there between Esther 1:20 and Esther 1:21? I do not think much. The king has a great opportunity to stand up and exert good leadership. He does not do so.

Queen dismissed, women oppressed

> "This word pleased the king and the princes, and the king did as Memucan proposed. So he sent letters to all the king's provinces, to each province according to its script and to every people according to their language, that every man should be the master in his own house and the one who speaks in the language of his own people" (Esther 1:21–22).

Where

Palace
The entire kingdom

When

If we started in 483 BC, the third year of the reign of Ahasuerus (Esther 1:3) and we add the 180 days for the state banquets, the seven day celebration banquet, the dismissal of Vashti, and the notification "to all the king's provinces, to each province according to its script, and to every people according to their language," I think we are close to the fourth year of the reign of Ahasuerus, 482 BC.

X 486 BC—Ahasuerus becomes king

X 483 BC—story begins

483 BC—after 180-day banquets X

482 BC—after Vashti dismissal and notification of empire X

490	485	480

"This word pleased the king and the princes, and the king did as Memucan proposed" (Esther 1:21).

This word is a figure of speech, metonymy, which is substituting one word for another. *This word* is a substitute for Esther 1:20. It "pleased the king." Why is the king pleased? The king thinks he has a way out. He will not have to deal with Vashti or the problems his wise men say will occur with her around.

"The king did as Memucan proposed." Memucan had great power and knew how to use it. This reveals a great flaw in the character of Ahasuerus. He agrees with the decision someone else makes, and the results of that decision have great national effect. Throughout the book of Esther look to see how many times Ahasuerus does what others want him to do. Some of the decisions are bad, and some of them are good. We will see what happens when Esther tells Ahasuerus what to do.

"So he sent letters to all the king's provinces, to each province according to its script and to every people according to their language, that every man should be the master in his own house and the one who speaks in the language of his own people" (Esther 1:22).

If Congress passes a law today and the President signs it, how long does it take before everyone in the country knows? With our system of communication, it is instantaneous. How was the system of communication in Persia in 482 BC? Actually, communication from the king to the rest of the empire was very good. Darius had built a highway in 515 BC, the Royal Road from North Africa to India, which was 1,500 miles long. There were 111 rest stops or inns, with one every eighteen miles. Information was carried by riders on horses. Within days to weeks, everyone in the empire could be informed of new laws. This fact is very important, as it enables events later in the book to occur (Esther 3:13, 8:10).

The logical connector of result, *so,* indicates that because the king liked the idea presented in Esther 1:19–20, making a new law, he had to notify everyone in the kingdom. "To each province according to its script" means the written language of each province. "To every people according to their language" means the spoken language of every person. Every person was made aware of the new edict.

What was it everyone was made aware of? That "every man should be the master in his own house and the one who speaks in the language of his own people." What is "master in his own house"? It means the man would be the authority in his own home. If the wife disobeys, she could be dismissed—just as Vashti had been dismissed. What is "one who speaks in the language of his own people"? The man of the house speaks in the language of his own people—not in the language of his wife's people if they were different from his.

The king agreed to what the wise men had suggested. On the surface, it was so that "every man should be the master in his own house." I think Memucan wanted to get the letters out as soon as possible before the king changed his mind. We will see in chapter two that the king may have had second thoughts about what he had done.

Theme Statement

Queen is dismissed; men remain masters at home.

Things to Remember

Paragraph Theme Statements

Esther 1:1–4—Ahasuerus gives banquets; obtains military and political support for war.

Esther 1:5–9—King gives banquet, shows wealth and thanks supporters.

Esther 1:10–12—Ahasuerus becomes drunk and summons Vashti, who refuses to appear.

Esther 1:13–20—Wise men exaggerate queen's disobedience and recommend her dismissal.

Esther 1:21–22—Queen is dismissed; men remain masters at home.

Principles

10. Making decisions when you are not in fellowship with God often leads to actions that are not in line with His plan.

11. Mental sins lead to bad decisions, which result in destructive behavior.

12. Respond with truth, honesty, and integrity in your relationships.

13. When governmental leadership puts self-interest before law and freedom, there is national decay.

14. Listening to false praise can lead to ungodly decisions.

Chapter Five

ESTHER 2:
A NEW QUEEN

A Plan to make the king happy

"After these things when the anger of King Ahasuerus had subsided, he remembered Vashti and what she had done and what had been decreed against her. Then the king's attendants, who served him, said, 'Let beautiful young virgins be sought for the king. Let the king appoint overseers in all the provinces of his kingdom that they may gather every beautiful young virgin to the citadel of Susa, to the harem, into the custody of Hegai, the king's eunuch, who is in charge of the women; and let their cosmetics be given them. Then let the young lady who pleases the king be queen in place of Vashti.' And the matter pleased the king, and he did accordingly" (Esther 2:1–4).

Where

The palace in Susa and the entire kingdom.

When

"After these things"—After the edict had been sent throughout the kingdom.

483–482 BC, before Ahasuerus leaves to invade Greece in 481 BC.

X 486 BC—Ahasuerus becomes king

X 483 BC—story begins

483 BC—after 180-day banquets X

482 BC—after Vashti dismissal and notification of empire X

Sometime after Vashti dismissal X

490	485	480

"After these things when the anger of King Ahasuerus had subsided, he remembered Vashti and what she had done and what had been decreed against her" (Esther 2:1).

"After these things" is a temporal connector, connecting Esther 1 with Esther 2. This is an interesting verse. When taken at face value, it does give us objective facts; however, I believe there are deeper meanings behind the facts the author does not tell us. The king has stopped being angry. We then become aware of what the king remembers. He remembers Vashti, her previous position as queen, her refusal to come when summoned, her punishment, that she can no longer come into the presence of the king, and the plan to find another queen. The verse does not tell us what the king thinks about those things he remembers.

Is the king happy or sad? Does he regret his decision to punish the queen? Does he accept the decision he made, and does he now want to move forward? What do you think the king is thinking? I think he regrets the events that have happened. I think he wishes Vashti were still around. I don't think this is about missing the queen because of sex. He had a harem full of women. I think he misses her because she was the queen, and he wants a queen—maybe for political reasons. He missed Vashti as his female counterpart in his role as king.

It does not say the king thinks he has made a mistake. Knowing Ahasuerus, he does not sound like the kind of person who would admit he was wrong. He makes no attempt to correct the error, nor does he give any solution to the thoughts he is having. Like before, he waits for advice from others on what to do.

Have you ever been angry and made a rash decision that ended up hurting yourself and others? When you come to your senses, you look back and see you have been foolish, thoughtless, and maybe even godless. It has happened to all of us. When it happens, how should you respond?

Principle 15: The solution to error is to admit, apologize, accept consequences, make restitution if possible, alter behavior, and move on.

The solution is not to cover up with another error or to live in guilt or self-pity. Since we all sin, make mistakes, and occasionally hurt others, there is tremendous application of this principle. Remember this in marriage, family, school, work, church, or wherever you are. Remember 1 John 1:9.

Failure to follow this principle is common in leadership—particularly in government. It seems that many times those in authority find it difficult to admit failure in their leadership ability and decision-making. Rather than face the truth of their own actions, they blame others, and then continue down the same wrong pathway. The embarrassment of admitting failure at the moment seems greater than the destructive effect of long-term deceit of continuing to deny truth. The result, however, is erosion of trust and confidence in leadership ability.

So does the king admit he was wrong—and does he try to correct his error? Not exactly! Instead of dealing with the problem he created, the king listens to advice from others on how to get himself out of a situation. He digs a deeper hole for himself and his country. If the king realized he had listened to bad advice to get rid of Vashti, why does he listen to more bad advice? I think Satan was watching this very closely—a king who had great power over God's chosen people was being led to do some crazy things.

"Then the king's attendants, who served him, said, 'Let beautiful young virgins be sought for the king'" (Esther 2:2).

Now, isn't this the most self-serving, arrogant "solution" to a self-inflicted situation? Well, enter the king's attendants. It does not say whether or not they were the same wise men who understood the law in Esther 1:13–14. It could have been the same wise men led by Memucan, but we don't know.

Why are they making this suggestion to the king? The king probably has 1,000 girls in his harem, so the answer is not more women. It is possible that they feared the king would bring Vashti back. If the king did so, Vashti would probably have them killed. I do not think they were thinking about the king. They were thinking only about themselves. The attendants go on:

"Let the king appoint overseers in all the provinces of his kingdom that they may gather every beautiful young virgin to the citadel of Susa, to the harem, into the custody of Hegai, the king's eunuch, who is in charge of the women; and let their cosmetics be given them" (Esther 2:3).

Remember, the king "reigned from India to Ethiopia over 127 provinces" (Esther 1:1). "Beautiful young virgins" would be brought from all over the kingdom. The Hebrew word for "gather" is *qabats* (kaw-bats'), which means to "collect, assemble, gather, heap, resort, surely, take up." The Hebrew word for "custody" is *yad* (yawd), which has many meanings, including "custody, debt, dominion, force." These words suggest that this was not a voluntary request. If families did not bring out their beautiful virgin daughters, overseers would come into homes and take them. Can you imagine the magnitude of what was being proposed? What national upheaval would result?

In Esther 1:17–18, the wise men worried about women showing contempt to their husbands if something was not done about Vashti's refusal to come when summoned. Here there does not seem to be much worry about the contempt women might now have toward the king. I wonder if the king's attendants had daughters who might be selected, or if they would be excluded.

Leaders who pass laws should be bound to the consequences of the laws—just as everyone is bound. There should be no exceptions.

Kings had harems in those times. It was a fact of life the king had many women with whom he could choose to have sex. The Hebrew words used for "harem" are *bayith* (bah'-yith) house, and *'ishshah* (ish-shaw') women," or "house of the women."

While the king had the authority to do what he wanted, the question is, "How many women does it take to satisfy the king?" Forcing virgins in the country to leave their families and go to the king is an act of extreme selfishness. Because the king got angry and listened to advisors who told him to dismiss the queen, and now probably regretted it, he was going to follow advice from his attendants that would devastate families throughout the entire kingdom.

About whom are the king's attendants now thinking? When making decisions or advising those who make decisions that affect others, of whom should you be thinking?

Principle 16: Making godly decisions and advising those who lead requires putting the interest of others over your own.

It is impossible for leaders in positions of authority to succeed without good advisors. The higher the level of authority, the more information is required for effective leadership, and the greater the importance of advisors. People who are advisors to those who make decisions are critical in the process of leadership and the correct application of authority. Those in leadership have to rely on others to give them accurate information and advice. Those who give advice have the responsibility to be truthful and honest in their communication and must present themselves with integrity.

On 6 June 1944, the greatest military invasion in history, D-Day, took place. Commander of Operation Overlord, the entering of Allied Forces into the continent of Europe, was Gen. Dwight D. Eisenhower. One of the most important advisors at the time of the invasion was meteorologist James Martin Stagg. The weather was a significant factor on the decision of whether to proceed with the invasion or wait. Rain, low clouds which lead to lack of visibility, and high winds threatened success. A wrong decision could have changed the outcome of World War II. With hundreds of thousands of lives in the balance, Stagg advised Gen. Eisenhower that although weather would remain marginal, visibility would improve, and winds would decrease. Gen. Eisenhower relied on this forecast, and the invasion was launched. Only the tried-and-tested trust Eisenhower had in his relationship with Stagg permitted such advice to determine this decision. Everyone involved in the decision process had one goal in mind—the successful invasion of Normandy.

This principle may be considered a follow-on to principle 12. If an advisor has an ulterior motive separate from that which the leader is addressing, wrong decisions may be made. If an advisor is simply wrong in his advice, catastrophic results may also occur.

Hegai, the eunuch in charge of the king's harem, is to oversee the women. Not much is said about him; however, he is a pivotal character. Although God is not mentioned, we will see how He grants Esther with the favor of Hegai, who promotes her to the lead position of all the girls. Because Hegai knows what will please Ahasuerus, I think Esther may have been given an inside track to gaining the king's favor and becoming queen.

The girls are not only taken from their families; they are required to undergo a process of beautification before they are considered worthy to go to the king. We will see the specifics of this process of beautification in Esther 2:12. It is quite interesting. Dads, can you imagine the ruler of the land making a law that takes your daughter away from you and makes her a slave in the king's harem? I have three daughters, and I would lay down my life before they were taken.

"'Then let the young lady who pleases the king be queen in place of Vashti.' And the matter pleased the king, and he did accordingly" (Esther 2:4).

What do you think "pleases the king" means? Beauty? Sexual pleasure? Emotional fulfillment? As we will see, each girl gets only one night to impress the king. What do you think "pleased the king" means? The king liked the idea of whatever was pleasing to him. He did not consider the effects this plan would have on his nation, however.

Again, we see character flaw and poor behavior on the part of the Ahasuerus. He gets in an emotional state, is manipulated by others, and the result is a bad decision. Let's compare and contrast the events in Esther 1 and Esther 2.

Esther 1:13–20	Esther 2:1–4
Initiated by drunken state and Vashti's refusal	Initiated by King's remembrance and result of first law
Seven wise men	King's attendants (same?)
Premise—Vashti had wronged the king	Premise—King is troubled
Argument—Other women will revolt	Argument—Need to make king feel better
Motive—Get rid of Vashti; increase power of men over women	Motive—Make king feel better; possibly to prevent the return of Vashti
Regard for men, no regard for women	Regard for men, no regard for women
Made a new law	Made a second law
Get rid of Vashti	Replace Vashti
Pleased the king, and he did it	Pleased the king, and he did it

So how and why did the events in Esther 1:13–20 and 2:1–4 happen? On one level, they occurred because the king could do anything he wanted to do. On a deeper level, these things happened because the king had a flawed personality. He was weak in character. History is full of leaders who were weak in character. The result has usually been disaster for the individual as well as for the nation he or she ruled.

Did God cause Ahasuerus and his attendants to gather the beautiful virgins in the land and bring them to the harem? Did God allow things to occur and then use them in His plan?

Theme Statement

King's remembrance leads to planned, enforced slavery of virgins.

Hero and heroine

It's time to switch gears and meet two new characters.

> "Now there was at the citadel in Susa a Jew whose name was Mordecai, the son of Jair, the son of Shimei, the son of Kish, a Benjamite, who had been taken into exile from Jerusalem with the captives who had been exiled with Jeconiah king of Judah, whom Nebuchadnezzar the king of Babylon had exiled. He was bringing up Hadassah, that is Esther, his uncle's daughter, for she had no father or mother. Now the young lady was beautiful of form and face, and when her father and her mother died, Mordecai took her as his own daughter (Esther 2:5–7).

Where

The citadel in Susa.

When

483–482 BC.

Think back to English Literature 101. If you have read through the book of Esther, who do you think is the protagonist? The *now* that begins this paragraph introduces the protagonist of the book of Esther—Mordecai. This paragraph is a pause between verse 4 and verse 8. It gives us facts, but it also leaves us with some uncertainties.

We first hear the term "Jew." What does it mean? It means "belonging to Judah" or "Judean." When was "Judean" first used?

> "At that time Rezin king of Aram recovered Elath for Aram, and cleared the Judeans out of Elath entirely; and the Arameans came to Elath and have lived there to this day" (2 Kings 16:6).

The word "Jew" came into use just before the Exile. It is found in Jeremiah.

> "And I gave the deed of purchase to Baruch the son of Neriah, the son of Mahseiah, in the sight of Hanamel my uncle's son and in the sight of the witnesses who signed the deed of purchase, before all the Jews who were sitting in the court of the guard" (Jeremiah 32:12).

It helped form a national identity and national principle for God's chosen people.

> "That each man should set free his male servant and each man his female servant, a Hebrew man or a Hebrew woman; so that no one should keep them, a Jew his brother, in bondage" (Jeremiah 34:9).

Those who were exiled were called Jews.

> "These are the people whom Nebuchadnezzar carried away into exile: in the seventh year 3,023 Jews" (Jeremiah 52:28).

A religious identity became associated with the Jews.

> "There are certain Jews whom you have appointed over the administration of the province of Babylon, namely Shadrach, Meshach and Abed-nego. These men, O king, have disregarded you; they do not serve your gods or worship the golden image which you have set up" (Daniel 3:12).

By the time of Esther, the word "Jew" had national, religious, and personal meaning.

When you read this paragraph, how do you make sense of the lineage? I read that it was Kish, a Benjamite, who was taken into exile from Jerusalem in 597 BC, during the reign of Nebuchadnezzar. Mordecai is a descendent of Kish, who was Mordecai's great-grandfather. Who was the son of a different Kish who lived 600 years earlier? King Saul.

Mordecai is the Hebrew form of a Babylonian name. It is based on the name Marduk, which is a Babylonian deity. "Idolatrous names for devout Jews grew out of a practice during the Diaspora of giving both a Babylonian and a Hebrew name to the same person (Daniel 1:6–7)."[1] The name Marduka has been found in a text that mentions Persian dignitaries from Susa. This could be proof of Mordecai's existence. Obviously all the descendants of Kish did not return to Judah when Cyrus freed the Jews from Babylonian rule. The name Mordecai is found in Ezra 2:2 and Nehemiah 7:7. They could possibly be the same person.

We are not told Mordecai's occupation. There is no wife or family mentioned other than his caring for Esther. We will see that he has access to the king's harem (Esther 2:11), and he is well-known at the king's gate (Esther 3:2–3). It is possible he worked in the palace and may even have been at the seven-day banquet (1:5–9).

What do you think of Mordecai? I think he is a man of responsibility and integrity. He assumed responsibility to care for his cousin, Hadassah, Esther. He acted as her father when her parents died. We will see he is a man of courage, vision, and faith. Do you think Mordecai had any faults? As the story goes on, we will see he has a tendency to arrogance and pride.

Hadassah is a Hebrew name that means "myrtle." Esther is Persian and means "star."[2] These are truly lovely names that seem to fit her well. Her father was Abihail (Esther 2:15, 9:29). She is cousin to Mordecai and is "beautiful of form and face." When the Bible says this of someone, she could have been the supermodel of all supermodels, even before the beautification process.

So we have a beautiful Jewish girl, who we believe is a virgin, and we have an edict requiring all beautiful virgins to report to the king's harem. We know where this is going and what is going to happen.

What do you think of Esther? As we go through the story, look for the following characteristics. In addition to physical beauty, we will see that her character reveals love, joy, peace, patience, kindness, goodness, faithfulness, gentleness, and self-control—at least, most of the time. Do you think Esther has any faults? She deals with adversity very well. She does

---

1   Huey, F. B. Jr. 1988. *The Expositor's Bible Commentary.* Grand Rapids: Zondervan Publishing House, Volume 4. 805.

2   Ibid.

show fear when presented with the possibility of death, but she overcomes it. She appears to be very street-smart. She understands the facts of life, she is able to think under pressure, she knows what to do in most situations, she does what is necessary, and she is extremely patient in waiting for the right time to act. She exhibits grace under pressure. When all is said and done, you will want to be on her side, not against her.

In closing this paragraph, I would like to ask several questions concerning our two newest characters. Should Mordecai and Esther have tried to go back to Jerusalem? Did Mordecai and Esther have a strong belief in God, and is there any proof? Did Mordecai and Esther practice their faith, in private and public, and is there any proof? Did most Jews practice their faith, in private and public, and what proof do we have?

In the book of Esther, we see Mordecai and Esther—and all the Jews in Persia—face situations in which they have to choose whether or not they will obey God. At the risk of bursting our impression of a perfect Mordecai and Esther, we will see our hero and heroine make decisions to obey man rather than God. Yet God still provides grace, mercy, and providential care—just as He does for us today.

As we go through Esther, look for examples of failure as well as success in our main characters. We need to hold to the facts of the story. Based on personalities, as well as thoughts, actions, and words revealed under extreme pressure, I believe Mordecai and Esther had a strong faith in God as well as tested characteristics that came from strong teaching and family.

Theme Statement

Mordecai, a Jew, acts as father to his beautiful cousin, Esther.

Expectations and Realities

We had a break in the story in Esther 2:5–7. We now go back to it:

> "So it came about when the command and decree of the king were heard and many young ladies were gathered to the citadel of Susa into the custody of Hegai, that Esther was taken to the king's palace into the custody of Hegai, who was in charge of the women. Now the young lady pleased him and found favor with him. So he quickly provided her with her cosmetics and food, gave her seven choice maids from the king's palace and

transferred her and her maids to the best place in the harem. Esther did not make known her people or her kindred, for Mordecai had instructed her that she should not make them known. Every day Mordecai walked back and forth in front of the court of the harem to learn how Esther was and how she fared" (Esther 2:8–11).

Where

The harem at the palace where a court was present.

When

482–479 BC.

X 483 BC—story begins
X 482 BC—after 180-day banquets, seven-day banquet, dismissal of Vashti and notification of empire
X sometime after Vashti dismissed

X----482–479 BC----X (Time in harem)

485	480	475

"So it came about when the command and decree of the king were heard and many young ladies were gathered to the citadel of Susa into the custody of Hegai, that Esther was taken to the king's palace into the custody of Hegai, who was in charge of the women" (Esther 2:8).

Esther 2:8 is a continuation from Esther 2:4. Beautiful young ladies were brought to the citadel of Susa. The Hebrew word for "young ladies" is *na'arah* (nah-ar-aw'), "a girl from infancy to adolescence, young woman." When it says Esther "was taken," the Hebrew word is *laqach* (law-kakh'), which means "to take (in the widest variety of applications)." Nothing is indicated that says whether the girls were taken forcefully or if they chose to go voluntarily. Josephus writes in *Antiquities of the Jews* that there were 400 girls.[3]

What do you think was going through the minds of the girls as they were being gathered? The reality of what was going to happen to them was very clear. They would spend a year of beautification, have sex with the king one time, and then spend the rest of their lives in a different harem with other girls who had sex with the king. If they did not *please* the king, they would probably not be called back to see him again (Esther 2:14). They certainly would not be eligible to then marry and have a family. Their life as they knew it or dreamed about was over.

So did the girls look forward to being taken to the harem? I think the answer depends on whether they thought it was a good thing or a bad thing. For some, the expected life of a young woman in 480 BC Persia may have been so hopeless the opportunity to spend her life in the king's harem was something to be looked on as a wonderful thing. Some may have considered this an opportunity to become the queen—or at least live in the palace where there was food, clothing, and shelter. Even if she had sex with the king only one time and then spent the rest of her life in another harem waiting for the king to ask for her, the quality of her life might be better than what she had. If this was a good thing, however, I would think there might be some indication families "volunteered" their daughters to be put in the king's harem. From a secular standpoint, I do not know if this is something girls aspired to do or be.

I think, however, that for most girls, the edict was probably a combination of terror, despair, and disbelief. They did not know if they would ever see their families again. They may have been betrothed, and now their plans had been terminated. A lot of these girls may have been Jewish. They might have thought, "God, why are you allowing this?"

What about the specific issue of Jewish girls going into the harem? Several questions come to mind. Were Mordecai and Esther following the laws of God? Why did Mordecai allow Esther to go or be taken to the harem? She would potentially marry the king, and God's Word was clear on marrying a heathen. It was not to be done (Deuteronomy 7:1–4; Ezra 9:1–4, 14; Ezra 10:3, 11, 18-44; Nehemiah 10:30, 13:23–27). She was not to have sexual relations with a man unless she was married to him (Exodus 20:14).

Was it possible to defy a powerful king and survive? Daniel refused to eat forbidden food (Daniel 1:5), yet we see in Esther 2:9 that Esther ate the

---

3   Antiquities of the Jews. http://www.earlyjewishwritings.com/text/josephus/ant11.html.

food from the citadel. Was Esther violating the laws of God by participating in the king's edict? Would she have been killed if she had refused?

Everyone in the land knew what had happened to Vashti when she refused to come before the king at his banquet. You might applaud Vashti on a moral basis for refusing to go to the king when she was summoned. Remember, he was drunk. Maybe he had immoral intentions—maybe not. If you do applaud, however, how do you respond to Mordecai and Esther as they rejected God's law and followed the king's command?

As we stated earlier, we are to obey the legal authority over us if the request is not illegal, immoral, or in violation of God's command. Old Testament law was a higher authority over the Jews than the king's authority or the laws of Persia. What would have happened if Esther had refused to follow the king's command? Is it possible God made it clear to Mordecai and Esther she was to obey the law of the king, or was God showing grace and mercy in spite of Esther's disobedience?

What violations against God's law did Mordecai and Esther commit? Here are a few that come to mind: go to harem, have sex with someone not her husband, marry a non-Jew, eat improper food, and not celebrate established Jewish feasts. We also see Esther hide her nationality and belief. Before you criticize Esther and Mordecai, ask yourself the question, "Would you have done the same?"

What beliefs do you have that you are willing to "fall on your sword" to uphold?

When authority over you contradicts your belief, what do you do? Missionaries face this dilemma in different countries all the time. What does God truly require of us, and what does God do when we fail to acknowledge His commands?

Paul tells us in Romans that we as church-age believers are no longer under the authority of the Mosaic Law.

"For sin shall not be master over you, for you are not under law but under grace" (Romans 6:14).

"For Christ is the end of the law for righteousness to everyone who believes" (Romans 10:4).

We are, however, under a royal law described by Jesus in Matthew.

"And He said to him, 'You shall love the Lord your God with all your heart, and with all your soul, and with all your mind.' This is the great and foremost commandment. The second is like it, 'You shall love your neighbor as yourself.' On these two commandments depend the whole Law and the Prophets" (Matthew 22:37–40).

James describes this as the law of liberty and the royal law.

"But one who looks intently at the perfect law, the law of liberty, and abides by it, not having become a forgetful hearer but an effectual doer, this man will be blessed in what he does" (James 1:24–25).

"If, however, you are fulfilling the royal law according to the Scripture, 'You shall love your neighbor as yourself,' you are doing well" (James 2:8).

Even though we are not under the Mosaic Law, many of the requirements under it are present in the royal law.

"You shall not steal, nor deal falsely, nor lie to one another. You shall not swear falsely by My name, so as to profane the name of your God; I am the Lord. You shall not oppress your neighbor, nor rob him. The wages of a hired man are not to remain with you all night until morning. You shall not curse a deaf man, nor place a stumbling block before the blind, but you shall revere your God; I am the Lord. You shall do no injustice in judgment; you shall not be partial to the poor nor defer to the great, but you are to judge your neighbor fairly. You shall not go about as a slanderer among your people, and you are not to act against the life of your neighbor; I am the Lord. You shall not hate your fellow countryman in your heart; you may surely reprove your neighbor, but shall not incur sin because of him. You shall not take vengeance, nor bear any grudge against the sons of your people, but you shall love your neighbor as yourself; I am the Lord" (Leviticus 19:11–17) ,

God expects (commands) us to be filled with the Spirit (Ephesians 5:18), learn His Word (2 Timothy 2:15), love one another (John 13:34), and grow in grace and knowledge of Jesus Christ (2 Peter 3:18). When we sin, we are to confess (1 John 1:9).

What is the purpose of this thought process? Esther and Mordecai did break some of God's laws. Nevertheless, God did show grace and mercy to both. God used them both for a very specific purpose—to save His people. The application for you and me is that even though we sin, God shows grace and mercy and uses us for His plan. The Bible is full of verses about trusting God. When we see examples of people that failed at times, yet see God's grace and providence, it is comforting. The purpose is not to beat on Mordecai and Esther, but rather to acknowledge the grace of God.

> "Now the young lady pleased him and found favor with him. So he quickly provided her with her cosmetics and food, gave her seven choice maids from the king's palace and transferred her and her maids to the best place in the harem" (Esther 2:9).

What has happened between Esther 2:8 and Esther 2:9? Quite a bit. We go from "Esther was taken to the king's palace into the custody of Hegai, who was in charge of the women" to "now the young lady pleased him and found favor with him." She may not have been following all of God's laws, yet somehow she "found favor" with the man "in charge of the women." I believe her character of grace, submission, joy, kindness, and perseverance was the reason. She did not disobey the king, even though his law was unjust. She did not let her circumstances dictate her thoughts and actions. The Hebrew word for "pleased him" is *yatab* (yaw-tab'), which means "make cheerful, find favor." The Hebrew word for "found favor" is *checed* (kheh'-sed), which means "favor, kindness, mercy." The two together can mean "she lifted up grace before his face."[4]

How did Esther find such favor with Hegai? In answering this question, think of who Hegai was and what he did. He was the overseer of hundreds—if not thousands—of beautiful women. Most likely, he was unimpressed by beauty in a sexual way, since he was a eunuch. He had probably heard hundreds of sad stories from young women over the years. I don't think he was impressed with self-pity. I don't think he could be bribed.

First, Esther trusted God, even though she was not following all of His laws. Remember, she was also following Mordecai's advice. She had trained her mind to think on God. She was not swayed by emotion brought on by environmental upheaval. No matter what the situation or environment, Esther knew God was looking out for her. Second, she had a unique character. She displayed poise, integrity, grace, thoughtfulness, respectfulness, perseverance,

---

4   Ibid., Huey, Volume 4. 806.

willingness to listen and learn, kindness, patience, a sense of loyalty, reverence, and obedience.

How easy it would have been to panic—to let fear and despair control her thoughts. Her trust in God and her character of grace resulted in blessing. She received cosmetics, food, seven maids, and the best room in the harem. Think of other Bible heroes or heroines who displayed the same character as Esther and received blessing. How about Joseph in Egypt and Paul in prison? What do you do when faced with circumstances that seem unfair?

The Hebrew word for "cosmetics" is *tamruwq* (tam-rook'), which means "soap or bath perfume, detergent, something for purification."

Principle 17: God commands the believer to trust, obey and rejoice, even when circumstances seem unfair.

This principle is true in work, school, family, church, the military, or any organization. Trust God in every situation, even when it seems hopeless. When we trust and obey God and display a character of grace, we are blessed—both on earth and in heaven. What is God's answer to life's unfairness?

"Trust in the LORD with all your heart and do not lean on your own understanding. In all your ways acknowledge Him, and He will make your paths straight" (Proverbs 3:5-6)

"This is the day which the Lord has made; Let us rejoice and be glad in it" (Psalm 118:24).

"Rejoice in the Lord always; again I will say, rejoice! Let your gentle spirit be known to all men. The Lord is near. Be anxious for nothing, but in everything by prayer and supplication with thanksgiving let your requests be made known to God. And the peace of God, which surpasses all comprehension, will guard your hearts and your minds in Christ Jesus" (Philippians 4:4–7).

There is nothing in these two verses that qualify or limit when we should rejoice. We should always be rejoicing. Does this mean, "I should report everything on my income tax form, even though I think it is not fair, and rejoice in the Lord?" Yes. Does this mean, "My boss is moving me to a job I do not want to do. Are you telling me I should be gracious about it and rejoice in the Lord?" Yes. Eleven and a half years in the Air Force taught me that when you are given a lawful order, you say, "Yes, sir," and do it to the best of your ability. God is telling us to not only do that, but to rejoice in Him as we do it.

I think it is important to understand what rejoicing is and what it is not. Rejoicing is not jumping up and down in an emotional high. When you lose a loved one or there is financial ruin in your life, you do not jump up and down. You mourn. Yet you can still rejoice in these situations, because your state of mind is not based on the environment, but on your relationship with Jesus Christ. Rejoicing is acknowledging the ever-present grace and mercy of God in your daily life.

The benefit of trusting and obeying is blessing. It was for Esther, and it is for us. Esther 2:9 describes the result of living a gracious life in adverse situations. I think Hegai wanted Esther to be the one to win the favor of the king.

"Esther did not make known her people or her kindred, for Mordecai had instructed her that she should not make them known" (Esther 2:10).

Mordecai wisely instructs Esther to not tell anyone she is Jewish. There was growing anti-Semitism throughout the empire, and if Esther had revealed her race, I do not think she would have been selected queen. Was this disobedience to God? Before you decide, recall how Abram lied regarding his wife, Sarai, when they travelled to Egypt (Genesis 12:10–20). What was God's response?

It is clear God used both Mordecai and Esther, and He protected them throughout the book. They were sinners, like you and me—and God protected them, just like He protects you and me. This situation may have been harder on Mordecai than Esther.

"Every day Mordecai walked back and forth in front of the court of the harem to learn how Esther was and how she fared" (Esther 2:11).

Parents, when our daughters, or sons, are going through difficult times, all of us would gladly take their places a thousand times so they would not have to suffer—right? Mordecai was responsible for Esther, even though his authority had been challenged and superseded by the king. He had to be very careful if he was going to protect her. I think his decision for Esther to not tell anyone she was Jewish was based on the idea of being careful in a precarious situation.

Theme Statement

Esther finds favor in the harem and is rewarded.

Closing thoughts

God knows we do not always follow His commands. We sin and fail. He has an ultimate plan that will not be thwarted, however. God blesses us and takes care of us, even when we do not always follow His commands. Even though we fail at times, it is important to seek Him, learn His Word, take joy in what He provides, look to Him for guidance, present ourselves as godly servants, and exhibit the fruit of the Spirit through the filling of the Holy Spirit as much as possible. There are rewards and blessing—both on earth and in heaven—when we do so.

As believers, we trust in God. Because we live in a fallen world ruled by Satan where temptation to sin is present, we need to be mindful of our actions and words. While our eternal salvation is protected once we believe in Jesus Christ, our daily sanctification is continually threatened. God watches over us and gives us spiritual armor for protection (Ephesians 6:10–20); however, we are subject to the consequences of our failures. There are many traps that can derail our spiritual lives. I know, because I have stepped in a few of them myself. It is important to be on guard for people and situations that may turn you away from God. Evil is present all around us. Peter tells us to be alert for Satan:

> "Be of sober spirit, be on the alert. Your adversary, the devil,
> prowls around like a roaring lion, seeking someone to devour"
> (1 Peter 5:8).

Living a spiritual life is not going through life with blinders on. It is being aware of everything around us, trusting and obeying God, and at the same time making godly decisions as we go through life.

Being filled with the Holy Spirit, reading God's Word daily, and praying are essential to ensure your words and actions are in line with His. Specific environments and situations will require specific words and actions, and what is right in one situation may not be right in another. If

God is the foundation of your faith and you practice trust and obedience to Him, you will say and do the right things.

It is especially important when sharing the Gospel and spiritual truth to communicate in love. A self-righteous, confrontational or condescending manner will turn people away from Jesus. Remember, you are glorifying Him, and if your words are rejected, do not react in anger or frustration. It is the Holy Spirit who instructs, teaches, convicts, and opens the hearts of people. Our job is to communicate in love. The emphasis is never on us, but on Jesus Christ and what the Holy Spirit is revealing.

I think Mordecai and Esther were trusting and obeying God as best they could under extreme pressure. And Esther was doing so with grace.

Principle 18: Maximum knowledge of Bible doctrine, filling of the Holy Spirit, and prayer are critical in making right decisions in your life.

As believers in Jesus Christ, we should focus our physical, mental, and spiritual time and energy in these areas. They are essential for spiritual growth and the ability to handle or deal with the adversities of daily life.

"Rejoicing in hope, persevering in tribulation, devoted to prayer" (Romans 12:12).

"And do not get drunk with wine, for that is dissipation, but be filled with the Spirit" (Ephesians 5:18).

"With all prayer and petition pray at all times in the Spirit, and with this in view, be on the alert with all perseverance and petition for all the saints" (Ephesians 6:18).

"Be diligent to present yourself approved to God as a workman who does not need to be ashamed, accurately handling the word of truth" (2 Timothy 2:15).

"But grow in the grace and knowledge of our Lord and Savior Jesus Christ. To Him be the glory, both now and to the day of eternity. Amen" (2 Peter 3:18).

Beautification and sex

> "Now when the turn of each young lady came to go in to
> King Ahasuerus, after the end of her twelve months under the
> regulations for the women—for the days of their beautification
> were completed as follows: six months with oil of myrrh and six
> months with spices and the cosmetics for women—the young
> lady would go in to the king in this way: anything that she desired
> was given her to take with her from the harem to the king's
> palace. In the evening she would go in and in the morning she
> would return to the second harem, to the custody of Shaashgaz,
> the king's eunuch who was in charge of the concubines. She
> would not again go in to the king unless the king delighted in her
> and she was summoned by name" (Esther 2:12–14).

Where

The harem of the king and the king's palace.

When

Time period of a couple of years—482–479 BC.

> **X** 483 BC—story begins
> **X** 482 BC—after 180-day banquets, seven-day banquet,
> dismissal of Vashti and notification of empire
> **X** sometime after Vashti dismissed
>
> **X----**482–479 BC**----X** (Time in harem)

485	480	475

This is how I look at the time period. Esther 1:1 began in Ahasuerus'
third year of reign, 483 BC. There was a 180 day banquet and a seven-day
banquet. There was the edict to remove Vashti and make men masters at
home. The king then remembers Vashti and an edict to gather virgins was
issued. Ahasuerus put down a major revolt in Babylonia in 482 BC. He spent

125

the winter in Sardis in 481–480 BC and then started the invasion in 480 BC. The Persians were defeated at the Battle of Salamis in 479 BC. Ahasuerus returned home in 479 BC. We will see in the next paragraph that Esther goes to Ahasuerus in 479 BC. We find out in this paragraph it took one year of beautification before a woman could go to the king. Because of the time requirements for each event, I think the women did not start going to the king until after he returned from his defeat in 479 BC.

> "Now when the turn of each young lady came to go in to King Ahasuerus, after the end of her twelve months under the regulations for the women—for the days of their beautification were completed as follows: six months with oil of myrrh and six months with spices and the cosmetics for women" (Esther 2:12).

The temporal connector *now* is used to introduce when a "young lady" was to go to the king. Prior to the big event, we have a pause in action to explain the process that all the women went through. The Hebrew word for "regulations" is *dath* (law), the same word used in Esther 1:8 and Esther 1:15. The Hebrew word for "beautification" is *maruwq* (maw-rook'), "a rubbing (with perfumery, purification)." Six months of *myrrh more* (mor) is a fragrant gum resin obtained from various shrubs. Six months with *spices besem* (beh'-sem) is a sweet-smelling spice.

I will probably get myself in trouble here. I know women like to take time to make themselves look good and smell nice. We men do appreciate this process. You go to the spa, get your hair done, your manicure, your pedicure, your facials, you soak in the tub, apply beauty creams, put on your perfumes, put on your face and take off your face—but *nothing* compares to what they were doing to these beautiful young virgins for twelve months.

Why did it take twelve months of beautification? Assuming the king would be with only one girl each night, what were the rest of them to do until they were called? Can you imagine the trepidation these girls had during this time period? Some of them may have been looking forward to their chance to become queen. Even for these, I think there had to be tremendous anxiety leading up to the night they would spend with the king.

Ladies, how were you the months leading up to your wedding? Just think, you were looking forward to being married—yet there were still some very anxious moments. For these girls, this was a one-time chance to become queen. In addition to the normal concerns a girl might have getting married, these girls had additional pressures. They knew the likelihood was that they would be sent to live with the hundreds of concubines under the custody of Shaashgaz, the king's eunuch.

> "The young lady would go in to the king in this way: anything that she desired was given her to take with her from the harem to the king's palace" (Esther 2:13).

When the girl was to go to the king, she could take something with her from the harem. It is not clear what this means. It may have been something to impress the king, or it may have been something to comfort the girl.

> "In the evening she would go in and in the morning she would return to the second harem, to the custody of Shaashgaz, the king's eunuch who was in charge of the concubines. She would not again go in to the king unless the king delighted in her and she was summoned by name" (Esther 2:14).

The girl would go in the evening and return in the morning. She went in to have sex with the king, whom she had likely never met and maybe never even seen. She knew what was required of her physically; however, it is unlikely she knew the peculiarities and mannerisms of the king. Girls who had already been to the king went to a different harem. It does not say if there was communication between girls in the first and second harems.

Was there competition between the girls? Most of them probably *wanted* to be selected as queen. I wonder what the girls felt like in the morning when they left the king and went to the second harem. Probably a lot of them thought, "So, this is the reason I was born?" In the second harem, the girls were called concubines. The Hebrew word for "concubine" is *piylegesh* (pee-leh'-ghesh) or *pilegesh* (pee-leh'-ghesh). It is "a woman with whom a man cohabits without being married."[5]

The likelihood was that a concubine would spend the rest of her life in the second harem. On rare occasions, she might be called back to the king for another night of sex; however, if he is seeing a new virgin each night until he finds the one he wants as queen, it is unlikely she will be called back. Certainly she will not be able to have a normal family life. It is not

5   Merriam-Webster, Inc. 2003. *Merriam-Webster's Collegiate Dictionary, Eleventh ed.* Springfield, Mass.: Merriam-Webster, Inc.

what most women look forward to regarding intimacy. With this reality, it is hard to judge Esther when she does occasionally fail in her faith.

What was the mental state of Ahasuerus when he came back home in 479 BC? Remember, he won at Thermopylae, beating the 300 Spartans. He burned Athens in a fit of rage and then regretted it. His navy was beaten at the Battle of Salamis. He then returned home. Mardonius, his second-in-command, was killed at the Battle of Plataea. Persia had lost against Greece. So coming home, Ahasuerus was probably not a happy guy. Wives, how do you like being around your husband when he has tried something and failed or has been beaten by something? So Ahasuerus gets home and has all these virgins lined up for him.

Theme Statement

Virgins are purified, have sex with the king, and become concubines.

Showtime for Esther

> "Now when the turn of Esther, the daughter of Abihail the uncle of Mordecai who had taken her as his daughter, came to go in to the king, she did not request anything except what Hegai, the king's eunuch who was in charge of the women, advised. And Esther found favor in the eyes of all who saw her. So Esther was taken to King Ahasuerus to his royal palace in the tenth month which is the month Tebeth, in the seventh year of his reign" (Esther 2:15–16).

Where

King's palace.

When

479 BC, tenth month of the year Tebeth (December/January), seventh year of reign.

X August, 480 BC—Battle of Thermopylae
X September, 480 BC—Battle of Salamis
X 479 BC—Ahasuerus returns to Persia

Esther goes to king 479 BC, tenth month, Tebeth, December/January X

| 480 | 479 | 478 |

The stage is set. Esther 2:12–14 gave the sequence of events for every girl in the harem. The beautification process lasted at least twelve months for each girl. In most cases, it may have been much longer. Remember, every beautiful young virgin was being gathered into the harem. If there were four hundred girls, as Josephus writes, and assuming the king slept with only one virgin per night and did not call any girls back for a second night, a girl might be in the first harem for up to two years before she was called.

> "Now when the turn of Esther, the daughter of Abihail the uncle of Mordecai who had taken her as his daughter, came to go in to the king, she did not request anything except what Hegai, the king's eunuch who was in charge of the women, advised. And Esther found favor in the eyes of all who saw her" (Esther 2:15).

The temporal connector *now* brings us to the point of time when Esther has completed her twelve months of beautification and is about to go to the king. I wonder how much time in advance Esther knew before she was going in to see the king. What was going through her mind as she prepared for her night?

Remember Esther 2:13—each girl could bring anything she wanted when she went to the king. What did Esther do? She asked Hegai for advice. In Esther 2:9, we learned that Esther had found favor with Hegai. Over twelve months, they probably developed a trusting relationship.

This is a good illustration that choices you make in life do make a difference. Esther was taken from her home and put in the harem. She had choices to make. Esther made a choice to trust God and show a character of grace, joy, and integrity. As a result, she was blessed with special care from Hegai, the man in charge of her. She trusted him in preparation for her night with the king, and Hegai responded. You get the feeling Hegai wanted Esther to become queen. He knew what would impress the king. The thing that set her apart from the other virgins was not physical beauty, although she was indeed beautiful. It was her character.

Principle 19: Godly character and integrity result in blessing.

Godly character and integrity should be an integral part of our personalities. Whether we are alone, fellowshipping with other believers, or relating to non-believers, we should exhibit this behavior. Whether we are living in prosperity or adversity, we should strive to present ourselves as Christ lived on earth. This is something we cannot do on our own, however. It comes only from daily sanctification. It is the transformation Paul speaks of in Romans.

"Therefore I urge you, brethren, by the mercies of God, to present your bodies a living and holy sacrifice, acceptable to God, which is your spiritual service of worship. And do not be conformed to this world, but be transformed by the renewing of your mind, so that you may prove what the will of God is, that which is good and acceptable and perfect" (Romans 12:1–2).

It is Christ who transforms us. Application of principle 18 is also necessary.

Esther and Hegai had a good relationship. They developed a trust which benefited them both. Esther probably built good relationships with the other girls as well. Even though she had a good relationship with Hegai, if she did not relate well with the other girls, they could have banded together and derailed her. In some ways, Esther was the teacher's pet. She was also the most popular kid in school. Esther's behavior shows the importance of having godly relationships with everyone—not just those you are trying to impress.

Was Esther's outward manifestation of her character a result of a motivation to be queen? I do not think so. Was her personality a true reflection of who she was? I do think so. Did her character result in blessing that included the king selecting her queen? I think so, as well. The grace and humility exhibited by Esther was based on her integrity and played a great part in her acceptance by those around her.

Think of your relationships. If they are built on godly character and integrity, they are meaningful and they are a blessing, whether they are with superiors, subordinates, or equals. The result for Esther is found in Esther 2:15. "And Esther found favor in the eyes of all who saw her." It does not get any better than that.

And now for a Literature 101 question: How does a storyteller describe someone in a narrative? The author can do so by 1) direct description by the author, 2) words and thoughts of the individual, 3) actions of the person, 4) response and assessment of others, and 5) self-characterization.[6] How does the author describe Esther?

For physical appearance, the author uses direct description—"the young lady was beautiful of form and face" (Esther 2:7). For personal character analysis, the author uses response and assessment of others— "the young lady pleased him and found favor with him" (Esther 2:9). Her relationships with Hegai and all the other girls in the harem reveal her integrity—"and Esther found favor in the eyes of all who saw her" (Esther 2:15). We also see the author uses her actions—"she did not request anything except what Hegai, the king's eunuch who was in charge of the women, advised" (Esther 2:15).

I think Esther went to the king with the radiance of her inner beauty. Her grace, humility, poise, and integrity were the ornaments she wore. Even though there must have been some anxiety, Esther went to the king with godly strength. She had godly character, she had a good relationship with the Hegai, and she had already won the favor of all who saw her. Where most girls would have anxiety about "being selected queen," I think Esther had a trust in God that He would provide for her—no matter what happened. If this was a Miss America contest, she would have won first place, as well as Miss Congeniality and Most Talented.

Theme Statement

Esther goes to king with poise and grace.

Esther wins crown

"The king loved Esther more than all the women, and she found favor and kindness with him more than all the virgins, so that

6   Hanna, Ken. 2007. BE101 class notes, Dallas Theological Seminary, 62.

he set the royal crown on her head and made her queen instead of Vashti. Then the king gave a great banquet, Esther's banquet, for all his princes and his servants; he also made a holiday for the provinces and gave gifts according to the king's bounty. When the virgins were gathered together the second time, then Mordecai was sitting at the king's gate. Esther had not yet made known her kindred or her people, even as Mordecai had commanded her; for Esther did what Mordecai told her as she had done when under his care" (Esther 2:17–20).

Where

King's palace.

When

Seventh year of reign, 479 BC.

X August, 480 BC—Battle of Thermopylae		
X September, 480 BC—Battle of Salamis		
	X 479 BC—Ahasuerus returns to Persia	
Esther goes to king 479 BC—tenth month, Tebeth, December/January **X**		
		Esther made queen X
480	479	478

So what happened between Esther 2:16 and Esther 2:17? Let's take a look. The king "loved"—*'ahab* (aw-hab')—"to have affection for (sexually or otherwise)." "Esther more than all the women." The king had been having sex with different virgins for months. He then had sex with Esther. The difference was that she found "favor"—*chen* (khane)—"favor, grace" and "kindness"—*checed* (kheh'-sed)—"favor, kindness, mercy" "with him more than all the virgins." From Esther 2:17, we see that the other virgins did find favor and kindness with the king. It is just that Esther found more favor and kindness. As a result, the king sets the royal crown on her head and makes her queen.

Was Ahasuerus a different person since his return from defeat in war? I previously said the king was probably not very happy when he came home. It might have been very difficult for those who tried to please him. It was also probably very painful for those who crossed him. Interestingly, we will see that the king shows signs of positive changes in this paragraph.

We have discussed Esther's physical beauty and beauty of soul. She found favor in the eyes of all who saw her, and God showed favor on her. Most of what we have seen in Esther suggests she honored God, and we are seeing the results of His blessings on her. Is there anything you or I can do to make God show us favor?

Principle 20: God shows favor based on His perfect character.

Remember, the Hebrew word for *favor* means "grace." People are not able to earn God's favor. We cannot make God do anything. God gives favor when He determines to do so. What does it mean to have God's favor?

"Trust in the Lord with all your heart and do not lean on your own understanding. In all your ways acknowledge Him, and He will make your paths straight" (Proverbs 3:5–6).

When we trust and obey God, He promises to "make our paths straight." I think this means He keeps us following His plan for us. This is favor. As believers in Jesus Christ, we should remember that we have already received the greatest favor from God, His Son. Without the work on the cross that Jesus accomplished, we all would spend eternity separate from God in the lake of fire (Revelation 20:15).

It is important to understand that favor does not necessarily mean prosperity, and adversity does not necessarily mean lack of favor. You can live in sin, engage in fleshly pleasures, maybe obtain human wealth, and be out of God's favor, which results in misery. You can also live a life without wealth, struggle with physical and financial adversity, and be filled with God's favor, which results in peace and joy. Ultimately, all we do should be for God's glory. We may be doing everything we should and still have hardships. This does not mean, however, we do not have God's favor.

God wanted Esther to be queen, because He had a plan for her to act in a certain way to protect His people. God granted Esther favor to fulfill His purpose. Did the king really make Esther queen after just one night with her? We have seen that he was very impulsive. The king sets the royal crown on Esther's head and stops looking for any other woman to become queen. Does this mean Ahasuerus stopped sleeping with virgins or using the harem?

For those following the hermeneutic outline, notice the connectors the author uses: in Esther 2:17, *so that*—logical connector of result of the king loving Esther; in Esther 2:18, *then*—temporal connector, after selecting Esther as queen; and in Esther 2:19, *when*—temporal connector, time period of the gathering of virgins.

Let's compare/contrast the banquet Vashti had with the one the king gave Esther.

Vashti's Banquet Esther 1:9	Esther's banquet Esther 2:18
A banquet	A great banquet
Queen gave the banquet for herself	King gave the banquet for Esther
Just for women	All princes and servants
Nothing given in honor of the queen	Made a holiday—*hanachah* (han-aw-khaw') No work, No taxes for provinces (entire country)
Nothing given in honor of the queen	Gave gifts—*mas'eth* (mas-ayth')—according to bounty—*yad* (yawd). King giving to people in honor of making Esther queen
Men got drunk at their banquet	No mention of drunkenness
Queen was summoned	Queen was honored
King fired (dismissed) the queen	King honored the queen

What are the differences in the motives and outcomes in the two banquets? Although the banquets were given for different reasons, I get the feeling the king values Esther more than he did Vashti—or maybe he had simply learned how to treat his queen.

> "When the virgins were gathered together the second time, then Mordecai was sitting at the king's gate" (Esther 2:19).

It is not clear what "the second gathering of virgins" means. Maybe the girls who had not been in to sleep with the king were gathered and then sent home. Maybe there were new virgins being gathered for the first harem. Maybe the king wanted to have another look at those with whom he might choose to have sex. Maybe Esther wanted to honor all the other virgins. It does not say how long after the banquet the gathering took place.

Why is Mordecai sitting at the king's gate (Esther 2:19, 3:2)? Mordecai probably has an official position in the king's administration, possibly in the judicial system. Officials who sat at the gate often settled disputes brought to the authority or king. What is the importance to the story of Mordecai being at the gate? He is able to know what is going on and have communication with Esther. He is able to be close to the king and Esther and not be questioned. He is able to uncover an assassination plot, which we will see in the next paragraph. His contact with and behavior in relation to Haman leads to a plot to destroy all Jews, which we will see in the next chapter.

> "Esther had not yet made known her kindred or her people, even as Mordecai had commanded her; for Esther did what Mordecai told her as she had done when under his care" (Esther 2:20).

Esther continues to obey Mordecai. She does not tell anyone she is Jewish. Esther did not let her worldly position change her character. She could easily have said, "I am queen now. I will do as I want." Does prosperity change one's character or simply bring out one's true character? How many times do we see money, power, and fame influence people to the point they change their values?

Principle 21: Worldly things can influence and change your relationship with God.

Have you ever been in a very difficult situation? Whatever adversity you were facing was severe—almost unbearable. Did you ever say to God that you would change your life and live the way He wanted you to live if only He would remove the pain from your life? What did you do when the trial was over and you were no longer suffering? Did you honor your promise to God?

Have you ever been presented with extreme prosperity? Maybe it was in the form of financial wealth, a job promotion, or a new, wonderful relationship. Did your values change in relation to God?

There is a great temptation to forget God when living in prosperity. I think this is one reason God does not give us everything we ask.

Theme Statement

God and king show favor on Esther, and she is made queen.

Final thoughts

I think Ahasuerus had been unhappy for a long time. This was due to a series of self-inflicted destructive decisions, listening to bad advice, and military defeat. It appears he has finally found something that was good and real. So they all lived happily ever after and had no more problems. The end. Not exactly.

Mordecai saves the king

"In those days, while Mordecai was sitting at the king's gate, Bigthan and Teresh, two of the king's officials from those who guarded the door, became angry and sought to lay hands on King Ahasuerus. But the plot became known to Mordecai and he told Queen Esther, and Esther informed the king in Mordecai's name. Now when the plot was investigated and found to be so, they were both hanged on a gallows; and it was written in the Book of the Chronicles in the king's presence" (Esther 2:21–23).

Where

King's gate.

When

Some time after Esther was made queen, seventh year of reign or later, 479 BC or later. It is not known how much time is between Esther 2:20 and Esther 2:21.

X August, 480 BC—Battle of Thermopylae

X September, 480 BC—Battle of Salamis

X 479 BC—Ahasuerus returns to Persia

Esther goes to king 479 BC—tenth month, Tebeth, December/January X

Esther made queen X

Mordecai uncovers plot to assassinate Ahasuerus X
(After Esther made queen)

480	479	478

Mordecai is sitting at the king's gate, probably in an official capacity. Bigthan and Teresh are two officials who are responsible to guard the door. For some reason, they became angry. We are not told why. They planned to assassinate the king. Esther 6:2 describes them as eunuchs who were guarding the king's door. Earlier I said that eunuchs were less likely to try to overthrow the king. This plot is an exception to that premise. Just because they were eunuchs did not mean they could not plot to assassinate the king.

Is it important to know why they wanted to kill the king? The author does not tell us why Bigthan and Teresh were so angry that they wanted to plot an assassination. Mordecai becomes aware of the plot. How? It does not say. Josephus writes that "Barnabazus, the servant of one of the eunuchs, being by birth a Jew, was acquainted with their conspiracy, and discovered it to the queen's uncle; and Mordecai, by the means of Esther, made the conspirators known to the king."[7] In addition to this particular event, it is important to know there is communication between Mordecai and Esther.

---

7   Antiquities of the Jews. http://www.earlyjewishwritings.com/text/josephus/ant11.html.

Esther tells the king about the plot and tells him it was Mordecai who uncovered it.

The plot was investigated and found to be true. The two plotters are hanged on the gallows. Being hanged on the gallows is not like being hanged from a rope in the Wild West—it means being impaled on a stake (Ezra 6:11; Esther 5:14, 7:10).

How common were assassinations in those days? They were a common way for kings to die. Because of this threat it is easy to understand why people were executed for minor disagreements. Kings feared for their own lives. Physical access to the king was restricted, and made available only to those who were trusted or invited. We will see the importance of this in Esther 4. Ahasuerus was eventually assassinated in 465 BC by Artabanus.

The entire episode was recorded in official records of the king, the Book of Chronicles, and the king was aware of everything that happened, as well as it being written down. We see later the king actually reads the record (Esther 6:1–2). Why does the king not reward Mordecai at this time? If the king had rewarded Mordecai, would the upcoming conflict have been averted, or would the king have forgotten about the events by that time?

Theme Statement

Mordecai discovers plot to assassinate king; plot thwarted.

> **Principle 22: God in His sovereignty is always in control of the circumstances in our lives.**
>
> After you read the entire book and look back at all of the minute details that have to fit in place for everything to work out, you see God's sovereignty. Don't you just love to see God at work? Hollywood could not write a script this good. This paragraph shows God's sovereignty in directing the lives and events in the story, and it gives clear evidence to progress the story line in favor of Mordecai and Esther.
>
> Can you look back on your life and see how God's sovereignty has been present through people and events? At the time, things may have seemed irrelevant, but in looking back, they make sense.

Things to Remember

Paragraph Theme Statements

Esther 2:1–4—King's remembrance leads to planned, enforced slavery of virgins.

Esther 2:5–7—Mordecai, a Jew, acts as father to his beautiful cousin, Esther.

Esther 2:8–11—Esther finds favor in harem and is rewarded.

Esther 2:12–14—Virgins are purified, have sex with king, become concubines.

Esther 2:15–16—Esther goes to the king with poise and grace.

Esther 2:17–20—God and the king show favor on Esther, and she is made queen.

Esther 2:21–23—Mordecai discovers plot to assassinate king; plot is thwarted.

Principles

15. The solution to error is to admit, apologize, accept consequences, make restitution if possible, alter behavior, and move on.

16. Making godly decisions and advising those who lead requires putting the interest of others over your own.

17. God commands the believer to trust, obey and rejoice, even when circumstances seem unfair.

18. Maximum knowledge of Bible doctrine, filling of the Holy Spirit, and prayer are critical in making right decisions in your life.

19. Godly character and integrity result in blessing.

20. God shows favor based on His perfect character.

21. Worldly things can influence and change your relationship with God.

22. God in His sovereignty is always in control of the circumstances in our lives.

Chapter Six

ESTHER 3:
A PLAN TO ANNIHILATE THE JEWS

Mordecai's pride and Haman's hatred

"After these events King Ahasuerus promoted Haman, the son of Hammedatha the Agagite, and advanced him and established his authority over all the princes who were with him. All the king's servants who were at the king's gate bowed down and paid homage to Haman; for so the king had commanded concerning him. But Mordecai neither bowed down nor paid homage. Then the king's servants who were at the king's gate said to Mordecai, 'Why are you transgressing the king's command?' Now it was when they had spoken daily to him and he would not listen to them, that they told Haman to see whether Mordecai's reason would stand; for he had told them that he was a Jew. When Haman saw that Mordecai neither bowed down nor paid homage to him, Haman was filled with rage. But he disdained to lay hands on Mordecai alone, for they had told him who the people of Mordecai were; therefore Haman sought to destroy all the Jews, the people of Mordecai, who were throughout the whole kingdom of Ahasuerus" (Esther 3:1–6).

Where

King's gate.

When

Sometime between the seventh year of reign, 479 BC, and the twelfth year, 474 BC.

Close to 474 BC, if not exactly.

X Esther goes to king—479 BC, tenth month, Tebeth, December/January

X Esther made queen

   X Mordecai uncovers plot to assassinate Ahasuerus—before Haman's edict in 474 BC

Haman promoted to second in command—479–474 BC
Mordecai refuses to bow to Haman—474 BC X

480	479	478	477	476	475	474	473

"After these events King Ahasuerus promoted Haman, the son of Hammedatha the Agagite, and advanced him and established his authority over all the princes who were with him" (Esther 3:1).

"After these events" means after Mordecai had saved the king from assassination in Esther 2:21–23. It is a nonspecific indicator of a period of time in the future. I think some time has passed since Mordecai had revealed the plot to kill the king.

In a suspense movie, this is where the music changes to a sinister tone. We are introduced to the antagonist of the story, Haman. What do we know about him? He is the son of Hammedatha the Agagite; he was in Ahasuerus's administration; and for some reason we do not know, he is promoted to a position where he had "authority over all the princes who were with him." He is second only to Ahasuerus himself. This is likely the position Mordecai later assumes in Esther 10:2. "Advanced him and established his authority" indicates promotion through the ranks or administrative positions. Over time, Haman was evidently given greater positions and power by the king. It may have been several years. We do not know why he was promoted.

From where did Haman come? "Jewish tradition considers him to have been a descendant of the Amalekite king, Agag."[1] For years, the Amalekites and Israelites were enemies (Exodus 17:8–14; Numbers 24:7; Deuteronomy 25:17–19). King Saul was commanded to destroy the Amalekites in 1 Samuel 15:1–35.

> "Now go and strike Amalek and utterly destroy all that he has, and do not spare him; but put to death both man and woman, child and infant, ox and sheep, camel and donkey" (1 Samuel 15:3).

"Saul failed to destroy the Amalekites completely as God had ordered him to do, and consequently the kingdom was taken from him."[2] Some have suggested the feud between king Agag and Saul is continued with Haman, a descendent of Agag, and Mordecai, a descendent of Saul. This is unlikely, as only Agag was spared, and he was later killed by Samuel. "Archeologists have uncovered an inscription which indicates that Agag was also the name of a province in the Persian Empire. This probably explains why Haman was called an Agagite."[3]

So what does it mean to be promoted to the highest position in the land, except for the king?

> "All the king's servants who were at the king's gate bowed down and paid homage to Haman; for so the king had commanded concerning him" (Esther 3:2).

Hebrew words:

> "Commanded"—*tsavah* (tsaw-vaw')—command, set in order
>
> "Bowed down"—*kara`* (kaw-rah')—to bend the knee, to bow
>
> "Paid homage"—*shachah* (shaw-khaw')—to prostrate, homage to royalty or God.

---

1   Huey, F. B. Jr. 1988. *The Expositor's Bible Commentary.* Grand Rapids: Zondervan Publishing House, Volume 4. 811.

2   Ibid.

3   Walvoord, John F. and Roy B. Zuck. 1983. *The Bible Knowledge Commentary.* Wheaton, IL: Victor Books, S. 1:705.

The king had commanded everyone to bow down to Haman when he came into view. This is respect deserving of the king himself. What does Mordecai do? "But Mordecai neither bowed down nor paid homage." Why did Mordecai not bow down to Haman? Was he bitter about not being rewarded for saving the king but seeing Haman rewarded? It may have been several years since he had saved the king. Did he think bowing down violated Jewish law or was an insult to God? Although not specifically stated, it is possible people were required to bow to Mordecai if he was acting in an official capacity at the gate.

Was Mordecai right in not bowing to Haman? Was Mordecai wrong in not bowing to Haman? Let's look at the issue of bowing to the king or his appointed representative. It was a legal command given by the king. It did not appear to be an act of worship, but rather an act of respect. There is no evidence Mordecai refused to bow to the king. Being stationed at the gate, Mordecai would certainly have come in contact with the king on many occasions. To not bow to the king probably would have resulted in death. So the issue of bowing to another human being does not appear to be the reason. Mordecai had not refused to let Esther go to the harem, and there is no evidence that Mordecai is following all Jewish laws. So the issue of violating God's law does not appear to be the reason.

It says in Esther 3:4 Mordecai replies, "for he had told them that he was a Jew." Does being a Jew have anything to do with legitimate refusal to pay respect to civilian authority? Was it against Jewish law to bow before kings or other superiors? There are several references in the Old Testament that show God's people bowing before kings or other superiors (Genesis 23:7, 27:29; 1 Samuel 24:8; 2 Samuel 14:4; 1 Kings 1:16).[4] Bowing before legal authority as a sign of respect is authorized and should not be confused with the commandment God gave the Israelites in Exodus 20.

> "You shall not make for yourself an idol, or any likeness of what is in heaven above or on the earth beneath or in the water under the earth. You shall not worship them or serve them; for I, the Lord your God, am a jealous God, visiting the iniquity of the fathers on the children, on the third and the fourth generations of those who hate Me" (Exodus 20:4–5).

I think we are seeing one of Mordecai's flaws—pride. He may have thought he should have been rewarded for saving the king's life. He may have been jealous of Haman. He may have thought he should have been given the position Haman was given. He was not being forced to worship Haman.

4   Ibid., Huey, Volume 4, 812.

He was to show respect in the same way he showed respect to the king—the same way "all the king's servants who were at the king's gate" were required to do. Would the rest of the story have happened if Mordecai had bowed down to Haman? It is my opinion, Mordecai was wrong in not bowing. The following principle addresses personal responsibility to legal authority—not just in showing respect, but in all aspects.

Principle 23: God expects us to follow the legal authority over us when it does not violate His commands.

How does this apply to you and me? Should we respect and follow the legal authority over us, even when we dislike the individual in the position of authority? There is a scene in the HBO series *Band of Brothers* toward the end of World War II where Major Winters and Capt. Sobel encounter each other. At one time, Major Winters was a lieutenant under the authority of Capt. Sobel. Through a chain of events, Winters rose in rank while Sobel did not. When they encounter each other, Capt. Sobel does not salute Major Winters. Major Winters corrects Capt. Sobel by telling him, "we salute the rank, not the person."

When someone with legitimate authority over you makes a demand, as long as it is not in violation of God's command, is not illegal or immoral, you are obligated to do that thing or suffer the consequences.

We see the importance of this principle in school, work, athletics, church, the military, the police force, government, the laws of our land, or any place where there is authority. When there is a refusal to follow legitimate authority, consequences arise. There were times in the Air Force when I did not have personal respect for a superior officer or I disagreed with a lawful order that was given; yet I always respectfully saluted when required to do so and followed the order to the best of my ability. Here, Mordecai refuses to follow the legal command of showing respect to Haman.

What does God say about personal responsibility to legitimate authority? Jesus said:

"Tell us then, what do You think? Is it lawful to give a poll-tax to Caesar, or not?" But Jesus perceived their malice, and said, "Why are you testing Me, you hypocrites? "Show Me the coin used for the poll-tax." And they brought Him a denarius. And He said to them, "Whose likeness and inscription is this?" They said to Him, "Caesar's." Then He said to them, "Then render to Caesar the things that are Caesar's; and to God the things that are God's." And hearing this, they were amazed, and leaving Him, they went away." (Matthew 22:17-22)

Regarding submission toward the authority of God:

"For the mind set on the flesh is death, but the mind set on the Spirit is life and peace, because the mind set on the flesh is hostile toward God; for it does not subject itself to the law of God, for it is not even able to do so, and those who are in the flesh cannot please God" (Romans 8:6–8).

"Furthermore, we had earthly fathers to discipline us, and we respected them; shall we not much rather be subject to the Father of spirits, and live?" (Hebrews 12:9).

Regarding submission toward the authority of government:

"Every person is to be in subjection to the governing authorities. For there is no authority except from God, and those which exist are established by God. Therefore whoever resists authority has opposed the ordinance of God; and they who have opposed will receive condemnation upon themselves. For rulers are not a cause of fear for good behavior, but for evil. Do you want to have no fear of authority? Do what is good and you will have praise from the same; for it is a minister of God to you for good. But if you do what is evil, be afraid; for it does not bear the sword for nothing; for it is a minister of God, an avenger who brings wrath on the one who practices evil. Therefore it is necessary to be in subjection, not only because of wrath, but also for conscience' sake. For because of this you also pay taxes, for rulers are servants of God, devoting themselves to this very thing. Render to all what is due them: tax to whom tax is due; custom to whom custom; fear to whom fear; honor to whom honor" (Romans 13:1–7).

"Remind them to be subject to rulers, to authorities, to be obedient, to be ready for every good deed" (Titus 3:1).

Regarding employment:

"Servants, be submissive to your masters with all respect, not only to those who are good and gentle, but also to those who are unreasonable" (1 Peter 2:18).

Regarding believers to each other:

"And be subject to one another in the fear of Christ" (Ephesians 5:21).

"Now I urge you, brethren (you know the household of Stephanas, that they were the first fruits of Achaia, and that they have devoted themselves for ministry to the saints), that you also be in subjection to such men and to everyone who helps in the work and labors" (1 Corinthians 16:15–16).

Regarding leadership in the local church:

"Obey your leaders and submit to them, for they keep watch over your souls as those who will give an account. Let them do this with joy and not with grief, for this would be unprofitable for you" (Hebrews 13:17).

Regarding wives to husbands:

"Wives, be subject to your own husbands, as to the Lord" (Ephesians 5:22).

"Wives, be subject to your husbands, as is fitting in the Lord" (Colossians 3:18).

Regarding husbands to wives:

"Husbands, love your wives, just as Christ also loved the church and gave Himself up for her," (Ephesians 5:25)

"Husbands, love your wives and do not be embittered against them." (Colossians 3:19)

Lest those in leadership or position of authority think the above verses give them the right to abuse their power, they should remember that responsibility and accountability are always present. Ultimately, Jesus Christ has authority on earth and in heaven:

> "And Jesus came up and spoke to them, saying, 'All authority has been given to Me in heaven and on earth'" (Matthew 28:18).

I believe those in authority will be accountable to Jesus Christ on how they lead (Hebrews 13:17 for church leaders).

> "For we know Him who said, "Vengence is mine, I will repay.' And again, 'The Lord will judge His people'" (Hebrews 10:30).

> "There is only one Lawgiver and Judge, the One who is able to save and to destroy; but who are you who judge your neighbor?" (James 4:12)

For Mordecai, following the legal authority over him meant showing respect to Haman's position and bowing to him. For us, it means following laws of our city, state, and nation, as well as founding principles of the US Constitution. We are required to follow these laws, even if we disagree with them. This does not mean we do not use every legal means to voice our opinion and challenge wrong laws and bad leadership. It does mean we are not to violate the law in disobedience. When we break the law and disobey the legal authority over us, we disobey God and do not glorify Him.

I do not believe in Christian activism. I believe in studying, learning, and communicating the truth—specifically, the entire realm of Bible doctrine.

Jesus was not an activist. He taught the absolute truth. New Testament believers should follow His example of obeying authority—first, the Father's, and then second, legally appointed human government. Believers have no excuse for not obeying legal authority or the legal laws of the land.

Principle 23 is true not only for citizens, but also for leaders. Those who make laws are responsible to follow the oaths they take as well as the constitution they are sworn to uphold. Leaders who violate the constitution and pass unjust laws govern as tyrants, not as statesmen.

There is a proper balance between legal authority and personal freedom that is required for a nation to attain and maintain greatness. We in the United States are blessed with a constitution which created a system that defined such a balance. Disruption of this balance tips the scale towards one of two destructive outcomes. On many occasions, I heard R. B. Thieme, Jr. state, "Freedom without authority is anarchy; authority without freedom is tyranny." We see the results of the latter throughout the book of Esther. My concern is that the second part of this quote seems to be the direction our country is taking. Governmental control in all aspects of our lives is decreasing our freedom.

What do we do when our government or legal authority passes laws that prohibit believers from following God's commands? Luke gives a response to this question in Acts. It is important to put this passage in context.

"When they had brought them, they stood them before the Council. The high priest questioned them, saying, 'We gave you strict orders not to continue teaching in this name, and yet, you have filled Jerusalem with your teaching and intend to bring this man's blood upon us.' But Peter and the apostles answered, 'We must obey God rather than men'" (Acts 5:27–29).

When government sets up any law that restricts believers from communicating the Word or obeying God's commands, believers are required to obey God rather than men. Missionaries throughout the world face this adversity on a daily basis. We are blessed that in America we have freedom of worship. There are those who would like to take that away.

Does this mean it is never okay to challenge the authority of those who govern or unjust laws? Of course not. We challenge authority in our nation through the election process. Free speech and freedom of the press are also ways in which we voice our opinion. Every believer should become knowledgeable in our system of government, both in the people who are elected or appointed, as well as in the laws that are passed. When the government attempts to direct the country away from the principles of the Constitution, believers need to voice a challenge. I do believe, however, Christians should focus on spreading the Gospel and teaching the Word of truth, rather than attempting to change the world through activism. I believe the pulpit should not be used for politics; however, teaching the application of God's Word in all aspects of our lives, including government and law is not only allowable, it is mandatory. Paul clearly tells us the Word is a "judge of the thoughts and intentions of the heart" (Hebrews 4:12), and is "profitable for teaching, for reproof, for correction, for training in righteousness" (2 Timothy 3:16). When governmental leadership fails to follow godly principles and the nation suffers, biblical truth needs to be presented.

How about in the Christian life? Do we challenge the authority of those who teach the Word? In the first century, after the death and resurrection of Jesus Christ, the Christian faith was growing. One of the early leaders, Peter, had legitimate authority to present the teaching of Christ through the ministry of the Holy Spirit. He was also charged with the early organization of the church. Soon after, Paul became the leader for the Christian faith, particularly for the Gentiles. When Peter began to teach legalism, rather than the grace of Jesus Christ, Paul publicly admonished him. Galatians 2 explains Paul's correction of Peter.

Not only did Paul have a right to challenge Peter, he had a responsibility to do so. The same is true of us today. When people teach or speak doctrine that is incorrect, they need to be challenged and corrected. My pastor, Mark Land, correctly states that when doing so, one should "do so in love, remove any personal animosity, seek the other person's good, make truth the issue, seek to honor and glorify God, and be ready for criticism." Remember, be like the Bereans.

"The brethren immediately sent Paul and Silas away by night to Berea, and when they arrived, they went into the synagogue of the Jews. Now these were more noble-minded than those in Thessalonica, for they received the word with great eagerness, examining the Scriptures daily to see whether these things were so." (Acts 17:10-11)

What caused Mordecai to stop trusting God to the point he violated God's command to follow the legal authority over him? What causes us to stop trusting God in situations when we disagree with those who have authority over us? What happens when we let the human viewpoint, our flesh patterns, and our sinful nature override our trust and obedience to God? The next principle answers these questions.

Principle 24: Replacing trust and obedience to God with human arrogance, stubbornness, and pride leads to conflict for you and those around you.

There is no excuse for believers who should trust and obey God and do not do so. Whether we are blessed with prosperity or faced with adversity, God wants us to trust and obey Him. The reality is that we all sin and fail in this area from time to time. When everything seems to be going our way, the tendency is to forget God, because we think we do not need Him. When things are going against us, we often blame God and try to escape from the situation by disobedience. All of us need help and encouragement to stay trusting and obedient.

"Then the king's servants who were at the king's gate said to Mordecai, 'Why are you transgressing the king's command?'" (Esther 3:3)

Mordecai's buddies said to him, "What in the world are you thinking? Are you blind; are you stupid?" Have you ever known someone who is doing something that seems out of character and is potentially dangerous? You want to shake them and get them to start thinking and doing what is right.

"Now it was when they had spoken daily to him and he would not listen to them, that they told Haman to see whether

Mordecai's reason would stand; for he had told them that he was a Jew" (Esther 3:4).

Mordecai's refusal to bow down to Haman was not a one-time thing. He was stationed at the gate where Haman passed every day. The king's servants told him daily, "You need to bow down to Haman." Maybe they did not care for Mordecai, maybe they feared for their own lives, or maybe they believed it was their responsibility to report what they believed was insubordination to their superior, Haman. Eventually they told Haman what Mordecai was doing, as well as Mordecai's reason—that he was a Jew.

Hold the horses. What is wrong here? What did you think when you first read this? Mordecai has been telling Esther to not tell anyone she was a Jew (Esther 2:10, 20). Here, Mordecai tells the king's servants at the gate he is a Jew. Mordecai had to know that by not bowing to Haman, he was causing a scene. Why did he then tell everyone he was a Jew? This is a flaw in Mordecai's character and decision-making. It is not clear if he thought his explanation of being a Jew would give him a legitimate reason to not have to bow down to Haman or whether he was just being arrogant. Regardless, it was very foolish. You can't make good decisions while under pressure when your mental attitude is in sin.

Remember Principle 10, "Making decisions when you are not in fellowship with God often leads to actions that are not in line with His plan." Because Mordecai was filled with pride his decision making ability was impaired.

> "When Haman saw that Mordecai neither bowed down nor paid homage to him, Haman was filled with rage" (Esther 3:5).

The Hebrew meaning of "rage" is *chemah* (khay-maw'), which means "heat, anger, poison, indignation, rage, wrath." It comes from *chem'ah* (khem-aw'), which means "curdled milk or cheese."

What do you think of Haman's response? While someone with legitimate authority should deal with insubordination, the reaction of Haman tells me he was not of sound mind. Being filled with emotional rage for this disobedience is psychologically abnormal.

> "But he disdained to lay hands on Mordecai alone, for they had told him who the people of Mordecai were; therefore Haman

sought to destroy all the Jews, the people of Mordecai, who were throughout the whole kingdom of Ahasuerus" (Esther 3:6).

Haman does not discipline Mordecai. When he learns Mordecai is a Jew, he decides to destroy all the Jews in the whole kingdom. We are not talking about simple anger because someone refuses to show you respect. We are talking about the annihilation of God's chosen people. "Throughout the whole kingdom of Ahasuerus" means the entire empire. Remember, this includes the Jews who returned to Palestine when they were freed by Cyrus in 538 BC. What Haman is proposing is like what Hitler tried to do in World War II—only on a much larger scale. This was anti-Semitism at its worst. Haman was trying to exterminate the Jewish race.

I believe this was Satanic. It is my opinion Haman was demon-possessed. For someone with the position, power, and wealth Haman possessed to then decide to exterminate the Jews could only mean an intense hatred of God's chosen people. This was a chance for Satan to disrupt the lineage of Christ. If he was successful, Christ could not be born as revealed in prophecy. Of course, God was not going to let this happen. The events that unfold in the rest of the book will show God's sovereignty in the progression of His perfect plan.

> "I know that You can do all things, and that no purpose of Yours can be thwarted" (Job 42:2).

As we close this paragraph, a new tension has developed—one that will solidify the main plot of the book. Someone of high authority is planning to exterminate all the Jews.

Theme Statement

Mordecai disrespects Haman, who then plans to exterminate the Jewish race.

A plot is hatched

> "In the first month, which is the month Nisan, in the twelfth year of King Ahasuerus, Pur, that is the lot, was cast before Haman from day to day and from month to month, until the twelfth month, that is the month Adar. Then Haman

said to King Ahasuerus, 'There is a certain people scattered and dispersed among the peoples in all the provinces of your kingdom; their laws are different from those of all other people and they do not observe the king's laws, so it is not in the king's interest to let them remain. If it is pleasing to the king, let it be decreed that they be destroyed, and I will pay ten thousand talents of silver into the hands of those who carry on the king's business, to put into the king's treasuries.' Then the king took his signet ring from his hand and gave it to Haman, the son of Hammedatha the Agagite, the enemy of the Jews. The king said to Haman, 'The silver is yours, and the people also, to do with them as you please'" (Esther 3:7–11).

Where

King's palace.

When

474 BC, first month of the year, Nisan (March/April); five years after Esther had become queen (Esther 2:16); twelfth year of the reign of Ahasuerus.

X 474 BC—month Nisan—Haman casts lot

474 BC—13th day Adar—when Jews are to be destroyed **X**

* * * * * * * * * * * * *

474

Nisan	Sivan	Av	Tishri	Chislev	Shebat	(Adar II)
(Ma/Ap)	(May/Jun)	(Jul/Aug)	(Sep/Oct)	(Nov/Dec)	(Jan/Feb)	(leap yr)
Iyyar	Tammuz	Elul	Cheshvan	Tebeth	Adar	
(Ap/May)	(Jun/Jul)	(Aug/Sep)	(Oct/Nov)	(Dec/Jan)	(Feb/Mar)	

What has Esther been doing for five years? Other than being queen, we do not know. It does not say if she is happy being queen. Knowing her character and ability to win favor and overcome difficult situations, I think she was happy. It does not say if she had become pregnant or if she had any children. We find evidence in chapter four that she and Mordecai have communicated. How secluded is the queen from everyday life? How secluded is the queen from what is going on with the king? At this point, we do not know if Esther is aware Mordecai has told the officials he is a Jew or if she knows Haman is angry. You would think she knows Haman is second in power in the kingdom. She has not told the king she is a Jew. We assume the king still loves her more than all the other women (Esther 2:17). We assume her character of grace has had a positive effect on their relationship. We will see in Esther 4 the relationship between the king and queen was based on things other than love.

"Pur, that is the lot, was cast before Haman from day to day and from month to month" to determine the day in which the Jews would be annihilated. What is the lot, and what does it mean? The Hebrew word for "pur" is *Puwr* (poor), which means "Pur." The Hebrew word for "lot" is *gowral* (go-rawl'), which means "a lot, small stones being used for that purpose, figuratively, a portion or destiny." It is why Jews recognize the Feast of Purim (Esther 9:26).

Many Persians, including Haman, were superstitious (Esther 6:13). They believed in fate and chance as part of their religious system.[5] Haman decided to allow fate to determine when and how he should carry out his plan. In casting lots, he came up with the twelfth month, Adar, which is February/March. We find in Esther 3:13 it is the thirteenth of the month of Adar (Esther 8:12, 9:1). This gives almost one year until the plan is to be carried out.

Jews and even early Christians used the system of casting lots (Leviticus 16:8; Numbers 26:55–56; Joshua 14:2; 1 Samuel 14:41–42; 1 Chronicles 26:14; Nehemiah 10:34; Psalm 22:18; Proverbs 16:18; Joel 3:3; Acts 1:26).[6] We have talked about sovereignty and free will, and we are seeing how they are presented in Esther. We now add the human viewpoint—the concept of chance. When people cast lots, was it truly chance—or was it divine input as to when and what occurred? When people cast lots, was it God directed they do so—or was it man's self doing? Was it really chance Haman was going to wait one year before attempting to kill all the Jews?

> "The lot is cast into the lap, but its every decision is from the Lord" (Proverbs 16:33).

> "And they drew lots for them, and the lot fell to Matthias; and he was added to the eleven apostles" (Acts 1:26).

---

5   Ibid., Walvoord, S. 1:705.

6   Ibid., Huey, Volume 4, 813.

God is sovereign, omniscient, and omnipotent. His timing is perfect. There is nothing left to chance. God determined Haman would choose the thirteenth of the month, Adar. By waiting a year for the event, what opportunity did this provide the Jews? It provided time for events to occur to thwart Haman's plan. It provided time for Jews to prepare to defend themselves. It provided testing for the Jews to trust God. It provided time for the Jews to watch His perfect plan unfold. It allowed the Jews, and us, to see God being glorified with His solution.

> "Then Haman said to King Ahasuerus, 'There is a certain people scattered and dispersed among the peoples in all the provinces of your kingdom; their laws are different from those of all other people and they do not observe the king's laws, so it is not in the king's interest to let them remain'" (Esther 3:8).

So if you want to do something evil and you have to get approval from your superior, what do you do? First, you tell half-truths, lies, and spin facts. What do you think of Haman's premise? Haman says "a certain people." Note that he does not tell the king it is the Jews who are to be destroyed. In Haman's mind, this included all Jews under Persian rule, including those in Judah as well. It was true the Jews were dispersed throughout the kingdom, and they had different customs. However, with the exception that Mordecai refused to bow to Haman, we have no evidence Jews did not observe the king's laws. The Jews had observed the laws of the Babylonians. They had impressed King Cyrus and had been told they could go home to Jerusalem. We have to think they were good citizens. They provided a buffer against Egypt. Haman has stated an untrue premise.

The logical connector of result, *so,* is used to make it sound like the expected conclusion to the untrue premise is that it is against the king's interest for them to *remain.* What do you think of Haman's conclusion? It appears to be illogical. To not "let them remain" serves no purpose for the kingdom.

Two erroneous statements have been presented. The premise is false, and the conclusion is illogical. Notice that Haman does not mention Mordecai by name. It is possible Haman knew Mordecai had saved the king's life, and if his name is mentioned, the king would side with Mordecai.

> The above exchange of words from Haman to Ahasuerus sounds like present-day government leaders trying to explain why certain legislation should be passed. Half-truths, lies, and facts that have been spun are presented in such a manner as to convince people to agree with bad decisions or laws.

I think Haman knows he is skating on thin ice. The king may reject his plan. He needs to sweeten the deal. Before the king has a chance to ask a question or even think about things, Haman continues.

> "If it is pleasing to the king, let it be decreed that they be destroyed, and I will pay ten thousand talents of silver into the hands of those who carry on the king's business, to put into the king's treasuries" (Esther 3:9).

We have seen the "if it pleases the king" method of communicating to the king before. When the wise men and Haman make this statement, it makes my skin crawl. Haman says, "Let's make a law to destroy this group of people (the Jews)," and by the way, "I will pay you money if you let me do this." Haman offers to pay the king 10,000 talents of silver if the king will let him kill all the Jews. By weight, this was about 750,000 pounds.

What does this say about Haman? He was very wealthy. He hated the Jews. I think he also had other selfish motives, like taking all the personal property and wealth of the Jews for himself (Esther 3:13). I am sure he believed he would come away with more than 10,000 talents of silver after killing all the Jews and taking their property.

The response of the king is almost beyond comprehension. The last several encounters with the king have been the banquet he gave for the queen five years earlier (Esther 2:17–18), the assassination plot uncovered by Mordedcai, the king's failure to honor him (Esther 2:21–23) and the promotion he gave to Haman (Esther 3:1). We really do not know how he has been acting for the last five years. We know Ahasuerus has been easily manipulated by his advisors (Esther 1:16–22; 2:2–4), but his actions in this situation reach new lows for poor leadership.

The king does two things. First:

> "Then the king took his signet ring from his hand and gave it to Haman, the son of Hammedatha the Agagite, the enemy of the Jews" (Esther 3:10).

Without saying anything, Ahasuerus gives his signet ring to Haman. This represented the king's authority (Esther 3:12; 8:2, 8; Genesis 41:42; Daniel 6:17; Haggai 2:23).[7] It is Ahasuerus's way of saying, "Do whatever you want." Write a letter saying whatever you want to do, sign my name to it, and it will become law. Notice what Haman is called by the author. He is called "the enemy of the Jews"—here as well as in Esther 7:6; 8:1; 9:10, 24.

Second:

> "The king said to Haman, 'The silver is yours, and the people also, to do with them as you please" (Esther 3:11).

You can tell the king's priority. He addresses the silver first. He then tells Haman the people belong to him to do with as he pleases. We do not know for sure what was going on in the mind of Ahasuerus; however, I think the king did not give a second thought as to what he told Haman.

How does the leadership of Persia go from Cyrus freeing the Jews in 538 BC (Ezra 1:1–4) to Ahasuerus signing an edict to have them destroyed in 474 BC, around sixty-five years later? It is like I mentioned in Chapter Four, Esther 1 under Principle 11, "Mental sins lead to bad decisions, which result in destructive behavior." Individually, we go from point A, being in fellowship with God, to point B, from B to C, and so on to Z. Here, a nation is going down a path of degeneracy, and is doing so one policy at a time. How could national policy change in such a short time? As you consider that, look back sixty-five years and see what national policy and public opinion were in America and how we have changed. Sometimes I think our culture has changed almost as much.

Two questions to close this paragraph: How can people in leadership make such horrible decisions? When you are in a position of authority, how can you prevent making horrible decisions?

---

7   Ibid., Walvoord, S. 1:706..

Theme Statement

Haman gains the king's approval to have a certain people destroyed.

Edict to annihilate is issued

"Then the king's scribes were summoned on the thirteenth day of the first month, and it was written just as Haman commanded to the king's satraps, to the governors who were over each province and to the princes of each people, each province according to its script, each people according to its language, being written in the name of King Ahasuerus and sealed with the king's signet ring. Letters were sent by couriers to all the king's provinces to destroy, to kill and to annihilate all the Jews, both young and old, women and children, in one day, the thirteenth day of the twelfth month, which is the month Adar, and to seize their possessions as plunder. A copy of the edict to be issued as law in every province was published to all the peoples so that they should be ready for this day. The couriers went out impelled by the king's command while the decree was issued at the citadel in Susa; and while the king and Haman sat down to drink, the city of Susa was in confusion" (Esther 3:12–15).

Where

Throughout the entire kingdom.

When

Shortly after Haman's conversation with the king; 474 BC, the thirteenth day of the first month of the year, Nisan (March/April); five years after Esther had become queen (Esther 2:16).

X 474 BC—month Nisan—Haman casts lot

X 474 BC—thirteenth day of Nisan—king's scribes summoned

474 BC—13th day Adar—when Jews are to be destroyed **X**

---

*   *   *   *   *   *   *   *   *   *   *   *   *

474

Nisan	Sivan	Av	Tishri	Chislev	Shebat	(Adar II)
(Ma/Ap)	(May/Jun)	(Jul/Aug)	(Sep/Oct)	(Nov/Dec)	(Jan/Feb)	(leap yr)

Iyyar	Tammuz	Elul	Cheshvan	Tebeth	Adar
(Ap/May)	(Jun/Jul)	(Aug/Sep)	(Oct/Nov)	(Dec/Jan)	(Feb/Mar)

We are getting into specific time periods now. I think Esther 3:12 occurs immediately after 3:11. Haman is not wasting any time. He did not want the king to change his mind. He knew once the law was written and authorized with the king's signet ring, it was irrevocable. Everyone in the kingdom was to be notified. See similarities in Esther 1:22 when everyone in the empire was notified "that every man should be the master in his own house and the one who speaks in the language of his own people."

The author uses the phrase "just as Haman commanded." This tells us several things. First, the edict that goes out has the express words directly from Haman. It has the king's authority; however, the words come from Haman. Second, there is a difference between what Haman told Ahasuerus and what he told the scribes. We will look at the differences in just a minute. Third, the king was not present when Haman dictated to the scribes. We will not know this for sure until Esther 9. Can you imagine the looks on the faces of the scribes, and the thoughts going through their heads when Haman dictated the letters? I imagine the scribes may have asked him to repeat himself to make sure they heard correctly.

Hebrew words:

"Satrap"—*'achashdarpan* (akh-ash-dar-pan') was a governor of a province in Persia. There were twenty major divisions in the empire. The governors were directly under the king.

"Governors" is *Pechah* (peh-khaw'), which is "a depute or governor." This was someone who had authority of a city or small district.

"Princes"—*Sar* (sar) means "general, governor, keeper" and was a local leader of people.

"Province"—*Mediynah* (med-ee-naw') means "province or jurisdiction." It was territory governed by a specific jurisdiction. Remember from Esther 1:1 that there were 127 provinces present.

"Script"—*Kathab* (kaw-thawb') means "register or writing." It included the language spoken as well as local rules or laws of the province.

"Language"—*Lashown* (law-shone') means "the language spoken." The letters were being written to the level of each person, so everyone could understand.

Haman was making sure every living and breathing human being under the authority of Ahasuerus was made aware of the edict.

The statement "being written in the name of King Ahasuerus and sealed with the king's signet ring" means the edict had the authority of the king. Haman had incredible power with the signet ring. There was no legislative branch to vote. There was no judicial branch to determine legality. There were not even the seven "wise men" to tell the king what the law said. This was an evil man with absolute power. What is being proposed here is unprecedented. It is the extermination of a race of people—God's chosen people.

Have you ever heard the quote, "Power tends to corrupt, and absolute power corrupts absolutely?"[8] It was written in 1887 by Lord John Emerich Edward Dalberg Acton, a historian and moralist. Haman was certainly guilty of monumental corruption. His use of power was without responsibility or concern for consequences. Haman thought only of his own hatred and personal gain. He had no concern for others. We will see how God gives Haman a long length of rope to hang himself.

If this were not so tragic, it would be almost comical. When the king wanted to know what to do with Vashti, who disobeyed a summons in Esther 1, he consulted the wise men to determine what the law said about the situation. As it turns out, it was a mockery of justice. But here, when there is discussion to exterminate the Jewish race, there is not even a mention of law.

The nation has surely degenerated. Who is to blame for the state of affairs? Blame has to go to the leaders, Ahasuerus and Haman, of course. Are

---

8   The Phrase Finder. http://www.phrases.org.uk/meanings/288200.html.

the people also to blame? Who is responsible for a nation's wrong decisions, policies, and actions? Is it just the leaders, or are all people responsible?

Principle 25: Every person has to bear some responsibility for the decisions, policies, and actions of the nation—as well as their consequences.

While leadership is primarily responsible, everyone in a nation has to be accountable for what they do or do not do in response to issues affecting the country, including decisions made by leadership. There is, of course, a difference in whether a person lives under a tyrannical dictatorship, or a republic where personal freedom is protected. Even when there are limited rights godly principles can and should be followed. Ultimately, they will have a positive effect on the nation.

This is true for a king, a president, or any national leader. It is true for advisors and for legislators. It is true for those in the judicial system. How about for all citizens of a nation? We have talked about personal responsibility to follow legal and moral authority. We have talked about obeying God and following His laws, even when the government attempts to make such activity illegal.

Look back at Chapter Three: Context when we stated Principle 1, "When a leader sins and rejects God's authority, all those under the leader's authority are affected." At that time, we discussed the Israelite's failure to trust God when He wanted them to go into Canaan. Eleven of twelve leaders chose to reject God's authority. Only Caleb believed God would lead them to victory. As a result, the Israelites had to wander in the desert forty years. All of the Israelites had to accept responsibility and bear the consequence of the decision of the eleven leaders. We should note the response of the people, as they certainly reflected the decision of the eleven leaders.

"Then all the congregation lifted up their voices and cried, and the people wept that night. All the sons of Israel grumbled against Moses and Aaron; and the whole congregation said to them, 'Would that we had died in the land of Egypt! Or would that we had died in this wilderness! Why is the Lord bringing us into this land, to fall by the sword? Our wives and our little ones will become plunder; would it not be better for us to return to Egypt?' So they said to one another, 'Let us appoint a leader and return to Egypt'" (Numbers 14:1–4).

What about government that usurps its authority and passes laws which restrict freedom and move the country towards tyranny? Is this principle relevant in America? Should people simply agree with what leaders say and do without challenging wrong decisions? If no one challenges wrong decisions by leaders, can anyone complain when the consequences of the wrong decisions present themselves? Everyone bears some responsibility for the direction our country is taking. Christians not only have the right, under our Constitution and our civil laws, but also have the responsibility to speak out and legally challenge tyranny.

What examples do we have in modern history of the government becoming tyrannical and restricting freedom? How about Germany in the 1930s? When Hitler was consolidating his power, where were the people to oppose his fascist ideology? I am sure they had no idea where things would lead. What is the answer to the following question, "How did the citizens of Germany allow Hitler to design and execute the mass extermination of 6 million Jews?" The answer is, "one day at a time." Just as in our illustration of the evolution of personal sin, "A to B, then B to C, ultimately to Z," so a nation goes from freedom to tyranny. Slowly giving up personal freedoms at the expense of fear, perceived security, or pleasure leads people and nations down a path resulting in loss of freedom.

How about things in the United States of America? At present, we have freedom to worship. I think we sometimes forget how precious this is. Throughout our history, millions of lives have been given so we would have this freedom. It might not always be this way. Christianity and our freedom to worship are under attack. Could our country go the route of Persia, from letting all the Jews go back to Jerusalem in 539 BC to planning to have all Jews killed in 4/4 BC? Meaning, could our country go from being founded on Judeo-Christian beliefs and a freedom of personal faith and worship in 1776 to not only an absence of such values, but an organized mentality to do away with the right to worship God?

Could anyone in Persia have prevented what Haman was trying to do? Had people allowed anti-Semitism to flourish to the point it was unstoppable? Did the people support what Haman was trying to do, or did they even care? Haman wants to kill all Jews. He deceived Ahasuerus by telling him what the king wanted to hear. We have already discussed the false premise made. In presenting his case, Haman gives a good example of how to convince someone to do something they would not do if the truth were known.

Where else in the Bible do we find deception used for evil means? We have no further to look than the Garden of Eden. Satan deceived the woman by telling her what she wanted to hear.

Deception, which results in bad decisions and loss of freedom, is just as present in our country as it was in Persia in 474 BC. Government leaders often spin truth to accomplish political gains. Manufacturing a crisis, or taking advantage of national adversity to push an agenda of government control is tyranny. Passing laws which result in fundamental changes to the Constitution and presenting them as "good" for America is deceptive.

Lest we think this process is only found in government, we should also look in many of our churches today. Pastors do not always teach God's truth. Emphasis is often on the human viewpoint, involving one person's idea of being good. Feel-good sermons that do not accurately state Bible truths often replace sound Bible doctrine that reveals God's truth. The reason may be due to ignorance on the part of the pastor, an intentional effort to not offend anyone, or to increase attendance. This is a tragedy. The entire realm of Bible doctrine should be taught.

"For the word of God is living and active and sharper than any two-edged sword, and piercing as far as the division of soul and spirit, of both joints and marrow, and able to judge the thoughts and intentions of the heart" (Hebrews 4:14).

"All Scripture is inspired by God and profitable for teaching, for reproof, for correction, for training in righteousness; so that the man of God may be adequate, equipped for every good work" (2 Timothy 3:16–17).

As we progress through the book of Esther, I hope you see the importance of critical Bible study and the application of God's Word to your life. You and I are responsible for our own thoughts, actions, and words, as well as the effect they have on others. I think that our spiritual walk has tremendous effect, not only on those closest to us, but on our nation as well.

In the USAF I was bound by law to follow all lawful orders. To disobey a lawful order could result in Court-martial. I was not bound to follow an unlawful order. In fact, if I was given an unlawful order, I was bound not to follow it. I was bound to do what was right, even if my superiors ordered me to do what was wrong. To the best of my knowledge, this never occurred. Sometimes it is easy to tell right from wrong. Sometimes it is not. To me, the most helpful thing is to remember what Peter said:

"You therefore, beloved, knowing this beforehand, be on your guard so that you are not carried away by the error of unprincipled men and fall from your own steadfastness, but grow in the grace and knowledge of our Lord and Savior Jesus Christ. To Him be the glory, both now and to the day of eternity. Amen" (2 Peter 3:17–18).

So what do we as believers in Jesus Christ do to help our country? I believe we are to stop sinful behavior and turn to God, learn His Word, mature spiritually as in 2 Peter 3:17–18, be transformed as in Romans 12:2, pray, live our lives as God intends us to live, present ourselves with honor and integrity in everything we do, and make right decisions based on our relationship with God. This process should be present in every walk of life; individuals with God, husbands with wives, parents and children, teachers and students, employees and employers, and all citizens with legitimate authority and leaders with those over whom they have authority. Remember what God told Israel.

"And My people who are called by My name humble themselves and pray and seek My face and turn from their wicked ways, then I will hear from heaven, will forgive their sin and will heal their land" (2 Chronicles 7:14).

"Letters were sent by couriers to all the king's provinces to destroy, to kill and to annihilate all the Jews, both young and old, women and children, in one day, the thirteenth day of the twelfth month, which is the month Adar, and to seize their possessions as plunder" (Esther 3:13).

Hebrew words:

"Destroy"—*shamad* (shaw-mad') means "to destroy, overthrow, or perish."

"Kill"—*harag* (haw-rag') means "to destroy, kill, murder, or slaughter."

"Annihilate"—*'abad* (aw-bad') means "to destroy, perish, not to escape, having no way to flee."

In simple terms, Haman wanted to exterminate the Jewish race. Let's compare what Haman told Ahasuerus to what he told the scribes.

Told to Ahasuerus	Told to the Scribes
People in land are different from all other people	Jews
Do not observe the king's laws (Lie)	No accusation made
Not in king's interest to let them remain	No reason for actions given in edict
If it is pleasing to the king, let it be decreed that they be destroyed	To destroy, to kill and to annihilate all the Jews, both young and old, women and children
No time period	One day, the thirteenth day of the twelfth month (Adar)
No property discussed	Seize their possessions as plunder (Haman wants to get rich as well)

Remember the state-of-the-art communication system in chapter two? They used it to gather virgins for the king. Now they use it to spread impending doom.

Who do you think was to do the killing? The edict indicates a command is being given. It is not clear if Haman is ordering the regular army or Persian citizens to kill the Jews.

> "A copy of the edict to be issued as law in every province was published to all the peoples so that they should be ready for this day" (Esther 3:14).

This is truly bizarre. Haman has issued a law, with the king's authority, that non-Jews will kill all Jews—men, women, and children—one year from the edict, and all their possessions will be taken. The law was copied and passed to every location in the empire. It was being published and placed in locations where everyone could read it.

What and who does "to all the peoples" relate? Are these the non-Jews doing the killing or the Jews being killed? Does it mean all non-Jews should be ready to kill the Jews? Does it mean all Jews should be ready to be killed? I think Haman wants to not only tell non-Jews they should be ready to kill Jews, he wants to frighten Jews. Remember, once a law is written, it cannot be repealed (Esther 1:19).

> "The couriers went out impelled by the king's command while the decree was issued at the citadel in Susa; and while the king and Haman sat down to drink, the city of Susa was in confusion" (Esther 3:15).

Hebrew words:

> "Impelled"—*Dachaph* (daw-khaf') means "to hasten." Haman wanted everyone to know immediately.

> "Confused"—*bawk* (book) means "perplexed."

This sounds like Adolf Hitler and Hermann Goering planning the extermination of Jews in World War II Germany and then going to a party. Ahasuerus and Haman sit down and have a drink after ordering the murder of the Jewish race. Both men are out of touch with reality. When I first read this, I was sure Ahasuerus was aware of what Haman had written in the edict. While I believe the king knew Haman planned to have a group of people killed, he did not know it was the Jews. We will see in Esther 7 and 8 that Ahasuerus implies he did not know Haman intended to kill the Jews. In Esther 9, we see it recorded that he did not know the Jews were to be destroyed until Esther told him. The rest of Susa—and possibly the country—is shocked. Non-Jews and Jews can't believe what the king has ordered. In the next chapter, we see the response of the Jews.

While it seems beyond comprehension that the king did not know it was the Jews to be killed, the same incredulous activity can be seen in our government leaders today. The 2009 Stimulus Bill and the 2010 Health Care Reform Bill, passed by Congress and signed by the President, were not, by their own admission, read or understood by many of those who voted for them.

I again ask the question I asked at the end of the last paragraph (Esther 3:7–11): How does the leadership of Persia go from Cyrus freeing the Jews in 538 BC (Ezra 1:1–4) to Ahasuerus signing an edict to have them destroyed in 474 BC, around sixty-five years later? I am sure most people knew of the generosity Cyrus showed to the Jews. Most likely, Haman's edict was a polarizing topic in Persia at the time. On one hand there were the Jews who were to be exterminated. On the other were the non-Jews. It is not clear how many non-Jews supported the edict. There does not seem to be any opposition and it does not appear anyone is willing to stand in the way of Haman's plan. Either because of fear or apathy, they did not do anything to stop it. It was not a normal activity to challenge the authority of the king. We will see in Esther 8 that many non-Jews change their minds and decide to support the Jews.

Present-day government often uses similar tactics in pursuing its agenda. A group of people, a business, or an entity is identified that the government wants to defeat or take over. Half-truths, lies, and facts are spun to demonize the targeted group. Class envy is used to gain the support of those not in the group. Economic policies and health care reform are recent examples of this type of governmental tyranny.

Christianity is under a similar attack in America. Christians are often labeled as people who hate others for standing on principles of Bible doctrine. Satan is certainly trying to stop the spread of the Gospel. Paul tells us:

"Indeed, all who desire to live godly in Christ Jesus will be persecuted" (2 Timothy 3:12).

It is very important for believers to live and act as Jesus Christ lived. Many of the principles found in this book will help you in your journey.

Theme Statement

Law to have the Jews destroyed is spread throughout the empire.

Things to Remember

Paragraph Theme Statements

Esther 3:1–6—Mordecai disrespects Haman, who then plans to exterminate the Jewish race.

Esther 3:7–11—Haman gains the king's approval to have a certain people destroyed.

Esther 3:12–15—Law to have Jews destroyed is spread throughout empire.

Principles

23. God expects us to follow the legal authority over us when it does not violate His commands.

24. Replacing trust and obedience to God with human arrogance, stubbornness, and pride leads to conflict for you and those around you.

25. Every person has to bear some responsibility for the decisions, policies, and actions of the nation—as well as their consequences.

Chapter Seven

ESTHER 4:
TRUST AND OBEDIENCE

Jews mourn

"When Mordecai learned all that had been done, he tore his clothes, put on sackcloth and ashes, and went out into the midst of the city and wailed loudly and bitterly. He went as far as the king's gate, for no one was to enter the king's gate clothed in sackcloth. In each and every province where the command and decree of the king came, there was great mourning among the Jews, with fasting, weeping and wailing; and many lay on sackcloth and ashes" (Esther 4:1–3).

Where

City of Susa and throughout the entire kingdom.

When

474 BC, after the edict had been sent out; five years after Esther had become queen (Esther 2:16).

X 474 BC—month Nisan—Haman casts lot
  X 474 BC—thirteenth day of Nisan—king's scribes summoned

  X 474 BC—sometime after the 13ᵗʰ day of the first month, Nisan—Mordecai mourns

      474 BC—13ᵗʰ day Adar—when Jews are to be destroyed **X**

---

*   *   *   *   *   *   *   *   *   *   *   *   *

474

Nisan	Sivan	Av	Tishri	Chislev	Shebat	(Adar II)
(Ma/Ap)	(May/Jun)	(Jul/Aug)	(Sep/Oct)	(Nov/Dec)	(Jan/Feb)	(leap yr)

Iyyar	Tammuz	Elul	Cheshvan	Tebeth	Adar
(Ap/May)	(Jun/Jul)	(Aug/Sep)	(Oct/Nov)	(Dec/Jan)	(Feb/Mar)

Time starts to speed up, with a lot of events occurring in the next several days. Does everyone in the kingdom know what is to happen on the thirteenth day of Adar, about one year from the present date? I think most Jews and non-Jews alike are aware; however, not everyone knows. As stated in the last chapter, the king knows a group is to be killed; however, he is not aware it is the Jews. There is another person who is not aware of what is to happen—Esther.

> "When Mordecai learned all that had been done, he tore his clothes, put on sackcloth and ashes, and went out into the midst of the city and wailed loudly and bitterly" (Esther 4:1).

Hebrew words:

"Sackcloth"—*saq* (sak), "coarse, loose cloth or sacking"

"Ashes"—*'epher* (ay'-fer), "ashes"

"Cried"—*za`aq* (zaw-ak'), "to publicly cry out in anguish"

"Cry"—*za`aq* (zah'-ak) and *ze`aqah* (zeh-aw-kaw'), "cry"

"Loud"—*gadowl* (gaw-dole'), "loud or mighty"

"Bitter"—*mar* (mar), "angry, bitter, discontented"

172

As a Jewish citizen in the city of Susa, "Mordecai learned all that had been done," meaning he became aware of the law to exterminate the Jews and the date it was to occur. What does he do? He responds with great emotion. He "tore his clothes, put on sackcloth and ashes, and went out into the midst of the city and wailed loudly and bitterly."

So what does all this mean? Wearing sackcloth and ashes and crying out in public is a sign of mourning. It is a legitimate form of expressing grief for the Jewish people (Genesis 37:29, 34; 1 Samuel 4:12; 2 Samuel 1:2, 3:31, 13:19; 1 Kings 20:31; 2 Kings 6:30; Job 1:20; Jeremiah 49:3; Daniel 9:3; Joel 1:13; Jonah 3:6). Mordecai was legitimately grieved and is expressing his feelings.

How do you respond to disappointment and grief? When you are sad, angry, or just feel life is unfair, what do you do? Do you respond the way Mordecai did? His was a very public, very emotional, very physical outpouring of his feelings. This was not a private mourning. It was letting the entire city know of his sorrow. It was cultural for the Jews of that period. In Esther 4:3, we see this behavior went on throughout the kingdom.

Mordecai knew what was going to happen and why. Did he feel responsible for the law that was issued to kill the Jews? He had refused to bow down to Haman. To further complicate the situation, Mordecai told people he was Jewish. It appears Mordecai did not have his faith and trust in God when he made his decisions in the previous chapter. Remember Principle 24: "Replacing trust and obedience to God with human arrogance, stubbornness, and pride leads to conflict for you and those around you." Mordecai's actions did contribute to the situation.

Would Haman have planned to kill the Jews if Mordecai had not refused to bow down to him? I believe Haman would have found another reason if he did not have Mordecai to blame. As I said in Esther 3:6, it is my opinion Haman was demon-possessed, and the plot against the Jews was satanic. What was happening to the Jews was premeditated. In addition, it was completely unfair.

Principle 26: Life is not fair. In our fallen world bad things will happen to you, whether you deserve them or not.

This is as true for us today as it was for Mordecai, Esther, and the Jews. Satan is the ruler of the world, and he wants to destroy what God has made, including your relationship with Him. Sin is in the world and has corrupted everything it touches. I know everyone reading this book has had something unfair happen to them. The question is not, "will something bad happen to you?" It is, "what will happen, when, what will be your response, and to whom will you turn for help?"

You will face adversity, whether you think you deserve it or not. Detailed reasons for adversity are beyond the scope of this book. Simply put, adversity may be the consequence of personal choices (deserved), or it may be through no fault of one's self (undeserved). Whether Satan is behind your suffering or not, God is ever-present. Your suffering will not be greater than God allows. The story of Job clearly defines Satan's attempt to inflict pain and God's authority in limiting the degree (Job 1:1–12, 2:1–6). As we saw in Chapter Three, the Israelites suffered greatly, usually due to sin and the resulting discipline. Nevertheless, God did not let them be destroyed (Exodus 20:20–21; Deuteronomy 8:1–3; Joshua 1:9; 1 Chronicles 29:17–18; Lamentations 3:37–38; Isaiah 41:8–10, 43:2–3, 51:7–8).

What does this mean for the New Testament believer? God tells us we will suffer, He is aware of it, it has a purpose, He will deliver us, and we have the potential for great blessing from it (Luke 12:4–7; 2 Corinthians 1:3–11; Philippians 1:29; 1 Thessalonians 3:1–5; 2 Timothy 3:10–13; James 1:1–5, 12; 1 Peter 1:5–8, 4:12–14, 19; Revelation 2:8–10). How we respond to suffering is critical. Just as we stated in Principle 8, "Disobedience to God in times of discipline leads to further discipline." Turning away from God in times of suffering negates the blessing He has for you.

"For this reason I also suffer these things, but I am not ashamed; for I know whom I have believed and I am convinced that He is able to guard what I have entrusted to Him until that day" (2 Timothy 1:12).

"Therefore be patient, brethren, until the coming of the Lord. The farmer waits for the precious produce of the soil, being patient about it, until it gets the early and late rains. You too be patient; strengthen your hearts, for the coming of the Lord is near. Do not complain, brethren, against one another, so that you yourselves may not be judged; behold, the Judge is standing right at the door. As an example, brethren, of suffering and patience, take the prophets who spoke in the name of the Lord. We count those blessed who endured. You have heard of the endurance of Job and have seen the outcome of the Lord's dealings, that the Lord is full of compassion and is merciful (James 5:7–11).

Temptation is often associated with adversity. At the beginning of His ministry, Jesus faced adversity and was tempted.

"And He was in the wilderness forty days being tempted by Satan; and He was with the wild beasts, and the angels were ministering to Him" (Mark 1:12).

For believers, God has promised that when we face adversity and are tempted, we will be able to resist turning away from Him and sinning.

"No temptation has overtaken you but such as is common to man; and God is faithful, who will not allow you to be tempted beyond what you are able, but with the temptation will provide the way of escape also, so that you will be able to endure it" (1 Corinthians 10:13).

When we submit to temptation and sin, we become active participants in the bad things that happen to us. Sin separates us from God which often results in self-induced misery or discipline from God. All of us are guilty of this from time to time.

"For all have sinned and fall short of the glory of God" (Romans 3:23).

"For the wages of sin is death, but the free gift of God is eternal life in Christ Jesus our Lord" (Romans 6:23).

Even when we try to do "good" in our human flesh, we are unable to meet God's standard.

"For all of us have become like one who is unclean, and all our righteous deeds are like a filthy garment; and all of us wither like a leaf, and our iniquities, like the wind, take us away" (Isaiah 64:6).

We have two strikes against us—our personal sin, and our inadequate "good deeds" that fail to measure up to God's righteousness. The amazing thing is that God blesses us, even though we do not deserve His favor. This includes salvation and everything else God does for us. Yes, it is true that life is not fair—and thankfully so. Why? Because God shows us grace and mercy when we do not deserve them.

What was behind Mordecai's mourning? Was it remorse? Was it pity? Was it concern for the Jewish population? Was it crying out for deliverance? Did he think God's chosen people would be destroyed? Did he regret telling people his nationality?

> "He went as far as the king's gate, for no one was to enter the king's gate clothed in sackcloth" (Esther 4:2).

Evidently no one was allowed inside the gate if they were dressed in sackcloth. I wonder if the king and those inside the palace saw Mordecai's mourning. I suspect Haman received satisfaction observing Mordecai's grieving.

> "In each and every province where the command and decree of the king came, there was great mourning among the Jews, with fasting, weeping and wailing; and many lay on sackcloth and ashes" (Esther 4:3).

The Jews in the empire were in mourning as well. There was weeping, wailing, and the wearing of sackcloth and ashes. We also see there was fasting, or *tsowm* (tsome). "In the Old Testament the fast was regarded as an act of self-renunciation designed to mollify God's wrath and move him to act in gracious disposition. In times of emergency, the people fasted to persuade God to spare them from impending calamity (Judges 20:26; 1 Samuel 7:6; 1 Kings 21:9; 2 Chronicles 20:3; Jeremiah 36:6, 9). Individuals fasted in the hope that God would liberate them from trouble (2 Samuel 12:16–20; 1 Kings 21:27; Psalms 35:13, 69:10). Fasting was regarded as concomitant to prayer to assure that God would answer the prayers (Ezra 8:21; Nehemiah 1:4; Jeremiah 14:12). Throughout the Old Testament, fasting is associated with a mournful attitude of importuning God to aid the supplicant."[1]

Although God is not mentioned here, fasting does suggest acknowledgement of God and the seeking of His grace. This is the first reference in Esther of the Jews seeking God. It does not say Mordecai fasted, just other Jews.

Look back to Esther 3:15. "The couriers went out impelled by the king's command while the decree was issued at the citadel in Susa; and while the king and Haman sat down to drink, the city of Susa was in confusion." I wonder what the king and Haman thought when they were told of the Jews morning, fasting, wailing, and weeping?

Theme Statement

Mordecai and Jews mourn impending destruction.

Esther learns of plan for Jewish destruction

"Then Esther's maidens and her eunuchs came and told her, and the queen writhed in great anguish. And she sent garments to clothe Mordecai that he might remove his sackcloth from him, but he did not accept them. Then Esther summoned Hathach from the king's eunuchs, whom the king had appointed to attend her, and ordered him to go to Mordecai to learn what this was and why it was. So Hathach went out to Mordecai to the city square in front of the king's gate. Mordecai told him

---

1   Elwell, Walter A. and Barry J. Beitzel. 1988. *Baker Encyclopedia of the Bible.* Grand Rapids: Baker Book House. S. 780.

all that had happened to him, and the exact amount of money that Haman had promised to pay to the king's treasuries for the destruction of the Jews. He also gave him a copy of the text of the edict which had been issued in Susa for their destruction, that he might show Esther and inform her, and to order her to go in to the king to implore his favor and to plead with him for her people" (Esther 4:4–8).

Where

Palace and the city square in front of the king's gate.

When

474 BC, after the edict had been sent out; five years after Esther had become queen (Esther 2:16).

X 474 BC—thirteenth day of Nisan—king's scribes summoned

X 474 BC—sometime after the 13th day of the first month, Nisan—Mordecai mourns

X 474 BC—Esther learns of Mordecai's mourning and edict to kill Jews

474 BC—13th day Adar—when Jews are to be destroyed X

* * * * * * * * * * * * *

474

Nisan	Sivan	Av	Tishri	Chislev	Shebat	(Adar II)
(Ma/Ap)	(May/Jun)	(Jul/Aug)	(Sep/Oct)	(Nov/Dec)	(Jan/Feb)	(leap yr)

Iyyar	Tammuz	Elul	Cheshvan	Tebeth	Adar
(Ap/May)	(Jun/Jul)	(Aug/Sep)	(Oct/Nov)	(Dec/Jan)	(Feb/Mar)

In chapter three, paragraph two (Esther 3:7–11), I asked the question of what Esther had been doing for five years. We now hear from her for the first time since she became queen. She has maidens and eunuchs to meet her needs. She lives in luxury expected for the queen and appears to be comfortable. We find out a little later she does not regularly see the king. How much information she knew about what was going on in the kingdom is not known. We are about to find out that she did not know what was going on with the king's edict.

"Then Esther's maidens and her eunuchs came and told her, and the queen writhed in great anguish. And she sent garments to clothe Mordecai that he might remove his sackcloth from him, but he did not accept them" (Esther 4:4).

Hebrew words:

"Writhed"—*chuwl* (khool), "writhe in pain, fear, shake, tremble"

"Great anguish"—*me'od* (meh-ode'), used as an intensive or superlative

Esther's maidens and eunuchs became aware of what Mordecai was doing and told her he was parading around the city in sackcloth, wailing as he went. Esther's response was that she "writhed in great anguish." She was truly upset, worried, and anxious.

I don't think Esther's maidens and eunuchs knew she and Mordecai were related, otherwise they would know she was Jewish, which would likely result in the king knowing. We do know there had been some communication between Mordecai and Esther. Prior to Esther becoming queen, Mordecai "walked back and forth in front of the court of the harem to learn how Esther was and how she fared" (Esther 2:11), and after she became queen, he was able to communicate with her (Esther 2:22).

Don't you just love the way the author describes how the Jews of 474 BC expressed feelings? Mordecai "tore his clothes, put on sackcloth and ashes, and went out into the midst of the city and wailed loudly and bitterly." Esther "writhed in great anguish."

Did Esther know what Mordecai had done, that he had refused to bow to Haman and then told people he was Jewish? Did Esther know about Haman's anger? Did Esther know about the edict to kill the Jews? I think the answer to all three questions is no. So why was she writhing in anguish? Esther was upset because she did *not* know why Mordecai was acting in such a manner. At this point, it does not say she is worried about herself. It would be natural for her to think people would know Mordecai was Jewish, since he was in sackcloth. Do you think it crossed Esther's mind people might make a connection between Mordecai and her?

What do you think of Esther's initial solution? She wants him to take off the sackcloth and put on good clothes. Maybe it is so he can come in the gate and talk with her directly. Maybe it is so he would stop making a scene and would not be an embarrassment. Maybe Esther did not want to have anyone know she was Jewish.

> "Then Esther summoned Hathach from the king's eunuchs, whom the king had appointed to attend her, and ordered him to go to Mordecai to learn what this was and why it was. So Hathach went out to Mordecai to the city square in front of the king's gate. Mordecai told him all that had happened to him, and the exact amount of money that Haman had promised to pay to the king's treasuries for the destruction of the Jews" (Esther 4:5–7).

Well, Mordecai refused the clothes. Esther could not go herself, so she sends Hathach, a eunuch, to find out what was going on and why. Hathach had to be somebody Esther could trust completely. What do you think of Mordecai's response to Hathach?

Hathach and Mordecai meet in the city square in front of the king's gate. Mordecai tells him everything: his refusal to bow to Haman, telling people he was Jewish, Haman's anger, the king's edict to exterminate the Jews, the amount of money Haman was to pay to the king to destroy the Jews, why he is wearing sackcloth and ashes, and why all other Jews in the country are fasting, weeping, and wailing.

> "He also gave him a copy of the text of the edict which had been issued in Susa for their destruction, that he might show Esther and inform her, and to order her to go in to the king to implore his favor and to plead with him for her people" (Esther 4:8).

Mordecai then drops the bombshell. Hathach is to give Esther a copy of the edict to educate her on the problem. Mordecai believes Esther is not aware of the things he has just told Hathach. Hathach is to order Esther to go to the king to implore his favor and to plead with him for her people. When Mordecai says to Hathach "her people," he is saying to him Esther is Jewish. He is telling Esther to tell the king she is Jewish.

What do you think about Mordecai at this point? It appears he has stopped his emotional wailing and has started to think. What do you think is going on with Esther?

She has to be on pins and needles waiting for Hathach to return.

Theme Statement

Mordecai confides in Hathach and instructs him to inform Esther of problem and solution.

Counting the costs

> "Hathach came back and related Mordecai's words to Esther. Then Esther spoke to Hathach and ordered him to reply to Mordecai: 'All the king's servants and the people of the king's provinces know that for any man or woman who comes to the king to the inner court who is not summoned, he has but one law, that he be put to death, unless the king holds out to him the golden scepter so that he may live. And I have not been summoned to come to the king for these thirty days.' They related Esther's words to Mordecai" (Esther 4:9–12).

Where

Palace and the city square in front of the king's gate.

When

474 BC, after the edict had been sent out; five years after Esther had become queen (Esther 2:16).

Hathach tells Esther everything. What does Esther now know that she did not know before? Mordecai refused to bow to Haman. Mordecai told everyone he is a Jew. Mordecai's actions resulted in Haman's anger. Haman has planned to kill all the Jews. The king has issued an edict calling for the destruction of the Jews. Hathach knows she is a Jew, and finally, that Mordecai wants her to tell the king she is a Jew and plead for all of her people.

I think there is quite a pause between the end of Esther 4:9 and the *then* in Esther 4:10. What do you think is going through Esther's mind? Have you ever told your children to not do something—and then later have done that thing yourself? Then have you gotten caught in doing that thing and gotten into trouble? What happens if your child becomes aware of what you have done? What do you think and feel at that moment? What does your child think and feel at that moment? Mordecai has been caught doing something he told Esther not to do.

Principle 27: Good leaders do what they tell others to do and do not do what they tell others not to do.

"Do what I say, not what I do" is not a legitimate way to lead. Effective leaders do not follow this principle. They deny themselves certain pleasures so that those under their authority have things better. They also lead by example, being the first to do those tasks which may be difficult or dangerous. This principle is critical in the military. A good example of this type of leadership is found in Steven Ambrose's *Band of Brothers*, particularly in the life of Major Dick Winters. It is also critical for parents in rearing children.

What do you think was going through Esther's mind between Esther 4:9 and 4:10? Mordecai had done exactly what he had told her not to do. Did Esther have fear for herself or others, doubt, or anger? When you hear bad news that involves you, what goes on in your mind, and what do you do? Do you think only of yourself, or do you think of others? Are you driven by emotion, or are you driven by sound thinking? Do you fear, or do you trust God? Do you try to escape from the situation, or do you sit tight, look to, and obey God? Esther does what most of us do from time to time when faced with a personal threat. She tries to reason things so she does not have to become involved. Her reply:

> "All the king's servants and the people of the king's provinces know that for any man or woman who comes to the king to the inner court who is not summoned, he has but one law, that he be put to death, unless the king holds out to him the golden scepter so that he may live. And I have not been summoned to come to the king for these thirty days" (Esther 4:11).

You cannot argue the facts Esther is presenting. If a man or woman goes to the king while he is in the inner court and that person has not been summoned, one of two things will happen. Either the king will hold out his golden scepter, and the person will live, or the king will not hold out his golden scepter, and the person will be put to death.

This was true for everyone—the queen included. If there was any doubt about the authority of the king, this shows his absolute power.

We also find out that Esther has not been summoned by the king in thirty days. No reason is given for this, and Esther's thoughts on why she has not been summoned are not stated. She could only imagine the king did not want to see her. Ladies, have you ever felt ignored by your husband, and were you afraid to bring a trouble to him? Men, have you ever felt ignored by your boss, and were you afraid to bring a trouble to that person? Children, have you ever felt ignored by your parents, and were you afraid to bring a trouble to them?

What was Esther thinking at this time? It is understandable she would need time to process all the information she had just received. It is also understandable she would want to give objective facts to Mordecai. Esther was, in fact, displaying a healthy acknowledgment of concern regarding the situation she was facing. It would not be expected for her or anyone to give a quick answer to Mordecai's command. Esther was counting the costs.

Taking into account the paragraph above, I do think after listening to what Hathach said, Esther felt fear. Instead of offering a solution to the problem or showing concern for all the Jews, she focused on the risk she would face personally in going to the king uninvited. Although she stated truth regarding her situation, she did not acknowledge faith in God. I also believe she did not truly understand the magnitude of the problem, nor the fact that God had chosen her for this position.

Principle 28: Fear comes from a failure to trust God. When facing adversity, trust and obey God.

I am not talking about the fear that keeps us from irrational actions. Fear of putting your hand in a fire or jumping off a tall building is normal. I am speaking of the fear of doing or saying what God wants of you. This type of fear results when there is a failure to trust Him.

The Bible is full of promises God has given us to combat the sin of fear. Knowing and understanding them is relatively easy. Applying them in adversity is sometimes difficult. Trust, obedience, and faith are required.

> "Do not fear, for I am with you; do not anxiously look about you, for I am your God. I will strengthen you, surely I will help you, surely I will uphold you with My righteous right hand" (Isaiah 41:10).
>
> "For God has not given us a spirit of timidity, but of power and love and discipline" (2 Timothy 1:7).
>
> "Therefore let us draw near with confidence to the throne of grace, so that we may receive mercy and find grace to help in time of need." (Hebrews 4:16)
>
> "Make sure that your character is free from the love of money, being content with what you have; for He Himself has said, 'I will never desert you, nor will I ever forsake you,' so that we confidently say, 'The Lord is my helper, I will not be afraid. What will man do to me?'" (Hebrews 13:5–6)

In fairness to Esther, I have to point out she did not have a strong support system for her faith. For five years, she had not been able to tell anyone she was Jewish. I assume that occasionally she would talk to Mordecai; however, she could not tell her husband of her beliefs. She had been lavished in luxury as queen. Did she have daily prayer with God? What a temptation to forget her faith.

> God tests us in many ways—sometimes with adversity and sometimes with prosperity. What do you do when God blesses you with success or wealth? Maybe you have worked hard and earned whatever you have attained, or maybe you became prosperous without any effort. In either case, do you thank God and keep your eyes on Him, or do you turn away from Him, forget it is He who sustains you, and sink into arrogant pride?

What is Esther saying to Mordecai? Her words do not say she will not go to the king. She is simply implying that if she were to go, there was a possibility she would be killed. From a human standpoint, this makes perfect sense, and I cannot criticize Esther for her response.

How do you respond when you are under stress and are faced with making a decision that will likely cause you to suffer? This is a trick question. It depends on whether or not you trust and obey God. Most of us respond like Esther at one time or another. Fear grips us, and we look for a way out. The result is making decisions that are against what God wants for us.

Principle 29: You cannot make right decisions while under stress unless you look to God for the solution and you trust and obey Him.

Your relationship with God has to be right. If there is sin in your life, confess it, turn away from the human viewpoint, and turn toward God. The Holy Spirit will direct you through the knowledge and application of God's Word. Trust God and obey Him.

"They related Esther's words to Mordecai" (Esther 4:12).

Do you notice something strange here? Mordecai told one person, Hathach. Hathach told Esther what Mordecai said. Esther told Hathach what to tell Mordecai. When Mordecai was told Esther's response, there were more people present than just Hathach. Why was this? I think Hathach said to Esther, "Now wait a minute, I want somebody else with me to make sure I do not mess this up. What you are telling me is critical."

Theme Statement

Esther tells Mordecai she may perish if she goes to the king.

Sovereignty and free will

"Then Mordecai told them to reply to Esther, 'Do not imagine that you in the king's palace can escape any more than all the Jews. For if you remain silent at this time, relief and deliverance

185

will arise for the Jews from another place and you and your father's house will perish. And who knows whether you have not attained royalty for such a time as this?' Then Esther told them to reply to Mordecai, 'Go, assemble all the Jews who are found in Susa, and fast for me; do not eat or drink for three days, night or day. I and my maidens also will fast in the same way. And thus I will go in to the king, which is not according to the law; and if I perish, I perish.' So Mordecai went away and did just as Esther had commanded him" (Esther 4:13–17).

Where

Palace and the city square in front of the king's gate.

When

474 BC, after the edict had been sent out; five years after Esther had become queen (Esther 2:16).

X 474 BC—month Nisan—Haman casts lot
  X 474 BC—thirteenth day of Nisan—king's scribes summoned
    X 474 BC—sometime after the 13th day of the first month, Nisan—Mordecai mourns
   X 474 BC—Esther learns of Mordecai's mourning and edict to kill Jews

  X 474 BC—Esther agrees to go to king

      474 BC, 13th day Adar—when Jews are to be destroyed **X**

*   *   *   *   *   *   *   *   *   *   *   *   *

474

Nisan	Sivan	Av	Tishri	Chislev	Shebat	(Adar II)
(Ma/Ap)	(May/Jun)	(Jul/Aug)	(Sep/Oct)	(Nov/Dec)	(Jan/Feb)	(leap yr)

	Iyyar	Tammuz	Elul	Cheshvan	Tebeth	Adar
	(Ap/May)	(Jun/Jul)	(Aug/Sep)	(Oct/Nov)	(Dec/Jan)	(Feb/Mar)

In heaven, I hope we get to go back and watch historical events occur. I would love to hear these words spoken. If not, I would at least like to sit down and talk with Esther about this next scene. It is one of my favorite paragraphs in the Old Testament. Although it is not the climax of the story, it is the significant moment in personal acknowledgement and resolution of mental conflict for both Mordecai and Esther. I believe this is the critical scene in the entire book. Both Mordecai and Esther face the reality of the situation and thoughtfully make decisions based on their trust and obedience to God.

Where else in the Bible do we see resolution of mental conflict in the soul that enables an individual to do God's will, even though the decision results in severe suffering? Think of the night and early morning hours before Jesus was crucified. Jesus struggled mentally before He went to the cross. Words such as *agony, deeply grieved,* and *sweat became like drops of blood* are used to describe Jesus in the Garden of Gethsemane. He asked God if the cup could pass from Him. Once He knew the Father was indeed requiring Him to go to the cross, Jesus accepted and went full speed ahead. We will see Esther come to grips with the reality of what she must do, both for herself and all the Jews. Once she does, she is unstoppable.

We look at Esther in terms of God's providence and the saving of His people. We should also see the glorification of God through individuals who choose His plan. God would have delivered the Jews from another source if Esther had not done what she was supposed to do. The fact she did trust and obey God glorified Him. We may think our lives are trivial in comparison to Esther's. God may not be asking us to save all believers from Satan's destruction, but He is just as glorified when we trust and obey Him in our daily lives as He was when Esther did so in 474 BC.

Trusting and obeying is not easy. In fact, it is so hard you cannot do it on your own. God intended it that way. If you could do it on your own, you would not need Him. When you turn to Him (Father), and rely on Him (Holy Spirit), to help you trust and obey, He (Father, Son, and Holy Spirit) is glorified. When faced with adversity, what is the harder thing to overcome—the mental or physical conflict?

> "Then Mordecai told them to reply to Esther, 'Do not imagine that you in the king's palace can escape any more than all the Jews. For if you remain silent at this time, relief and deliverance will arise for the Jews from another place and you and your father's house will perish. And who knows whether you have not attained royalty for such a time as this?'" (Esther 4:13–14)

Mordecai tells the messengers to tell Esther three truths. I think they either said them very slowly, or said them over and over, or maybe both. First, "do not imagine that you in the king's palace can escape any more than all the Jews." Mordecai makes things very personal. He gets right to the point. He reminds Esther she is a Jew, just like everyone else, and will be found out. I am sure Esther remembered what the king did to her predecessor. He had her dismissed just because she would not come to his party. He has since signed an edict saying all Jews will be killed. Even though she is queen, she knows she will be included.

Second, "for if you remain silent at this time, relief and deliverance will arise for the Jews from another place and you and your father's house will perish." It is time to bring God into the picture. Mordecai does not mention God's name, but he might as well have. Of course, He has been present, directing the events from the beginning. It is nice, however, to point the finger a little more clearly toward Him. Although He is not mentioned by name, Mordecai is speaking of Yahweh.

Esther has two options—she can speak up and go to the king or remain silent. Mordecai acknowledges that Esther has volition. She has a choice. It is clear the right thing for her to do is to speak up. God wants Esther to go to the king, and if she "remains silent," she will be disobeying. Esther's trust and obedience are being put to the test. Mordecai gives two reasons which describe the result of disobedience in order to convince Esther to do the right thing. If she does not act, God will provide another source for deliverance for the Jews. If she does not act, she and her father's house will perish. That means Mordecai. If she disobeys God, He will deliver the Jews, but she and her house will be destroyed.

Mordecai is convinced God will deliver the Jews. He believes deliverance will come from the king because of what he is telling Esther to do. Since Mordecai tells Esther "relief and deliverance will arise for the Jews from another place" if she does not go to the king, he has to believe if Esther fails to convince the king, and is put to death, the Jews will still be rescued.

Third, "and who knows whether you have not attained royalty for such a time as this?" Mordecai is playing hardball. He is saying to her, "It is not enough you will be killed and God will find someone else to go to the king, you need to know, Esther, God has sustained you your entire life so you would be in this position to go to the king and save your people." I am sure Esther thought about her entire life and all the events that led up to her present position as queen. Why was Vashti dismissed? Why were all beautiful virgins forced into the harem? How did she find favor with Hegai? Why was she selected to be queen? Why had she been protected for the last five years? Why had everything happened the way it did?

The three truths which Mordecai has stated are pivotal in the outcome of our story as well as in characterizing an important biblical doctrine. In the book of Esther, it means the beginning of the resolution of the conflict facing the Jews. On a much bigger scale, it is one of the best examples of God's sovereignty and man's free will working together. God knew in eternity past that Satan would try to annihilate the Jews. In God's perfect plan He provided for Esther to be in this position for the express purpose of going to the king and pleading for the Jews. Esther has volition; she can choose to do what Mordecai says, or she can refuse. If she trusts God and obeys Him, she will be used by God. If she does not trust God and disobeys Him, God will deliver the Jews in another manner. Remember God's foreknowledge. He knew exactly what Esther would do. Think of the implications these verses have for us. The following verse was presented in the introduction under the discussion of sovereignty and free will.

"For we are His workmanship, created in Christ Jesus for good works, which God prepared beforehand so that we would walk in them" (Ephesians 2:10).

In eternity past, God designed specific works for each one of us in which we are to walk. I think Esther is seeing the specific work God has designed for her. If she does not walk in it, God will find someone else. If we do not walk in the works God has designed for us, He will find someone else. Just as Esther would have suffered if she did not go to the king, we will suffer if we do not do the things God has designed for us. I think this means there will be suffering on earth as well as loss of blessings in heaven.

How do you know when God is asking you to do something? What are the works God has for you? It seems clear in the Bible when God is asking men and women to act. Mordecai simply tells Esther what she is supposed to do, and we believe that it is one of the works God has planned for her. There are many times in the Bible when we read, "God said ..." Think of Noah, Moses, and many of the prophets. Well, how do things work for you and me? The simple answer is the filling of the Holy Spirit, knowledge of God's Word, and prayer. It is also a daily personal relationship with Jesus Christ and spiritual growth.

Have you ever been sure God had something for you to do—and you said no to Him? Do you ever wonder whom God used in your place? Do you ever wonder how they were blessed and what opportunities you missed? I believe these questions will be answered in heaven.

If the example of Mordecai and Esther does not convince you of the coexistence of God's sovereignty and people's free will, let's look at the person of Jesus Christ. He existed on earth as a true man and undiminished deity. This is known as the doctrine of the hypostatic union. As a man, Jesus was tempted—I believe far more than we will ever know.

"Jesus, full of the Holy Spirit, returned from the Jordan and was led around by the Spirit in the wilderness for forty days, being tempted by the devil. And He ate nothing during those days, and when they had ended, He became hungry" (Luke 4:1–2).

If Jesus was really tempted, then he must have had an opportunity to say yes to the temptation. Free will had to be present. In eternity past, God's divine plan determined Jesus would become man and be our substitutionary sacrifice on the cross. Divine sovereignty had to be fulfilled. Jesus would not fall into temptation. Jesus clearly stated His purpose on earth.

"For I have come down from heaven, not to do My own will, but the will of Him who sent Me" (John 6:38).

When He was in the garden of Gethsemane, He asked the Father if the cross could be taken away.

"Father, if You are willing, remove this cup from Me; yet not My will, but Yours be done" (Luke 22:42).

In His humanity, I believe Jesus had free will to refuse to do the Father's will. He, of course, did not refuse, and we are eternally grateful for his decision. Once again, God's sovereignty remains perfect.

How much time elapsed between the end of Esther 4:14 and the beginning of Esther 4:15? Before you read Esther 4:15, go back and re-read verse 11. This is what we last heard from Esther. When she opens her mouth to speak in 4:15, she is a different person. The words that come out of her mouth are incredible. I think they come from the strength of godly virtue and integrity. Listen to what she says:

"Go, assemble all the Jews who are found in Susa, and fast for me; do not eat or drink for three days, night or day. I and my maidens also will fast in the same way. And thus I will go in to the king, which is not according to the law; and if I perish, I perish" (Esther 4:15).

I can see her saying these words. There is strength, peace, conviction, and determination. Esther has her mind made up. She knows what she needs to do. But before she does anything, she is going to God. Remember, fasting signifies going to God. Prayer is not specifically mentioned; however, it would be expected of Jews during fasting (1 Samuel 1:7–10; 2 Samuel 12:16–17; Ezra 8:23; Isaiah 58:2–5; Jeremiah 14:12; Daniel 9:3; Zechariah 7:3–5). She is asking all Jews in Susa to fast for three days and nights and to pray to God. She and her maidens will do the same. If they did not know she was Jewish, they will now.

For what and for whom were the Jews praying? One would think they prayed that Esther would have strength, wisdom, and courage. Hopefully they would also be praying for Ahasuerus to receive Esther. Prayer was needed to prevent distractions to the king and to prevent satanic influence. This leads to a very important principle for all of us.

Principle 30: We should pray for our leaders, whether we agree or disagree with them.

We have said quite a bit about leaders and the responsibility of authority. The fact is that leadership is difficult. There are tremendous pressures on those who are responsible for others. Leaders need all the good help they can get. This includes prayer from believers. For what should we pray? We should pray that our leaders seek God's will, have wisdom in making decisions, speak truthfully, and do not become distracted with personal gain. We should pray for their health and safety. We should pray the same for those who influence our leaders. Should we pray for our leaders even when they make wrong decisions that result in harm to us? Do so especially in those situations. Believers have no excuse for not praying for their leaders, even when they disagree with those in authority. Listen to what Jesus said:

"Bless those who curse you, pray for those who mistreat you" (Luke 6:28).

Paul also has some good words concerning this issue:

> "First of all, then, I urge that entreaties and prayers, petitions and thanksgivings, be made on behalf of all men, for kings and all who are in authority, so that we may lead a tranquil and quiet life in all godliness and dignity. This is good and acceptable in the sight of God our Savior, who desires all men to be saved and to come to the knowledge of the truth" (1 Timothy 2:1–4).

Finally, when you pray, do so fervently, as Elijah (James 5:16-18).

The logical connector of result, *and thus,* indicates a positive action. After three days of fasting and prayer, Esther was going to the king. She was doing so with full awareness the law said if the king does not hold out his scepter, she would be put to death. Even so, she was stating her plans with peaceful conviction. She knew God wanted her to do this. If she was to be killed as a result, she knew God would be with her.

Was there a real possibility Esther would be put to death? Esther thought so. She did not know what the king would do. Do we need to know the outcome when we walk in the works God has prepared for us?

Principle 31: It is not necessary to know the outcome when you walk in the works God has prepared for you.

"Trust in the Lord with all your heart. And do not lean on your own understanding. In all your ways acknowledge Him, and He will make your paths straight" (Proverbs 3:5–6).

If we trust God, follow His ways, and live our lives in obedience to Him, all of those works He prepared for us in eternity past will be laid out for us in such a way that we can walk in them. There will be no reason to be concerned with outcome, because God will direct things. Does it mean we will always be successful? No—at least not from a human viewpoint, however, if we walk in the path God has for us, we will be successful from a His viewpoint.

So the messengers, including Hathach, tell Mordecai. What was his response? "So Mordecai went away and did just as Esther had commanded him." The word got out, and every Jew in Susa fasted for three days and nights. I think there was a lot of praying going on as well. Not only did God prepare Esther to go to the king to plead for the Jews, He prepared Esther so she would lead a national revival of the Jews. It began with the Jews in Susa. Because of her, they were all fasting and praying.

Theme Statement

Esther trusts and obeys God and agrees to go to the king. "Victory is snatched from the jaws of defeat."

Things to Remember

Paragraph Theme Statements

Esther 4:1–3—Mordecai and Jews mourn impending destruction.

Esther 4:4–8—Mordecai confides in Hathach and instructs him to inform Esther of problem and solution.

Esther 4:9–12—Esther tells Mordecai she may perish if she goes to the king.

Esther 4:13–17—Esther trusts and obeys God and agrees to go to the king. "Victory is snatched from the jaws of defeat."

Principles

26. Life is not fair. In our fallen world bad things will happen to you, whether you deserve them or not.

27. Good leaders do what they tell others to do and do not do what they tell others not to do.

28. Fear comes from a failure to trust God. When facing adversity, trust and obey God.

29. You cannot make right decisions while under stress unless you look to God for the solution and you trust and obey Him.

30. We should pray for our leaders, whether we agree or disagree with them.

31. It is not necessary to know the outcome when you walk in the works God has prepared for you.

Chapter Eight

ESTHER 5:
GRACE UNDER PRESSURE

Faith in Action

"Now it came about on the third day that Esther put on her
royal robes and stood in the inner court of the king's palace
in front of the king's rooms, and the king was sitting on his
royal throne in the throne room, opposite the entrance to the
palace. When the king saw Esther the queen standing in the
court, she obtained favor in his sight; and the king extended
to Esther the golden scepter which was in his hand. So Esther
came near and touched the top of the scepter. Then the king
said to her, 'What is troubling you, Queen Esther? And what
is your request? Even to half of the kingdom it shall be given
to you.' 4 Esther said, 'If it pleases the king, may the king and
Haman come this day to the banquet that I have prepared for
him'" (Estjer 5:1–4).

Where

Inner court of the king's palace and the throne room.

When

474 BC, after the edict had been sent out; five years after Esther had become queen (Esther 2:16); third day of fasting (fasting had been completed—Esther 4:16); third day (part of a day is counted as a whole—Matt 12:40).

X 474 BC—month Nisan—Haman casts lot

X 474 BC—thirteenth day of Nisan—king's scribes summoned

X 474 BC—sometime after the 13th day of the first month, Nisan—Mordecai mourns

X 474 BC—Esther learns of Mordecai's mourning and edict to kill Jews

X 474 BC—Esther agrees to go to king

X 474 BC—Esther goes to king after three days of fasting

474 BC—13th day Adar—when Jews are to be destroyed **X**

| * | * | * | * | * | * | * | * | * | * | * | * | * |

474

Nisan	Sivan	Av	Tishri	Chislev	Shebat	(Adar II)
(Ma/Ap)	(May/Jun)	(Jul/Aug)	(Sep/Oct)	(Nov/Dec)	(Jan/Feb)	(leap yr)

Iyyar	Tammuz	Elul	Cheshvan	Tebeth	Adar
(Ap/May)	(Jun/Jul)	(Aug/Sep)	(Oct/Nov)	(Dec/Jan)	(Feb/Mar)

Have you ever found yourself doing things you never thought of doing or things you said you would never do? When I started medical school, I had plans of becoming a cardiovascular surgeon. The last thing I envisioned myself doing was primary care medicine—particularly geriatrics. The reality today is that my practice is primarily clinic medicine for the elderly. It is a practice I dearly love. In looking back I can clearly see the events that lead me to where I am today. What does this have to do with Esther? I do not believe Esther ever thought growing up she would be risking her life to speak to the king in order to save the entire Jewish race. The reality is that God provided the events in her life to lead her to this very event.

So what has happened in Susa between the end of Esther 4 and the beginning of Esther 5? There were probably growling stomachs and a lot of prayer. What do you think the king and Haman were doing? Do you think God was listening?

"Now it came about on the third day." What do you think Esther's state of mind was at this time? She had known about Haman's plan to exterminate the Jews for at least three days.

> "Esther put on her royal robes and stood in the inner court of the king's palace in front of the king's rooms, and the king was sitting on his royal throne in the throne room, opposite the entrance to the palace" (Esther 5:1).

When Esther went to the king, she did so respectfully, putting on her "royal robes" in order to look as nice as possible. I am sure she wanted to make the best impression she could. After putting on her best clothes, she stood in a place where the king could see her. At that point, she had done all she could do. In presenting herself to the king, she had passed the point of no return; she had exposed herself to death (Esther 4:11). It was left up to the king whether he would acknowledge her or not. There was no whining or pleading on the part of Esther. She was simply relying on God. How much time elapsed between verse 1 and verse 2? For Esther, it probably seemed like an eternity.

> "When the king saw Esther the queen standing in the court, she obtained favor in his sight; and the king extended to Esther the golden scepter which was in his hand. So Esther came near and touched the top of the scepter" (Esther 5:2).

Why/how did Esther find favor in the king's sight? Did the fasting and praying of the Jews help? It put them in line with God's will, which glorified Him. First and foremost, it was God. In addition, maybe the king missed her, because he had not seen her in thirty days. Maybe Esther looked especially pleasing. Maybe the king was in a good mood. When he extended his golden scepter (Esther 4:11, 8:4), I think Esther breathed a big sigh of relief, at least inwardly. She probably felt like she was walking on air as she went forward to touch the top of the scepter.

When you have faced some trial and you reach a point when the adversity is overcome, how do you feel? Relief? Thankfulness? Elation? Do you thank God? Is your faith in Him strengthened?

> "Then the king said to her, 'What is troubling you, Queen Esther? And what is your request? Even to half of the kingdom it shall be given to you'" (Esther 5:3).

"Troubling" is not in the original text; it has been added for clarification, however, it would be natural for the king to assume Esther is troubled. He knew Esther had taken a very great risk in coming to see him without being invited. He then senses she wants something and asks what it is. What a turn of events. In thirty seconds, Esther goes from not knowing if she would be killed to the king offering to give her half of the kingdom.

The statement "even to half of the kingdom it shall be given to you" is an idiom meaning Esther could ask for anything and it would be given to her (Esther 5:6, 7:2; Mark 6:23).[1] Would Ahasuerus actually have given Esther anything she wanted? In Mark 6:23, Herod make this statement to Herodias, the wife of his brother Philip, whom he had married. Herodias asked for the head of John the Baptist, and Herod complied. If you were Esther, what would be your response?

> "Esther said, 'If it pleases the king, may the king and Haman come this day to the banquet that I have prepared for him'" (Esther 5:4).

Esther's response is fascinating. Again we see "if it pleases the king." This statement by Esther says a lot about her character, her wisdom, her cunning, her patience, and her absolute resolve to overthrow Haman and save the Jews. Mordecai told her in Esther 4:8 to "go in to the king to implore his favor and to plead with him for her people." Esther says in verse 16, "I will go into the king." Her response here reveals she is no longer simply doing what Mordecai is telling her to do. She is thinking on her own and possibly being lead by the Holy Spirit. She is taking charge of the situation. What she says now is only the tip of the iceberg of what she is planning. It is the beginning of the presentation and unfolding of a plan that is simply perfect in its design and execution, with the result that Haman is exposed, overthrown, and killed, and the Jews are saved.

I would not want to play poker with Esther. The saying that a person has "ice water in their veins" would fit her. This is not meant as a negative statement, but rather as a positive characteristic of someone who can think, act, and speak with poise and grace, even in the midst of extreme pressure. What if she had blurted out, "You cannot have all the Jews killed, because I am a Jew"? If she had done so, the king may have

---

1   Walvoord, John F. and Roy B. Zuck. 1983. *The Bible Knowledge Commentary.* Wheaton, IL: Victor Books. S. 1:708.

honored her request, yet Haman may still have remained in power. She had to tell the king at the right time and in the right way.

Have you ever seen the movie *Stalag 17?* It is a 1953 movie directed by Billy Wilder about American POWs in a World War II German prison camp. William Holden plays Sgt. J. J. Sefton, an American POW. Otto Preminger plays Col. Von Scherbach, the German commandant. Peter Graves plays Price, a German spy pretending to be an American POW. Almost all the POWs hate Sefton, because they think he is giving information to the Germans. Sefton finds out it is Price who is the spy. His dilemma is, how to expose the true spy? He realizes if he tells the other prisoners who it is, they might not believe him—or if they do, and they all kill Price, the German, everyone in the barracks might be executed. If he tells the other prisoners and they expose Price and have him thrown out of the barracks, he will probably be sent to another camp and cause problems for other American prisoners. Sefton has to wait for the right time to expose Price as the German, which he does. After doing so, he and all the other prisoners in the barracks devise a plan that results in the Germans killing their own comrade.

What Esther devises is simply perfect. She bides her time; she entices her husband, the king; she further gains his trust and increases his desire to please her; she brings Haman into the web, making him feel comfortable, even swelling with false pride; and she waits for just the right time to spring her trap. What better way to do so than at a banquet?

It is not clear whether Haman was present during any or all of the conversation between the king and Esther. When we read ahead in Esther 5:5, it appears he was not present. Assuming he was not, when he does find out what is happening, he has to be elated. He must have been beaming inside. The king trusts him completely, as he has given Haman his signet ring. The king has just offered the queen half of the kingdom, and she has just said she wants to have the king and him attend her banquet that she had "prepared for him." I think "him" means the king, although Haman's presence at the banquet was necessary.

Note that she says "that I have prepared." She does not say "will prepare." She had faith in God to see her through. She has already prepared the banquet.

Principle 32: Be patient as God leads you.

There is a right time for everything. There are certainly times when you need to rush to accomplish things you are doing. I think there are as many or more times when you need to be patient and methodical in your endeavors. When God is leading you in something, wait on His timing. We will see in the next chapter under Principle 37 that God's timing is perfect. This principle is true for individuals, businesses, governments, and churches.

Theme Statement

Esther obtains the king's favor and invites him and Haman to banquet.

Esther's First Banquet

"Then the king said, 'Bring Haman quickly that we may do as Esther desires.' So the king and Haman came to the banquet which Esther had prepared. As they drank their wine at the banquet, the king said to Esther, 'What is your petition, for it shall be granted to you. And what is your request? Even to half of the kingdom it shall be done.' So Esther replied, 'My petition and my request is: if I have found favor in the sight of the king, and if it pleases the king to grant my petition and do what I request, may the king and Haman come to the banquet which I will prepare for them, and tomorrow I will do as the king says'" (Esther 5:5–8).

Where

Banquet room in king's palace

When

474 BC; five years after Esther had become queen (Esther 2:16); immediately after Esther gave request to king (verse 5 follows verse 4).

> "Then the king said, 'Bring Haman quickly that we may do as Esther desires.' So the king and Haman came to the banquet which Esther had prepared" (Esther 5:5).

It was an honor to be asked to have dinner with the king and his queen. It would be like the president and first lady asking you to have a private dinner with them in the White House. I am sure Haman was ecstatic. I am sure Esther felt some comfort hearing the king say "do as Esther desires."

> "As they drank their wine at the banquet, the king said to Esther, 'What is your petition, for it shall be granted to you. And what is your request? Even to half of the kingdom it shall be done' (Esther 5:6).

What is a banquet without wine? Esther was not trying to get anyone drunk. It was just common courtesy. I am sure it helped put everyone at ease. I don't think Haman was worrying about what the king said to Esther. He had no fear or anxiety at this point. Remember this, as we will see a much different Haman at the next banquet. The king's words in Esther 5:6 are very similar to those in Esther 5:3 and in 7:2, but not exactly the same.

> "What is troubling you, Queen Esther? And what is your request? Even to half of the kingdom it shall be given to you" (Esther 5:3).

Again, "troubling" is not in the original text.

Hebrew words:

> "Request"—*baqqashah* (bak-kaw-shaw'), is "a petition or request."

> "Given"—*nathan* (naw-than') means "to give," and is used with greatest latitude, of application (put, make, etc.): "add, apply, appoint, ascribe, assign, avenge."

> "The king said to Esther, 'What is your petition, for it shall be granted to you. And what is your request? Even to half of the kingdom it shall be done'" (Esther 5:6).

Hebrew words:

"Petition"—*she'elah* (sheh-ay-law') is "a petition; by implication, a loan, or request."

"Granted"—*nathan* (naw-than'), "to give," used with greatest latitude of application (put, make, etc.): "add, apply, appoint, ascribe, assign, avenge." This is the same word used in verse 3 (given).

"Request"—*baqqashah* (bak-kaw-shaw') is "a petition—request." Also used in verse 3.

"Shall be done"—*'asah* (aw-saw') means "to accomplish, advance, appoint, apt, be at, become, bear, bestow, bring forth."

Esther 5:3 and 5:6 are similar; however, the king seems to be making a greater offer in Esther 5:6. He goes from the request being given in 5:3 to the petition being granted and the request being accomplished. The king had used the same word *'asah* in Esther 3:11 when he told Haman that whatever Haman wanted to be done with the Jews would be done. Remember, Haman's request became law. You get the feeling the king is going to grant Esther's request, and it will become law. The difference in Esther 5:6 and 3:11 is that the king is granting to the queen whatever she wants without knowing anything of what she wants or will ask.

To me, this is another example of the king's impulsivity. Remember the results of previous emotional decisions: he dismissed Vashti, kidnapped the virgins, made Esther queen, and agreed to have a group of people killed (Jews). He is granting this request of the right person, Esther; however, remember that he had not seen her in thirty days. I can understand a husband wanting to give his wife whatever she wants, but for the king to make this statement to Esther when he had not even wanted to see her for thirty days is unusual. Is this God controlling what the king is saying and doing? Is this the king simply doing what he normally does?

> "So Esther replied, 'My petition and my request is: if I have found favor in the sight of the king, and if it pleases the king to grant my petition and do what I request, may the king and Haman come to the banquet which I will prepare for them, and tomorrow I will do as the king says'" (Esther 5:7–8).

Why did Esther not tell the king her request? It does not say. I think she believes it is still not the right time. Esther is a great communicator, and we can learn much of what to say, how to say it, and when to say it by watching her. She knows when to be tough and when to show charm. She has the king on her side. However, her request will require major upheaval in the empire. She is still not ready to reveal her intentions. So she needs to strengthen her position with the king. She has probably heard people say to the king, "if I have found favor in the sight of the king" many times and seen how it works. Maybe God is instructing her to wait until the king realizes what one particular Jew, Mordecai, has done for him, and waiting for Haman to reveal himself.

What is important about how Esther is presenting herself? She shows humility and respect to the king, and it is extremely effective. She knows she has found favor in the sight of the king, otherwise she would be dead. She does not flaunt her position, but rather, in a very unpretentious manner acknowledges it. She adds, "if it pleases the king to grant my petition." The king has already said he will do so. Her response simply acknowledges the king's gracious offer.

She requests the king and Haman come to another banquet the next day.

Again, she shows respect by saying she will do as the king says—that is, tell him her petition and request. Esther's way of communicating is a good example of the fact that humility does not mean weakness. Esther had extreme strength, but presented it in a humble way.

This next principle has a multitude of applications, from individuals to relationships; from marriage to ministry; in children, adolescents, and adults.

Principle 33: Grace and humility are effective tools in leadership and communication.

Leadership and communication do not require one to be overbearing, loud, or pushy. In fact, arrogance and rudeness destroy leadership effectiveness and communication to those under one's authority. Being gracious and humble does not mean watering down the truth. Tony Dungy, previous coach of the Indianapolis Colts, is a soft-spoken, gracious man who is a very effective communicator, leader, and football coach. Jesus showed extreme grace and humility during His three years of ministry, yet was a great leader, communicating His truth to all. In the parable of the Pharisee and the Publican He says:

> "I tell you, this man went to his house justified rather than the other; for everyone who exalts himself will be humbled, but he who humbles himself will be exalted." (Luke 18:14)
>
> Remember this principle when you communicate the Word.

Theme Statement

Esther impresses the king and plans another banquet.

Arrogance and Evil

"Then Haman went out that day glad and pleased of heart; but when Haman saw Mordecai in the king's gate and that he did not stand up or tremble before him, Haman was filled with anger against Mordecai. Haman controlled himself, however, went to his house and sent for his friends and his wife Zeresh. Then Haman recounted to them the glory of his riches, and the number of his sons, and every instance where the king had magnified him and how he had promoted him above the princes and servants of the king. Haman also said, 'Even Esther the queen let no one but me come with the king to the banquet which she had prepared; and tomorrow also I am invited by her with the king. Yet all of this does not satisfy me every time I see Mordecai the Jew sitting at the king's gate.' Then Zeresh his wife and all his friends said to him, 'Have a gallows fifty cubits high made and in the morning ask the king to have Mordecai hanged on it; then go joyfully with the king to the banquet.' And the advice pleased Haman, so he had the gallows made" (Esther 5:9–14).

Where

King's gate and Haman's house.

When

474 BC; five years after Esther had become queen (Esther 2:16); immediately after first banquet with Esther, king, and Haman.

We have not spent much time discussing literary laws. In looking at the last paragraph and this paragraph, we do see contrast as the author presents characteristics of Esther and Haman. As we go through this paragraph, we will look at some of their differences. Esther 5:5–8 shows grace and humility on the part of Esther. Esther 5:9–14 shows pride and arrogance on the part of Haman.

> "Then Haman went out that day glad and pleased of heart; but when Haman saw Mordecai in the king's gate and that he did not stand up or tremble before him, Haman was filled with anger against Mordecai" (Esther 5:9).

"Then Haman went out that day glad and pleased of heart." "Pleased of heart" is a euphemism for "happy." As far as he knows, Haman is "on cloud nine"—he is "made in the shade." What is Haman's "pleased of heart" feeling based on? He has had a couple glasses of wine. He has had a personal audience with the king and queen. He is being invited to another banquet with the two. Is this true happiness? I do not think so. His feelings of pleasure are based on his warped human emotion and his perceived environment. As we will soon see, there is no stability in his human emotion or his environment.

Here comes the dreaded *but*. Remember, *but* is a logical connector of contrast. In Esther 1:12, we saw *but* when Queen Vashti refused the king. We said if this *but* had not been present, the rest of the story might not have happened. The threat to the Jews would probably have occurred, but there may have been a different plot and different characters. Here is another *but* that changes the events in the story. Maybe it does not affect what will happen to the Jews, but it sure does affect what will happen to Haman.

> "But when Haman saw Mordecai in the king's gate and that he did not stand up or tremble before him, Haman was filled with anger against Mordecai" (Esther 5:9b).

Here we see one reason Haman's presence at Esther's banquet was necessary. His pride and false sense of self-importance were inflated. In his present state of mind, he reacts irrationally. The result is that he devises a plan that ultimately results in his death.

What is it Haman expects from Mordecai? It is not the normal respect for his position of authority that Mordecai refused to give him in Esther 3:2. In that situation, everyone was to bow down and pay homage to Haman. Here Haman expects Mordecai to "stand up and tremble." Haman is planning on having Mordecai and all the Jews killed. He is now "filled with anger" because Mordecai does not show fear. This is deranged mental thinking. Haman is filled with hatred, pride, and arrogance. Haman, who has tremendous wealth and position, has enjoyed a private banquet with the king and queen and has been invited back to a second feast, and now he lets his hatred of a single individual change his mental attitude.

What is Mordecai thinking? His response is based on different thoughts than when he previously did not bow down to Haman. Before, I think Mordecai was prideful and arrogant. Now I think he has a resolve against the man who has planned to kill him and all the Jews. Was his refusal to "stand up and tremble" a sign of disrespect to the position of authority Haman had? I think it was more like righteous indignation.

Have you ever been on top of the world, and then you let something or someone affect you in a negative way and your joy turned into sorrow? We are about to see an example of someone "snatching defeat from the jaws of victory." This was Haman's personal life. He reacted to everything that did not make him happy. In some ways, he was like the king, who was also impulsive. We as believers do not have an excuse for such behavior. If this was a scene in a movie, I would expect to hear Frank Sinatra sing, "That's Life" with the lyrics, "riding high in April, shot down in May." If Haman only knew how low he was going to fall.

We said in principle 24 that "replacing trust and obedience to God with human arrogance, stubbornness, and pride leads to conflict for you and those around you." Fear, worry, and anxiety, as well as any emotion that replaces trust, are sins. Haman did not believe in God. He was filled with extreme pride and arrogance, as well as hate. The result of this sin pattern is self-induced misery and self-destruction. It was for Haman in 474 BC, and is for present-day believers and non-believers as well.

Principle 34: Pride, arrogance, and hate will destroy you.

We sometimes emphasize the overt sins of lasciviousness (see principle 11); however, mental attitude sins of pride, arrogance, and hate are just as deadly, and they are very insidious. Remember, it was pride that caused Lucifer to challenge God and be thrown out of heaven.

I believe one of the main reasons so many people reject Jesus Christ as Savior is because of pride. For some, it is hard to accept that they are not good enough to earn their way to heaven. For some, it is a refusal to believe in something other than themselves.

"Pride goes before destruction, and a haughty spirit before stumbling" (Proverbs 16:18).

"Haman controlled himself, however, went to his house and sent for his friends and his wife Zeresh" (Esther 5:10).

To his credit, Haman does not react, at least not until he gets home. "Haman controlled himself, however, went to his house and sent for his friends and his wife Zeresh." Zeresh is "a Persian name that perhaps means 'golden' or 'one with disheveled hair.'"[2] When he gets home, what does he do? He gets everyone together who thinks he is great, and they talk about how good he is and how bad Mordecai is to him.

Have you ever been filled with such anger that all you can think about is hurting the other person and exalting yourself? Maybe you have been mistreated, maligned, criticized, misunderstood, or hurt in some way by someone else—or you simply think you have. Have you ever been tempted to go down the path Haman is going? When your feelings are hurt, do you try to fill yourself with false praise and then get even? As believers, we have no excuse for this type of mental or physical behavior. Our Father knows everything that happens to us. He provides for us. He protects us. When it says, "cast your burden upon the Lord and He will sustain you" (Psalm 55:22), it includes those times when you think you have been unfairly treated. It is easy to tell someone else to do these things, but it is hard to do when you are the one in the hot seat.

---

2   Huey, F. B. Jr. 1988. *The Expositor's Bible Commentary.* Grand Rapids: Zondervan Publishing House. Volume 4. 820.

Esther 5:11–14 is hard to read with a straight face. "Then Haman recounted to them the glory of his riches, and the number of his sons, and every instance where the king had magnified him and how he had promoted him above the princes and servants of the king" (Esther 5:11). Here Haman is filled with pride and arrogance. He is stating facts, yet boasting.

"Haman also said, 'Even Esther the queen let no one but me come with the king to the banquet which she had prepared; and tomorrow also I am invited by her with the king'" (Esther 5:12). There is nothing wrong with telling others good things that have happened to you, however it is best to glorify God and acknowledge His presence in those good things. Haman, however, is totally self-centered and self-absorbed. Everything is about him.

"Yet all of this does not satisfy me every time I see Mordecai the Jew sitting at the king's gate" (Esther 5:13). With all Haman has, he cannot be happy because Mordecai does not stand up or tremble before him.

Remember principle 10, "do not make decisions when you are not in fellowship with God. Your ability to think clearly is negatively affected. Your decisions will not be right, and they will not be in line with God's plan," and principle 14, "don't be pressured into making ungodly decisions, and don't listen to false praise." Combining these two gives us a new principle.

Principle 35: When you are full of pride and arrogance, you are vulnerable to ungodly influence, following bad advice, and making wrong decisions.

This principle goes along with principle 34. When filled with pride, it is easy to be fooled by those who can do you harm.

"Then Zeresh his wife and all his friends said to him, 'Have a gallows fifty cubits high made and in the morning ask the king to have Mordecai hanged on it; then go joyfully with the king to the banquet'" (Esther 5:14).

Fifty cubits is seventy-five feet. The purpose here is not just to kill Mordecai; it is to make an example of him. It is possible Mordecai was a leader in the Jewish community, and Haman recognized him as such. If he was hanged on the gallows, what would it do to all the other Jews in the country—and what would it do to Esther? Hanging Mordecai would prevent other Jews from trying to resist Haman.

Isn't Zeresh a lovely wife? I think Zeresh took a chapter out of the book of Jezebel. With a wife like Zeresh and the friends Haman had, he would have been better off being single and friendless. In reality, Zeresh and Haman's friends are just like him. In Esther 3, Haman's answer to Mordecai's snub is to have all Jews killed. Here Haman's wife and friends answer to Mordecai's perceived snub is to have him publicly impaled.

"Then go joyfully with the king to the banquet." Do you remember the first time you ever read Esther? What did you think was going to happen? At this point, you were probably thinking, "What else could go wrong?" How in the world could God fix things at this point? Is Mordecai really going to be killed? Will Esther be able to convince the king? If she cannot, will the Jews be killed? Will the line to Jesus Christ be broken? We, of course, know the outcome. At the time the events occurred, however, I think Satan believed he had a chance to disrupt the prophecy regarding the birth of Christ.

> Have you ever seen the movie *Dave?* Kevin Klein plays a look-alike to the president named Dave. When the president has a stroke, Dave steps into the role. The chief of staff wants to run the country a certain way. Dave disagrees and fires the chief of staff, who then plots to destroy Dave and pave the way for himself to become president. The chief of staff has a big meeting at his house with family and friends. They hope to see Dave self-destruct on national TV while giving a speech to Congress. It reminds me of the atmosphere in Esther 5:14. Remember this when we get to Esther 6:13.

For now, everyone in Haman's household has these great ideas to kill Mordecai, make Haman happy, and further advance his position. Note that Haman knew he had to ask the king if he could hang Mordecai.

Theme Statement

Haman's pride leads him to plan Mordecai's murder.

Things to Remember

Theme Statements

Esther 5:1–4—Esther obtains the king's favor and invites him and Haman to a banquet.

Esther 5:5–8—Esther impresses the king and plans another banquet.

Esther 5:9–14—Haman's pride leads him to plan Mordecai's murder.

Principles

32. Be patient as God leads you.

33. Grace and humility are effective tools in leadership and communication.

34. Pride and arrogance will destroy you.

35. When you are full of pride and arrogance, you are vulnerable to ungodly influence, following bad advice, and making wrong decisions.

Chapter Nine

ESTHER 6:
THE TABLES ARE TURNED

A sleepless night

"During that night the king could not sleep so he gave an order to bring the book of records, the chronicles, and they were read before the king. It was found written what Mordecai had reported concerning Bigthana and Teresh, two of the king's eunuchs who were doorkeepers, that they had sought to lay hands on King Ahasuerus. The king said, 'What honor or dignity has been bestowed on Mordecai for this?' Then the king's servants who attended him said, 'Nothing has been done for him.' So the king said, 'Who is in the court?' Now Haman had just entered the outer court of the king's palace in order to speak to the king about hanging Mordecai on the gallows which he had prepared for him. The king's servants said to him, 'Behold, Haman is standing in the court.' And the king said, 'Let him come in.' So Haman came in and the king said to him, 'What is to be done for the man whom the king desires to honor?' And Haman said to himself, 'Whom would the king desire to honor more than me?' Then Haman said to the king, 'For the man whom the king desires to honor, let them bring a royal robe which the king has worn, and the horse on which the king has ridden, and on whose head a royal crown has been placed; and let the robe and the horse be handed over to one of the king's most noble princes and let them array the man whom the king desires to honor and lead him on horseback through the city square, and proclaim before him, "Thus it shall be done to the man whom the king desires to honor"" (Esther 6:1–9).

Where

King's palace.

When

474 BC; five years after Esther had become queen (Esther 2:16); the night after the first banquet and morning of the next day.

X 474 BC—month Nisan—Haman casts lot
  X 474 BC—thirteenth day of Nisan—king's scribes summoned
    X 474 BC—sometime after the 13th day of the first month, Nisan—Mordecai mourns
    X 474 BC—Esther learns of Mordecai's mourning and edict to kill Jews
   X 474 BC—Esther agrees to go to king
    X 474 BC—Esther goes to king after three days of fasting

    X day after Esther went to king

               474 BC—13th day Adar—when Jews are to be destroyed **X**

*   *   *   *   *   *   *   *   *   *   *   *   *

474

Nisan	Sivan	Av	Tishri	Chislev	Shebat	(Adar II)
(Ma/Ap)	(May/Jun)	(Jul/Aug)	(Sep/Oct)	(Nov/Dec)	(Jan/Feb)	(leap yr)
Iyyar	Tammuz	Elul	Cheshvan	Tebeth	Adar	
(Ap/May)	(Jun/Jul)	(Aug/Sep)	(Oct/Nov)	(Dec/Jan)	(Feb/Mar)	

Notice the pace has quickened.

"During that night the king could not sleep so he gave an order to bring the book of records, the chronicles, and they were read before the king" (Esther 6:1).

Why was the king having trouble sleeping? Men, has your wife ever called you in the middle of the day and told you something is troubling her and then put off telling you what it is? What if she says you have to wait until the next day before she will tell you? Is it easy to concentrate and go back to work? Is it easy to sleep that night?

So why did Ahasuerus have trouble sleeping? Was it intrigue concerning Esther? The events that occurred in the last twenty-four hours were certainly enough to cause insomnia in the king. Ultimately we know it was God who prevented Ahasuerus from sleeping.

Where else in the Old Testament do we see where a king who has power over one of God's chosen has difficulty sleeping? On the night Daniel was cast into the lion's den, Darius, king of Babylon, is described in the following:

> "Then the king went off to his palace and spent the night fasting, and no entertainment was brought before him; and his sleep fled from him" (Daniel 6:18).

What does the king do regarding his inability to sleep? I find his solution quiet interesting. How many of you, when you can't sleep, pull out house or business records from five years previous and start to read them?

Remember, Ahasuerus became king in 486 BC, and it is now 474 BC. That means there are twelve years of records for the king to review. Those would be the records during his reign only. I am sure there were records from his father as well. It is not clear if the king is really interested in what was being said in the chronicles or if he was trying to get sleepy. At least he is making an attempt to refresh his memory of what has gone on in the kingdom. This is certainly a lesson for government and business leaders. The Book of the Chronicles (Esther 2:23) or records were important documents for kings. Reference is made in Ezra 4:15, 6:1–2 and Malachi 3:16.

Look back at 479 BC. "Now when the plot was investigated and found to be so, they were both hanged on a gallows; and it was written in the Book of the Chronicles in the king's presence" (Esther 2:23). Now back to the present, when it is 474 BC. "It was found written what Mordecai had reported concerning Bigthana and Teresh, two of the king's eunuchs who were doorkeepers, that they had sought to lay hands on King Ahasuerus" (Esther 6:2). The king is being read state records from events occurring five years prior which point to Mordecai as a hero.

Is it a coincidence that on this night the king is being reminded it was Mordecai who saved him five years prior? What is the likelihood that, of all the chronicles recorded in the twelve years of Ahasuerus' reign, he would be read the record regarding Mordecai? It is time to present one of the overriding principles existing today. We have seen it throughout the book of Esther, we will see it in the remainder of the story, and we see it in our own lives.

Principle 36: Jesus Christ controls history.

God's perfect plan has been present from eternity past, is currently being progressed through human history, and will be ongoing throughout eternity. We have glimpses of this revealed in Scripture. Jesus Christ created the universe and everything in it. He maintains everything. Nothing occurs without His knowledge and consent.

"He is the image of the invisible God, the firstborn of all creation. For by Him all things were created, both in the heavens and on earth, visible and invisible, whether thrones or dominions or rulers or authorities—all things have been created through Him and for Him. He is before all things, and in Him all things hold together. He is also head of the body, the church; and He is the beginning, the firstborn from the dead, so that He Himself will come to have first place in everything. For it was the Father's good pleasure for all the fullness to dwell in Him, and through Him to reconcile all things to Himself, having made peace through the blood of His cross; through Him, I say, whether things on earth or things in heaven" (Colossians 1:15–20).

"And He is the radiance of His glory and the exact representation of His nature, and upholds all things by the word of His power. When He had made purification of sins, He sat down at the right hand of the Majesty on high" (Hebrews 1:3).

To this point in our story, it is evident events are occurring in such a way we know there is divine influence. When we try to understand this paragraph (Esther 6:1–9), we cannot help but believe these events are following God's explicit plan. We previously asked the question, "Why was Mordecai not rewarded five years earlier?" What would have happened if he had been rewarded? Possibly the king would have forgotten the significance of what Mordecai had done by this time. Possibly the events that are about to unfold might not have occurred.

Principle 37: God's timing is perfect.

Not only does Jesus Christ control history, but the timing of all events fits perfectly in God's plan. We have seen God's perfect timing through the lives and events in the book of Esther. It is the same today for you and me. Have you ever asked God for something, not received it when you asked for it, and then questioned God and His timing? Every time we do not get what we want when we want it, our tendency is to complain. I think at one time or another we all are guilty of this. What we see here is a wonderful example of God's perfect timing.

"The king said, 'What honor or dignity has been bestowed on Mordecai for this?' Then the king's servants who attended him said, 'Nothing has been done for him'" (Esther 6:3).

At this point, do you think the king knows Mordecai is a Jew and has been mourning? In Esther 2, we said Mordecai is a Hebrew form of a Babylonian name. The king should know he is a Jew. We will find out in the next paragraph that the king knows Mordecai is someone who works at the gate. I am not sure the king could pick him out of a crowd. There is no evidence that Haman has told the king about his hatred for Mordecai. After hearing the facts written in the book, I think the king does remember the events five years earlier. He may very well feel personally embarrassed he did not honor Mordecai at that time.

> "So the king said, 'Who is in the court?' Now Haman had just entered the outer court of the king's palace in order to speak to the king about hanging Mordecai on the gallows which he had prepared for him" (Esther 6:4).

I don't know if the king is looking for someone to go and pay honor to Mordecai or if he hears Haman coming in. Nevertheless, right on cue, Haman enters the outer court. He could not be happier. He has a full day ahead. He believes he is going to get permission from the king to hang Mordecai and then go to a banquet the queen is throwing for him and the king. Life could not be any better.

> "The king's servants said to him, 'Behold, Haman is standing in
> the court.' And the king said, 'Let him come in'" (Esther 6:5).

I am guessing it has to be about 8:00 in the morning. The king knows it
is Haman, and he wants Haman to come in. He wants to ask someone to help
him honor Mordecai. Who would be better than the highest ranking person
directly below the king? This is a classic example in which two people have
completely opposite thoughts regarding the same topic.

If you are like me and like to see the bad guy get what he deserves, this is
so good. The only thing that could have been better is if Haman had spoken
up first and told the king what he wanted to do with Mordecai. How do you
think the king would have responded if Haman had done so? Would the king
have had Haman killed or would Haman have talked his way out of things?
I do not know if it is God's sense of humor or justice that the story continues
on a little longer.

> "So Haman came in and the king said to him, 'What is to be
> done for the man whom the king desires to honor?' And Haman
> said to himself, 'Whom would the king desire to honor more than
> me?'" (Esther 6:6).

Two consistencies are presented here. First, the king has to ask someone
else what he should do. Second, true to form, Haman thinks only of himself.
Remember Principle 34, "pride and arrogance will destroy you," as we go
through the next couple of verses.

> "Then Haman said to the king, 'For the man whom the king
> desires to honor, let them bring a royal robe which the king has
> worn, and the horse on which the king has ridden, and on whose
> head a royal crown has been placed" (Esther 6:7–8).

As Haman is thinking of these things, you know he is picturing himself
wearing the robe, riding the horse with a royal crown on his head. What
Haman is proposing is a truly noble honor. Everyone who would witness the
event would know the significance. The king is elevating Mordecai to a very
high position. Being honored by the king would likely carry the ongoing
privilege of position and respect.

> "And let the robe and the horse be handed over to one of the
> king's most noble princes and let them array the man whom the
> king desires to honor and lead him on horseback through the city

square, and proclaim before him, 'Thus it shall be done to the man whom the king desires to honor'" (Esther 6:9).

What is it Haman craves? Is it wealth? He is already extremely wealthy. Is it power? He is already the second most powerful person in the empire. Haman lusted after personal acknowledgement and a warped, illegitimate sense of praise. What is obtained through normal position and accomplishment is not good enough for Haman. He has created in his mind what he thinks he deserves. He is filled with approbation lust and is trying to change his environment to fulfill his desires and irrational expectations.

Principle 38: Lust for personal acknowledgment and praise is destructive.

The TV show and song, *Cheers,* touted the bar where you could go and "everyone knows your name." There is nothing wrong with wanting to be around people who know who you are and with whom you are comfortable. There is something wrong when lust for recognition rules your thoughts, actions, and words.

We see Haman's failure to follow this principle in Esther 3:2, 5 and Esther 5:9, 13. Basing happiness on praise from others and lusting for approbation keeps our focus from the true source of happiness. Lives are wasted and sometimes destroyed when this principle is not understood and followed. God is the source of true peace, joy, and happiness.

As events of the day unfold, remember—the king has not slept; is probably tired, as well as confused by Esther; and is concerned he has not honored Mordecai. The king is thinking about something other than Haman's sense of self-importance.

Theme Statement

The king plans to honor Mordecai; Haman lusts for acknowledgement.

As we close this paragraph, we now see the purpose of Esther waiting another day before revealing her requests. God was going to have it placed in the king's mind that Mordecai was to be honored. At this point, the king knows Mordecai is a Jew, Mordecai saved his life, and Haman plans to destroy a group of people in the empire. He does not know the group of people are the Jews.

In Esther 6:1–9, the king has asked what should be done for the person the king wants to honor. Haman, thinking the king means him, eloquently says:

> "For the man whom the king desires to honor, let them bring a royal robe which the king has worn, and the horse on which the king has ridden, and on whose head a royal crown has been placed; and let the robe and the horse be handed over to one of the king's most noble princes and let them array the man whom the king desires to honor and lead him on horseback through the city square, and proclaim before him, 'Thus it shall be done to the man whom the king desires to honor'" (Esther 6:7–9).

Surprise and humiliation

I would love to have been looking at Haman's face when the king said the following:

> "Then the king said to Haman, 'Take quickly the robes and the horse as you have said, and do so for Mordecai the Jew, who is sitting at the king's gate; do not fall short in anything of all that you have said.' So Haman took the robe and the horse, and arrayed Mordecai, and led him on horseback through the city square, and proclaimed before him, 'Thus it shall be done to the man whom the king desires to honor'" (Esther 6:10–11).

Where

King's palace and city square.

When

474 BC; five years after Esther had become queen (Esther 2:16); the big day.

> "Then the king said to Haman, 'Take quickly the robes and the horse as you have said, and do so for Mordecai the Jew,

who is sitting at the king's gate; do not fall short in anything of all that you have said'" (Esther 6:10).

The king orders Haman to do for Mordecai exactly as Haman wanted done for himself as described in Esther 6:8–9. What do you think was going through Haman's mind as the king gave him these orders? How did he keep his composure? The king makes it known he is aware of two things concerning Mordecai. Mordecai is a Jew, as we have already said, and he is sitting at the king's gate, which means the king knows he works there.

Is the king aware of Haman's personal hatred of Mordecai? I do not think so. He is certainly not aware of Haman's desire to have Mordecai hung on this day. Did you delight in reading Esther 6:10? I did. I also cheered when I read the next verse.

> "So Haman took the robe and the horse, and arrayed Mordecai, and led him on horseback through the city square, and proclaimed before him, 'Thus it shall be done to the man whom the king desires to honor'" (Esther 6:11).

Remember how the king's servants at the gate questioned Mordecai as to why he did not bow down to Haman in Esther 3:3? I think many of the people in the city square knew about the conflict between Mordecai and Haman. To now see Mordecai being lead through the streets by Haman, who was shouting honor to Mordecai, would certainly have caused quite a scene.

Theme Statement

The king honors Mordecai instead of Haman.

Haman's mourning

> "Then Mordecai returned to the king's gate. But Haman hurried home, mourning, with his head covered. Haman recounted to Zeresh his wife and all his friends everything that had happened to him. Then his wise men and Zeresh his wife said to him, 'If Mordecai, before whom you have begun to fall, is of Jewish origin, you will not overcome him, but will surely fall before him'" (Esther 6:12–13).

Where

King's gate and Haman's home.

When

474 BC; five years after Esther had become queen (Esther 2:16); the big day.

> "Then Mordecai returned to the king's gate. But Haman hurried home, mourning, with his head covered" (Esther 6:12).

Remember ABC's *Wide World of Sports* several years ago, in the opening scene where the guy is going down the ski jump and falls off? All we need now is to have Jim McKay say, "The thrill of victory and the agony of defeat". Can you imagine how Mordecai felt? Do you think he was humble when he saw his peers at the king's gate? Do you think he was thanking God? Was he still concerned about Esther and all the Jews? What do you do when you are at your highest? Do you thank God? Do you remember others in need?

Can you imagine the way Haman felt? What do you do when you are at your lowest? You probably don't want to be seen. Do you still thank God, and do you still think of others? Haman decides to go home, where he thinks it might be safe.

> "Haman recounted to Zeresh his wife and all his friends everything that had happened to him. Then his wise men and Zeresh his wife said to him, 'If Mordecai, before whom you have begun to fall, is of Jewish origin, you will not overcome him, but will surely fall before him'" (Esther 6:13).

As far as a safe place, he is out of luck. Haman goes home and tells his wife and friends what has happened. Zeresh and his wise men hit the nail directly on the head. They are aware Haman wants to kill all the Jews in Persia. They now tell him that if Mordecai is a Jew, he will be destroyed by the king.

I bet the room clears out pretty quickly. Zeresh will probably stay, but all the "friends" will leave. They will not want to be associated with Haman. They do not seem to take any of the responsibility for the actions of Haman, even though it was their advice to have Mordecai hanged. Remember the movie *Dave?* This is the scene near the end of the movie where the chief of staff is sitting by himself in his home. Everyone has left him after he has been implicated in corruption.

Principle 39: Everyone is responsible for their own actions, even when advice has been taken from others.

The saying "You made your bed, now you have to lie in it" rings true. The day of reckoning for Haman is here. What has happened to Haman is a great example of an evil person getting his just reward. On a grander, scale God is saying evil forces that try to disrupt His plan will be destroyed.

Can you think of anything worse than what happened to Haman? I can. Let me tell you something that is much worse than what Haman faced: Living one's life *not* believing in the saving faith of Jesus Christ. Maybe you were not presented with the Gospel as a child; maybe you rejected salvation as an adult. Ultimately you decided on your own you would not believe. At the moment just after death occurs, you realize that you are separated from God and you will spend eternity in the lake of fire. Talk about wishing to go back and change things.

For believers, there will be that moment just after death when one is face-to-face with Jesus Christ. Will you hear, "Well done, good and faithful servant" (Matthew 25:21, 23; 1 Corinthians 13:12; 2 Corinthians 5:8), or will there be regret for absent works on earth which God had prepared for you (Ephesians 2:10)? At the Bema Seat Judgment (1 Corinthians 3:10–15; 2 Corinthians 5:10), will there be honor for good works accomplished through the filling of the Holy Spirit, or the realization that you neglected to do what God had prepared for you to do in eternity past?

Theme Statement

Haman mourns his demise.

From bad to worse

> "While they were still talking with him, the king's eunuchs arrived and hastily brought Haman to the banquet which Esther had prepared" (Esther 6:14).

Where

Haman's home and the banquet.

When

474 BC; five years after Esther had become queen (Esther 2:16); the big day.

Just when he thought his day could not get any worse, the king sends his eunuchs to bring Haman to the banquet. Was this a pleasant formality—escorting him to the banquet—or was the king in some way showing displeasure to Haman? Possibly, he had delayed going until he was summoned. We can just imagine what Haman is thinking on his way.

Theme Statement

Haman is brought to the second banquet.

Things to Remember

Theme Statements

Esther 6:1–9—The king plans to honor Mordecai; Haman lusts for acknowledgement.

Esther 6:10–11—The king honors Mordecai instead of Haman.

Esther 6:12–13—Haman mourns his demise.

Esther 6:14—Haman is brought to the second banquet.

Principles

36. Jesus Christ controls history.

37. God's timing is perfect.

38. Lust for personal acknowledgment and praise is destructive.

39. Everyone is responsible for their own actions, even when advice has been taken from others.

Chapter Ten

ESTHER 7:
SHOWTIME

For what we have been waiting

"Now the king and Haman came to drink wine with Esther the queen. And the king said to Esther on the second day also as they drank their wine at the banquet, 'What is your petition, Queen Esther? It shall be granted you. And what is your request? Even to half of the kingdom it shall be done.' Then Queen Esther replied, 'If I have found favor in your sight, O king, and if it pleases the king, let my life be given me as my petition, and my people as my request; for we have been sold, I and my people, to be destroyed, to be killed and to be annihilated. Now if we had only been sold as slaves, men and women, I would have remained silent, for the trouble would not be commensurate with the annoyance to the king.' Then King Ahasuerus asked Queen Esther, 'Who is he, and where is he, who would presume to do thus?' Esther said, 'A foe and an enemy is this wicked Haman!' Then Haman became terrified before the king and queen" (Esther 7:1–6).

Where

The queen's banquet at the palace.

When

474 BC- five years after Esther had become queen (Esther 2:16); the big day.

X 474 BC—month Nisan—Haman casts lot
   X 474 BC—thirteenth day of Nisan—king's scribes summoned
      X 474 BC—sometime after the 13th day of the first month, Nisan—Mordecai mourns
         X 474 BC—Esther learns of Mordecai's mourning and edict to kill Jews
        X 474 BC—Esther agrees to go to king
         X 474 BC—Esther goes to king after three days of fasting

      X day after Esther went to king, second banquet

              474 BC—13th day Adar—when Jews are to be destroyed **X**

*   *   *   *   *   *   *   *   *   *   *   *   *

474

Nisan	Sivan	Av	Tishri	Chislev	Shebat	(Adar II)
(Ma/Ap)	(May/Jun)	(Jul/Aug)	(Sep/Oct)	(Nov/Dec)	(Jan/Feb)	(leap yr)

Iyyar	Tammuz	Elul	Cheshvan	Tebeth	Adar
(Ap/May)	(Jun/Jul)	(Aug/Sep)	(Oct/Nov)	(Dec/Jan)	(Feb/Mar)

It is difficult to ascertain exactly when the king came to a full understanding of the relationships of Esther, Haman, Mordecai, and the edict to kill all the Jews. Once the king begins to speak, this paragraph and the next unfold quickly. The king is bombarded with information. At the end of the next two paragraphs, he has a new understanding of people and events.

We are now at Esther's second banquet in the palace. We have been anticipating this climax for some time. Let's take a minute to set up the scene. How would you define tension? In relation to personal experience, tension is "inner striving, unrest, or imbalance often with physiological indication of emotion or a state of latent hostility or opposition between individuals or groups."[1] Who likes tension? Is tension a good thing or a bad thing?

---

1   Merriam-Webster, Inc. 2003. *Merriam-Webster's Collegiate Dictionary, Eleventh ed.* Springfield, Mass.: Merriam-Webster, Inc.

The 1966 movie *The Good, the Bad, and the Ugly* is filled with tension. Clint Eastwood plays "the good"—Blondie; Lee Van Cleef plays "the bad"—Angel Eyes; and Eli Wallach plays "the ugly"—Tuco. It was directed by Sergio Leone, and Ennio Morricone composed the musical score. Most of you know the theme song. After the movie came out, everyone went around whistling it.

Do you remember the final gunfight scene in the cemetery? It is a classic. The gunfight is not between two men, it is among three—it is called a Mexican standoff. This is a fight among three people where each is fighting the other two. If one person tries to shoot another, he leaves himself open to attack from the third. It is a mind game with life-and-death consequences.

In the movie, who has the advantage in the fight, and who has the disadvantage? Clint Eastwood has a distinct advantage. He knows Eli Wallach (who has the disadvantage) does not have bullets in his gun, because Eastwood had removed them the night before. All Eastwood has to do is concentrate on shooting Lee Van Cleef. If he can get Lee Van Cleef to concentrate on trying to shoot Eli Wallach, he is in a no-lose situation. This is exactly what happens.

What we have in Esther 7:1 is not exactly a Mexican standoff; however, there are distinct similarities with *The Good, the Bad, and the Ugly*. Three people are present; there is definitely tension; there is a life-and-death situation for one individual, Haman; one person has a disadvantage, Haman; and one person has the greatest advantage, Esther.

> "Now the king and Haman came to drink wine with Esther the queen" (Esther 7:1).

What is the king thinking regarding Haman and Esther? He knows he has honored Mordecai, a Jew. He knows Haman wants to kill a group of people, but not which group. He does not know Esther is a Jew. Does he have any negative thoughts about Haman? Has he given any indication he wants to hurt Haman? Does he have any thoughts about Esther other than a desire to fulfill her requests?

What is Haman thinking regarding the king and Esther? Does he fear the king? Prior to the king deciding to honor Mordecai, I believe Haman had no fear of the king. Because of the king's decision to honor Mordecai and Haman's plan to kill Mordecai, I believe Haman had a very real fear of the king. Does he think there is any danger from Esther? I don't think so. He might even think he can rely on her if the king is angry with him. This is his disadvantage. He is not aware of the threat Esther is to him. Does he want to be at the banquet? Probably not. Is he looking for a way out? I bet he would take it if he could find one.

What is Esther thinking regarding the king and Haman? She knows she has the favor of the king. Twice he has told her that he will do whatever she wants (Esther 5:3, 6). Does she think she can convince the king to change an edict that has already been written and is therefore law? She knows she has to plead for her people. She knows she has to tell the king she is a Jew. There is no indication she knows the king has honored Mordecai or that the king knows he is a Jew.

What do you think of the way Esther has handled Haman to this point? It reminds me of the quote by Sun-tzu, a Chinese general and military strategist, around 400 BC, "Keep your friends close, and your enemies closer."[2] This is the second banquet in which Esther has invited Haman. She has definitely kept him close. I believe Esther is interested in not only saving her people; she is interested in exposing Haman and having him destroyed.

Esther has her offensive weapon—the king—primed, loaded, and pointed at Haman. The king has said twice he will give her whatever she wants. She has her prey, Haman, sitting there, afraid of the king, not her. And what is her advantage? She has the knowledge of Haman's plan to kill all the Jews, the king's commitment to granting her petition and request, and God's favor. God has lined up things perfectly for her. It is time for Esther to pull the trigger.

> "And the king said to Esther on the second day also as they drank their wine at the banquet, 'What is your petition, Queen Esther? It shall be granted you. And what is your request? Even to half of the kingdom it shall be done'" (Esther 7:2).

This is a quote from Esther 5:6, the first banquet. A *petition* is something more personal for oneself. A *request* is something you want someone to do for you. It is show time for Esther. She does not waste any more time. She gets right to the point.

---

2   The Quotations Page. http://www.quotations page.com.

Principle 40: When God calls you to act, do not hesitate.

Athletes prepare both physically and mentally to compete. At the time of competition, an athlete must be ready to unleash the physical and at the same time be in control of the mental. If there is mental fear or doubt, the athlete does not perform well. In football games, I always looked forward to the first "hit" on defense. It had a way of removing all jitters and helped me concentrate on playing.

There can be a tendency to freeze when you are called on to walk in those works that God has prepared for you. Satan likes nothing better than to stop you from doing God's Will. Fear, self-doubt, and anxiety can destroy your ministry. These temptations are just as destructive as those that turn you toward overt sins of degeneracy. We need to remember what God has told us in His Word. First, He will not let us be tempted beyond what we can resist.

"No temptation has overtaken you but such as is common to man; and God is faithful, who will not allow you to be tempted beyond what you are able, but with the temptation will provide the way of escape also, so that you will be able to endure it" (1 Corinthians 10:13).

Second, He has provided very specific principles in His Word that tell us not to worry, be afraid, or be anxious.

"For God has not given us a spirit of timidity, but of power and love and discipline" (2 Timothy 1:7).

"Rejoice in the Lord always; again I will say, rejoice! Let your gentle spirit be known to all men. The Lord is near. Be anxious for nothing, but in everything by prayer and supplication with thanksgiving let your requests be made known to God. And the peace of God, which surpasses all comprehension, will guard your hearts and your minds in Christ Jesus" (Philippians 4:4–7).

"Then Queen Esther replied, 'If I have found favor in your sight, O king, and if it pleases the king, let my life be given me as my petition, and my people as my request'" (Esther 7:3).

The first part of the verse is a quote from Esther 5:8a. What strikes me is that even in the midst of this highly charged, emotional moment, Esther has the poise to show respect to the king. Esther finally states her *petition* and *request*. The *petition* is for herself, to save her own life. The *request* is for the king to do something for others, to save all the Jews.

This statement by Esther must have been quite a shock to both the king and Haman. Up to this point, the king did not know there was a threat to the queen's life. He was also not aware she was a part of a group she referred to as "my people." After her statement, I think he began to understand the relationship of Esther and the edict to have a group of people killed.

> "For we have been sold, I and my people, to be destroyed, to be killed and to be annihilated. Now if we had only been sold as slaves, men and women, I would have remained silent, for the trouble would not be commensurate with the annoyance to the king" (Esther 7:4).

Without even taking a breath of air, Esther completes her response to the king. She gives the reason for her *petition* and *request*. The first part of this verse, "for we have been sold, I and my people, to be destroyed, to be killed and to be annihilated" says several things. Part of this is a quote from Esther 3:13 in the letter sent out by Haman telling what was going to happen to the Jews. The king had not read the letter; however, as Esther makes this statement, he begins to further understand the problem facing the queen. It may be at this time he comes to realize she is a Jew, and it is the Jews who are to be killed. When Esther says "if we had only been sold," she is referring to Haman's attempt to bribe the king with the silver (Esther 3:9; 4:7).

What do you think of the second part of the response? Have you ever asked someone for something you did not think you had a right to ask? You then ask for less, because you do not want to ask for more than you should. Esther's second response is a humbling acknowledgement of herself to the king. She has the king's favor. She has told the king someone is trying to kill her and her people. She believes the king will be on her side. By expressing her desire to not bother the king if her fate was less than death, I think she is showing humility to the king and respect for his position. She knows the king will respond in her favor even more.

Remember the prodigal son? After realizing what he had done, he went to acknowledge his sin to his father. He did not ask to be reinstated as a son. He was prepared to lower himself to the status of a hired hand—which, of course, was not necessary. His father had already forgiven him. Nothing else had to be done.

If you are a parent, has one or your children ever disobeyed you, been punished, and then come to apologize? When they have sorrow in their soul, they often times say things like, "You can take my toys away from me for a long time, I am really sorry." It is a form of humility before your authority. They want to be back in your good graces. This action is not necessary, as they have already been forgiven, but the thought is understandable in some circumstances.

Esther had not done anything wrong. But she was still responding with humility to her authority, the king. Esther's words were not necessary; however, I think they showed her true feelings to the king. What was the effect of Esther's words on Haman and the king? I think Haman probably choked on his wine when he heard Esther speak. He probably tried to withhold outward emotion, but inside he was scared to death. The king was a little more open with his emotion. I think he put anger and force in his next response.

> "Then King Ahasuerus asked Queen Esther, 'Who is he, and where is he, who would presume to do thus?'" (Esther 7:5).

With all the information the king has received, I can understand this question. He knows Haman wants to kill a group of people. He knows Mordecai is a Jew. He knows he has just honored Mordecai. He has just learned that Esther and her people are supposed to be killed. If left alone, he could probably figure out Haman is guilty. The normal response is to ask who and where.

> "Esther said, 'A foe and an enemy is this wicked Haman!' Then Haman became terrified before the king and queen" (Esther 7:6).

Hebrew words:

> "Foe"—*tsar* (tsar); "adversary, afflicted"
> "Enemy"—*'oyeb* (o-yabe'), "hating, enemy, foe"
> "Wicked"—*ra`* (rah); "bad, evil (natural or moral)"

Esther does more than simply tell the king *who* and *where*. She personifies the guilty person, Haman, in a most explicit and negative manner. There was force and emotion in her voice. This was not whining. This was a deliberate, calculating, deadly statement which sealed Haman's fate. When it says, "Haman became terrified before the king and queen," he was afraid he would be killed on the spot.

Theme Statement

Esther tells the king Haman plans to kill her and Jews.

What goes around, comes around

> "The king arose in his anger from drinking wine and went into the palace garden; but Haman stayed to beg for his life from Queen Esther, for he saw that harm had been determined against him by the king. Now when the king returned from the palace garden into the place where they were drinking wine, Haman was falling on the couch where Esther was. Then the king said, 'Will he even assault the queen with me in the house?' As the word went out of the king's mouth, they covered Haman's face. Then Harbonah, one of the eunuchs who were before the king said, 'Behold indeed, the gallows standing at Haman's house fifty cubits high, which Haman made for Mordecai who spoke good on behalf of the king!' And the king said, 'Hang him on it.' So they hanged Haman on the gallows which he had prepared for Mordecai, and the king's anger subsided" (Esther 7:7–10).

Where

Queen's second banquet at the palace.

When

474 BC, the big day.

> "The king arose in his anger from drinking wine and went into the palace garden; but Haman stayed to beg for his life from Queen Esther, for he saw that harm had been determined against him by the king" (Esther 7:7).

Why did the king go outside? He had been drinking wine and had just been told by his wife that the second most powerful person in the empire had plans to kill her and her people. I am sure he needed time to process all the information and decide what to do. Remember, the king has always asked others for advice before making important decisions.

We have seen the king's failures throughout the book. When he goes outside to think, he realizes that even though it was Haman who wrote the edict, it had the king's signet ring on it. The king was aware of what was going to happen to the Jews and had to accept that he was responsible. And now he finds out the queen was Jewish and was to be killed as well.

Even for someone who can think clearly, this would cause some stress. For someone who could not think clearly, who had a self-centered personality, drank a lot of wine, and could not make decisions, this was overwhelming. The king was probably trying to think what he was going to do. Should he have Haman killed for wanting to do something the king gave Haman the authority to do? I do not think he has decided to have Haman killed at this point. He needs a little more convincing evidence to condemn Haman.

Haman, on the other hand, did not have a problem in knowing what to do. He knows he is in big trouble. He has to plead for his life.

> "Now when the king returned from the palace garden into the place where they were drinking wine, Haman was falling on the couch where Esther was. Then the king said, 'Will he even assault the queen with me in the house?' As the word went out of the king's mouth, they covered Haman's face" (Esther 7:8).

Now this verse is just too good. You have to know God has a great sense of humor. Haman was falling on the couch, pleading with Esther, and the king thinks he is assaulting her. Additional translations have suggested physical divine intervention. "A Targum adds that the angel Gabriel pushed

Haman as the king entered the room!"[3] "The most elementary meaning of the word *targum* is 'translation' or 'interpretation,' but it is quite often connected with the various Aramaic translations of the Old Testament."[4] As far as the king was concerned, this was the final straw.

I do not know if Haman started to defend himself, or if he started to cry out. Regardless, his mouth was covered. Evidently the king's eunuchs were present. Haman did not have a chance to escape.

> "Then Harbonah, one of the eunuchs who were before the king said, 'Behold indeed, the gallows standing at Haman's house fifty cubits high, which Haman made for Mordecai who spoke good on behalf of the king!' And the king said, 'Hang him on it'" (Esther 7:9).

Where have we heard the name Harbonah before? In Esther 1:10. He was one of the eunuchs who went to fetch Vashti for the king. That was in 483 BC, nine years ago. It is obvious the eunuchs knew what was going on in the palace. We see that Harbonah knows Haman was planning on killing Mordecai. Not only that—he could think and come up with some pretty good ideas as well. Can't you just see the look on Haman's face when Harbonah mentions the gallows?

I have to think that Esther played some role in this. Back in Esther 2:8–11, she had found favor with Hegai, the eunuch in charge of the first harem. Over the past five years as queen, I think she had found favor with the other eunuchs in the palace. They had loyalty to the king. But I think they had a good relationship with Esther and wanted to protect her as well.

> "So they hanged Haman on the gallows which he had prepared for Mordecai, and the king's anger subsided" (Esther 7:10).

In literature, we would say this is poetic justice. Haman is impaled on the gallows he meant for Mordecai. It does not say when, but I think it was immediately.

---

3   Huey, F. B. Jr. 1988. *The Expositor's Bible Commentary.* Grand Rapids: Zondervan Publishing House. Volume 4. 826.

4   Bromiley, Geoffrey W. 2002. *The International Standard Bible Encyclopedia, Revised.* S. 4:727.

> **Principle 41: When you plan evil for others, God may allow that evil to be turned on you.**
>
> Here we have application of principle 39 in its most harsh form. "What goes around, comes around" is often true.

What does it mean, "the king's anger subsided"? "Anger," or *chemah* (khay-maw'), means "wrath." "Subsided," or *shakak* (shaw-kak'), means "to appease or pacify." The king is the authority in the land. The king has been personally attacked by way of attacking the king's people and Esther. He has anger. The death of the perpetrator makes this anger go away. The same word, *shakak,* is used in describing how the water receded after the flood in Genesis 8:1.[5]

> "But God remembered Noah and all the beasts and all the cattle that were with him in the ark; and God caused a wind to pass over the earth, and the water subsided" (Genesis 8:1).

Is there any relation between "the king's anger subsided" after "they hanged Haman on the gallows" and Christ's death on the cross as an act of propitiation? God has wrath against sin. When Jesus Christ paid our debt for sin, God's justice was satisfied. There is satisfaction of God's righteousness and the turning away of His wrath.

Theme Statement

Haman is hanged on the gallows.

Points to Remember

Theme Statements
Esther 7:1–6—Esther tells the king Haman plans to kill her and Jews.

Esther 7:7–10—Haman is hung on the gallows.

---

5   Ibid., Huey, Volume 4. 827.

Principles

40. When God calls you to act, do not hesitate.

41. When you plan evil for others, God may allow that evil to be turned on you.

Chapter Eleven

ESTHER 8:
ONE DOWN, ONE TO GO

Transfer of power

"On that day King Ahasuerus gave the house of Haman, the enemy of the Jews, to Queen Esther; and Mordecai came before the king, for Esther had disclosed what he was to her. The king took off his signet ring which he had taken away from Haman, and gave it to Mordecai. And Esther set Mordecai over the house of Haman" (Esther 8:1–2).

Where

The king's palace.

When

474 BC; same day (Queen's second banquet, Haman hanged).

X 474 BC—month Nisan—Haman casts lot

  X 474 BC—thirteenth day of Nisan—king's scribes summoned

    X 474 BC—sometime after the 13th day of the first month, Nisan—Mordecai mourns

   X 474 BC—Esther learns of Mordecai's mourning and edict to kill Jews

  X 474 BC—Esther agrees to go to king

   X 474 BC—Esther goes to king after three days of fasting

X day after Esther went to king, second banquet, Haman exposed, hanged

474 BC—13th day Adar—when Jews are to be destroyed **X**

*   *   *   *   *   *   *   *   *   *   *   *   *

474

Nisan	Sivan	Av	Tishri	Chislev	Shebat	(Adar II)
(Ma/Ap)	(May/Jun)	(Jul/Aug)	(Sep/Oct)	(Nov/Dec)	(Jan/Feb)	(leap yr)

Iyyar	Tammuz	Elul	Cheshvan	Tebeth	Adar
(Ap/May)	(Jun/Jul)	(Aug/Sep)	(Oct/Nov)	(Dec/Jan)	(Feb/Mar)

> "On that day King Ahasuerus gave the house of Haman, the enemy of the Jews, to Queen Esther; and Mordecai came before the king, for Esther had disclosed what he was to her" (Esther 8:1).

What a day this has been. It started with the king planning to honor Mordecai and Haman thinking he was going to hang Mordecai. Instead, Haman leads Mordecai around on a horse. The queen has her second banquet. Haman is found out and hanged. Without any break in the action, the king gives the house of Haman to Esther. What does "gave the house of Haman" mean? It means that all Haman possessed—including money, property, and authority over possessions and lives of the people—have been transferred from Haman to Esther. Persian law did allow for property of criminals to be seized and given to others. Herodotus records that after Oroetes murdered Polycrates, king Darius had Oroetes killed and his wealth seized and distributed.[1] Giving away "the house of Haman" would suggest he was considered to be a criminal for his actions.

The author again qualifies Haman as "the enemy of the Jews." Forever he will be known as such. The other thing we find in this verse is that Esther tells the king she is Mordecai's cousin. There is now no doubt the king knows Esther and Mordecai are Jewish and are related.

---

1   Iran Chamber Society, Histories of Herodotus. http://www.iranchamber.com.

"The king took off his signet ring which he had taken away from Haman, and gave it to Mordecai. And Esther set Mordecai over the house of Haman" (Esther 8:2).

Two things happen in this verse. Mordecai gets the king's signet ring. We know the power it represents. Why do you think Mordecai was given the ring? Was it a continuation of the honor to Mordecai for saving the king's life? Was it the realization Mordecai is related to the queen? The second thing that happens is that Esther sets Mordecai over the house of Haman. He now has authority over what the king had given Esther regarding Haman.

The relationship between Mordecai and Haman turned out to be quite ironic. Haman is forced to honor Mordecai in the way he thought he was to be honored. Haman wanted to hang Mordecai, yet ends up being hanged on the same gallows. Now Haman's household is being given to Mordecai.

Theme Statement

Mordecai is given the king's ring and authority over Haman's house.

A request to save the Jews

"Then Esther spoke again to the king, fell at his feet, wept and implored him to avert the evil scheme of Haman the Agagite and his plot which he had devised against the Jews. The king extended the golden scepter to Esther. So Esther arose and stood before the king. Then she said, 'If it pleases the king and if I have found favor before him and the matter seems proper to the king and I am pleasing in his sight, let it be written to revoke the letters devised by Haman, the son of Hammedatha the Agagite, which he wrote to destroy the Jews who are in all the king's provinces. For how can I endure to see the calamity which will befall my people, and how can I endure to see the destruction of my kindred?' So King Ahasuerus said to Queen Esther and to Mordecai the Jew, 'Behold, I have given the house of Haman to Esther, and him they have hanged on the gallows because he had stretched out his hands against the Jews. Now you write to the Jews as you see fit, in the king's name, and seal it with the king's signet ring; for a decree which is written in the name of the king and sealed with the king's signet ring may not be revoked'" (Esther 8:3–8).

Where

We assume it is in the king's palace.

When

474 BC; after the above events, probably in month of Sivan. Esther 8:9 records what happens after Esther 8:3–8: "So the king's scribes were called at that time in the third month (that is, the month Sivan), on the twenty-third day."

X 474 BC—month Nisan—Haman casts lot
  X 474 BC—thirteenth day of Nisan—king's scribes summoned
    X 474 BC—sometime after the 13th day of the first month, Nisan—Mordecai mourns
      X 474 BC—Esther learns of Mordecai's mourning and edict to kill Jews
        X 474 BC—Esther agrees to go to king
          X 474 BC—Esther goes to king after three days of fasting
            X day after Esther went to king, second banquet, Haman exposed, hanged

X 23rd day of third month, Sivan—Esther implores king to save Jews

474 BC—13th day Adar—when Jews are to be destroyed **X**

---

*   *   *   *   *   *   *   *   *   *   *   *

474

Nisan	Sivan	Av	Tishri	Chislev	Shebat	(Adar II)
(Ma/Ap)	(May/Jun)	(Jul/Aug)	(Sep/Oct)	(Nov/Dec)	(Jan/Feb)	(leap yr)

Iyyar	Tammuz	Elul	Cheshvan	Tebeth	Adar
(Ap/May)	(Jun/Jul)	(Aug/Sep)	(Oct/Nov)	(Dec/Jan)	(Feb/Mar)

What do you think went on in Susa, and throughout Persia, between the hanging of Haman and Esther 8:3? One obstacle has been overcome, and one crisis has been averted. Esther has spoken and made her petition and request to the king. Haman has been killed. The real issue still needs to be addressed—the edict to kill the Jews.

> "Then Esther spoke again to the king, fell at his feet, wept and implored him to avert the evil scheme of Haman the Agagite and his plot which he had devised against the Jews. The king extended the golden scepter to Esther. So Esther arose and stood before the king" (Esther 8:3–4).

Do you notice a difference in this exchange between Esther and the king and that found in Esther 5:1–4? Was Esther risking her life as she did in 5:1–4? Here, Esther is already in the presence of the king and gives her plea before the scepter was extended. This may mean extending the scepter in this case was not being used to determine whether she lived or died, but rather to encourage her.[2] Esther is very emotional in her plea to the king. She does show the king respect. This must have occurred in the inner court of the king's palace in front of the king's rooms with the king sitting on his royal throne in the throne room (Esther 5:1). Esther humbles herself before the king—"fell at his feet, wept and implored."

After all that has happened, why does Esther come before the king in this way? We know the king does not always make good decisions, he can be swayed to make bad decisions, and he follows his emotions when making decisions. We also know it can be risky going to the king if he does not want to see you. Esther knows it will take a new law to undo Haman's edict. I think she is simply showing her true emotion concerning the lives of the Jews. Esther reminds the king of Haman's plot to kill the Jews and implores him to stop it.

> "Then she said, 'If it pleases the king and if I have found favor before him and the matter seems proper to the king and I am pleasing in his sight, let it be written to revoke the letters devised by Haman, the son of Hammedatha the Agagite, which he wrote to destroy the Jews who are in all the king's provinces'" (Esther 8:5).

Esther would make a good attorney. She knew that all of her *if* questions were really true statements. She also knew the king would have to issue some decree to resolve the issue with the Jews. She puts the blame on Haman and not the king. She emphasizes the magnitude of the problem when she reminds the king of two things. First, the Jews are in all of the provinces, meaning the entire kingdom. They serve a great purpose in defending the kingdom from Egypt. Second, they are all under the authority and responsibility of the king. The king can make a decision that will be good for the kingdom. "Revoke," or *shuwb* (shoob), means "a primitive root; to turn back (hence, away)."

> "For how can I endure to see the calamity which will befall my people, and how can I endure to see the destruction of my kindred?" (Esther 8:6)

---

2 Huey, F. B. Jr. 1988. *The Expositor's Bible Commentary.* Grand Rapids: Zondervan Publishing House. Volume 4. 829.

If the king was not personally interested in the Jews, Esther was letting him know their destruction would devastate her. She was counting on the fact the king would not allow her to be sad. This verse reveals Esther's heartfelt concern for the Jews throughout the land.

> "So King Ahasuerus said to Queen Esther and to Mordecai the Jew, 'Behold, I have given the house of Haman to Esther, and him they have hanged on the gallows because he had stretched out his hands against the Jews'" (Esther 8:7).

We see that the king responds to both Esther and Mordecai. He starts out by stating facts. He has given the house of Haman to Esther. Haman has been hanged on the gallows. Haman was killed for trying to kill the Jews. Is the king reminding Esther and Mordecai of their new position and power? Is he reminding himself? Is he justifying himself? Is he simply laying the groundwork for his next statement?

> "Now you write to the Jews as you see fit, in the king's name, and seal it with the king's signet ring; for a decree which is written in the name of the king and sealed with the king's signet ring may not be revoked" (Esther 8:8).

Let's take the second part of the verse first: "for a decree which is written in the name of the king and sealed with the king's signet ring may not be revoked." This is both a curse and a blessing. They cannot repeal Haman's edict. However, if they write a new edict, it as well cannot be repealed. The solution is to write a new law which will alter the outcome of the first. In the first part of the verse, the king tells Mordecai to write a law as he sees fit, which will result in the Jews not being destroyed.

Theme Statement

Esther implores the king to save the Jews.

Before we go on with this chapter, I would like to discuss responsibility for the attempt to annihilate the Jews. First, a review of passages in Esther revealing who knew what and when:

- Haman tells the king he wants to kill a group of people who are different (Esther 3:8).

- Haman sends out letters stating Jews will be killed (Esther 3:13). The king is not aware Haman is speaking of Jews.

- The king wants to honor Mordecai (Esther 6:3–6).

- The king knows Mordecai is a Jew (Esther 6:10).

- The king knows Haman is planning to kill Esther and her people (Esther 7:3–6).

- The king knows Haman wanted to have the Jews killed (Esther 7:3–10 by way of Esther 8:7).

- The king knows Esther is a Jew (Esther 7:3–10).

It is incredible Haman could send out a letter with the king's seal on it, and everyone in the empire would become aware it was the Jews who were to be killed—with the exception of the king and Esther. This strengthens our impression that the king was detached from the daily activities of the kingdom.

In not knowing, did Ahasuerus fail in his responsibility as a leader? I believe he did. The magnitude of the order with which he allowed Haman to initiate required the king to know what was going on. While a good leader does not need to know all of the minute details in an organization, he or she should be aware of decisions that have such national repercussions. Ahasuerus had given Haman the authority and right to have a "certain people" killed. He must accept responsibility for that decision.

When the king says, "Behold, I have given the house of Haman to Esther, and him they have hanged on the gallows because he had stretched out his hands against the Jews" (Esther 8:7), he is putting all the blame on Haman. Although he does have Haman executed, the king does not take personal responsibility for what Haman tried to do.

In no way am I trying to take blame away from Haman. He was evil and received his just end. Would you still consider him a criminal, however, if he was doing what the king said he could do?

I believe the king is responsible (and guilty) for allowing Haman to arrange the extermination of a race of people without knowing who they were as well as putting the blame solely on Haman. This leads to a principle which is applicable in every walk of life, particularly in leadership.

> **Principle 42: Personal failure demands the acceptance of responsibility for failure.**
>
> This is similar to Principle 15, "the solution to error is to admit, apologize, accept consequences, make restitution if possible, alter behavior, and move on." It is somewhat broader in application, however, and is desperately needed in most organizations, including business, church, and government. How many times have you seen "the little guy" take the fall for the leader? Sometimes the subordinate is a willing participant, sometimes not. An organization that protects the leader at the top at all costs, regardless of failure, is corrupt.
>
> Where is the first recorded event of a failure to follow this principle? How about the actions of Adam and Eve in the Garden of Eden?
>
> "And He said, 'Who told you that you were naked? Have you eaten from the tree of which I commanded you not to eat?' The man said, 'The woman whom You gave to be with me, she gave me from the tree, and I ate.' Then the Lord God said to the woman, 'What is this you have done?' And the woman said, 'The serpent deceived me, and I ate'" (Genesis 3:11–13).
>
> Not admitting and accepting responsibility for personal failure does not lessen the failure. One is just as guilty whether there is admission or denial. Remember, God knows the thoughts and intents of the heart (Hebrews 4:12).

A new law

> "So the king's scribes were called at that time in the third month (that is, the month Sivan), on the twenty-third day; and it was written according to all that Mordecai commanded to the Jews, the satraps, the governors and the princes of the provinces which extended from India to Ethiopia, 127 provinces, to every province according to its script, and to every people according to their language as well as to the Jews according to their script and their language. He wrote in the name of King Ahasuerus, and sealed it

with the king's signet ring, and sent letters by couriers on horses, riding on steeds sired by the royal stud. In them the king granted the Jews who were in each and every city the right to assemble and to defend their lives, to destroy, to kill and to annihilate the entire army of any people or province which might attack them, including children and women, and to plunder their spoil, on one day in all the provinces of King Ahasuerus, the thirteenth day of the twelfth month (that is, the month Adar). A copy of the edict to be issued as law in each and every province was published to all the peoples, so that the Jews would be ready for this day to avenge themselves on their enemies. The couriers, hastened and impelled by the king's command, went out, riding on the royal steeds; and the decree was given out at the citadel in Susa" (Esther 8:9–14).

Where

The king's palace; the citadel in Susa; the entire kingdom.

When

474 BC, twenty-third day, third month (month of Sivan—June/July)

X 474 BC—month Nisan—Haman casts lot
   X 474 BC—thirteenth day of Nisan—king's scribes summoned
      X 474 BC—sometime after the 13th day of the first month, Nisan—Mordecai mourns
         X 474 BC—Esther learns of Mordecai's mourning and edict to kill Jews
         X 474 BC—Esther agrees to go to king
            X 474 BC—Esther goes to king after three days of fasting
               X day after Esther went to king, second banquet, Haman exposed, hanged

                  **X 23rd day of third month, Sivan—Esther implores king to save Jews—
                  Edict written to save Jews, sent by couriers**

                  474 BC—13th day Adar—when Jews are to be destroyed **X**

*	*	*	*	*	*	*	*	*	*	*	*	*

474

Nisan	Sivan	Av	Tishri	Chislev	Shebat	(Adar II)
(Ma/Ap)	(May/Jun)	(Jul/Aug)	(Sep/Oct)	(Nov/Dec)	(Jan/Feb)	(leap yr)

Iyyar	Tammuz	Elul	Cheshvan	Tebeth	Adar
(Ap/May)	(Jun/Jul)	(Aug/Sep)	(Oct/Nov)	(Dec/Jan)	(Feb/Mar)

When was the edict Haman wrote sent out? It was sent the thirteenth day of the first month, Nisan, which is March/April. This paragraph occurs two months and ten days after Haman prepared his edict (Esther 3:12). The Jews still have about nine months before the first edict is to occur.

This paragraph has similarities with other parts of Esther. The edict is being written to everyone in Persia (Esther 1:1; 1:22; 3:12). In comparing this paragraph with Esther 3:12–15, I found the following:

Esther 3:12–15	Esther 8:9–14
King's scribes summoned (*qara*)	King's scribes called (*qara*)
Thirteenth of first month	Twenty-third day of third month
Just as Haman commanded	According to all that Mordecai commanded
To the king's satraps, to the governors who were over each province and to the princes of each people	*To the Jews,* the satraps, the governors and the princes of the provinces which *extended from India to Ethiopia, 127 provinces*
To each province according to its script, each people according to its language	To every province according to its script, and to every people according to their language as well as *to the Jews according to their script and their language*
Written in the name of King Ahasuerus and sealed with the king's signet ring.	He wrote in the name of King Ahasuerus, and sealed it with the king's signet ring,
Letters were sent by couriers to all the king's provinces	Sent letters by couriers on *horses, riding on steeds sired by the royal stud.*

To destroy, to kill, and to annihilate all the Jews, both young and old, women and children	*In them the king granted the Jews who were in each and every city the right to assemble and to defend their lives*, to destroy, to kill and to annihilate the *entire army of any people or province which might attack them*, including children and women
To seize their possessions as plunder.	To plunder their spoil
In one day, the thirteenth day of the twelfth month, which is the month Adar	On one day in all the provinces of King Ahasuerus, the thirteenth day of the twelfth month (that is, the month Adar)
A copy of the edict to be issued as law in every province was published to all the peoples	A copy of the edict to be issued as law in each and every province was published to all the peoples,
So that they should be ready for this day.	*So that the Jews would be ready for this day to avenge themselves on their enemies.*
The couriers went out impelled by the king's command	The couriers, *hastened and* impelled by the king's command, went out, *riding on the royal steeds*
While the decree was issued at the citadel in Susa; and *while the king and Haman sat down to drink, the city of Susa was in confusion.*	And the decree was given out at the citadel in Susa.
Purpose—to kill the Jews	Purpose—to save the Jews

Look back at Esther 8:8, where the king says to Esther and Mordecai, "Now you write to the Jews as you see fit, in the king's name, and seal it with the king's signet ring; for a decree which is written in the name of the king and sealed with the king's signet ring may not be revoked." In writing "to the Jews," the king was not allowing Mordecai to order Persian resources (men) to defend the Jews. We will see in Esther 9:3 that many of the leadership in Persia did help the Jews, even without an order to do so.

Why did the Jews need this new edict in order to defend themselves and fight those who were going to kill them? If they did not have the new law, would they have simply stood by and let themselves be slaughtered? Wouldn't the normal response have been to fight those who were killing them? What would you have done?

I believe the Jews would have fought back as individuals if the new edict had not been written. Would they have been as successful? They would not have been organized and would not have had the support from the second-in-command in the country, who at this time was Mordecai.

The critical section in Mordecai's edict giving them hope is found in the words "the right to assemble." Without this ability, they could not organize resistance against those who would destroy them. With this ability, and the fact they had nine months to prepare, they would be able to develop their plans.

Being able to assemble was a tremendous freedom the Jews were given. It was unusual for a king to allow such activity. It most certainly sent a message to everyone in the kingdom that the king supported the Jews.

Who was "the entire army of any people or province which might attack them, including children and women" in Esther 8:11? Were those who were planning on killing the Jews part of the king's regular army, part of a secret army organized by Haman, or were they regular citizens of Persian who hated the Jews? Do you find it strange the king allows the Jews to kill so many of his subjects? Was there any other way for the Jews to escape massacre? Do you think the king read the edict this time?

Remember the Theme Statement for Esther 3:12–15, "Law to have Jews destroyed is spread throughout empire."

Theme Statement for 8:9–14

Law to allow Jews to destroy attackers is spread throughout empire.

It is good to be a Jew

"Then Mordecai went out from the presence of the king in royal robes of blue and white, with a large crown of gold and a garment of fine linen and purple; and the city of Susa shouted and rejoiced. For the Jews there was light and gladness and joy and honor. In each and every province and in each and every city, wherever the king's commandment and his decree arrived, there was gladness and joy for the Jews, a feast and a holiday. And many among the peoples of the land became Jews, for the dread of the Jews had fallen on them" (Esther 8:15–17).

Where

City of Susa; the entire kingdom.

When

474 BC, after the twenty-third day, third month (month of Sivan—June/July).

X 474 BC—month Nisan—Haman casts lot
  X 474 BC—thirteenth day of Nisan—king's scribes summoned
    X 474 BC—sometime after the 13th day of the first month, Nisan—Mordecai mourns
    X 474 BC—Esther learns of Mordecai's mourning and edict to kill Jews
    X 474 BC—Esther agrees to go to king
    X 474 BC—Esther goes to king after three days of fasting
   X day after Esther went to king, second banquet, Haman exposed, hanged
       X 23rd day of third month, Sivan—Esther implores king to save Jews—
       Edict written to save Jews, sent by couriers

--------Time period from second edict to 13th day of Adar--------

474 BC, 13th day Adar—when Jews are to be destroyed X

*   *   *   *   *   *   *   *   *   *   *   *   *

474

Nisan	Sivan	Av	Tishri	Chislev	Shebat	(Adar II)
(Ma/Ap)	(May/Jun)	(Jul/Aug)	(Sep/Oct)	(Nov/Dec)	(Jan/Feb)	(leap yr)

Iyyar	Tammuz	Elul	Cheshvan	Tebeth	Adar
(Ap/May)	(Jun/Jul)	(Aug/Sep)	(Oct/Nov)	(Dec/Jan)	(Feb/Mar)

249

This paragraph says a great deal:

> "Then Mordecai went out from the presence of the king in royal robes of blue and white, with a large crown of gold and a garment of fine linen and purple; and the city of Susa shouted and rejoiced" (Esther 8:15).

Mordecai already has the king's signet ring. He has the authority to make laws as if it were the king making them. Now he is dressed in clothes that identify him as having a position of royalty. Look back to Esther 1:6 and see how it discusses royal colors. Wherever Mordecai appeared, people saw him as a Jew with the honor of royalty. This had a tremendous impact on the entire nation.

Compare "and the city of Susa shouted and rejoiced" with "the city of Susa was in confusion" in Esther 3:15. These were not only the Jews in the city. The whole city—Jews and Persians—were elated.

We will talk about the Jews in minute. For now, think about why the Persians in Susa were happy. Jews now had freedom to protect themselves. Haman was now dead. I am sure it seemed like order was now back in the city. Were the people rejoicing because Haman was dead or because Mordecai was now second in command? Probably for both reasons.

> "For the Jews there was light and gladness and joy and honor" (Esther 8:16).

Hebrew words:

"Light"—*'owrah* (o-raw'); "prosperity, light"
"Gladness"—*simchah* (sim-khaw'); "exceeding gladness"
"Joy"—*sasown* (saw-sone'), "joy, rejoicing"
"Honor"—*yeqar* (yek-awr'), "value, honor, precious"

Why were the Jews happy? They knew Haman's edict, which said they were going to be attacked, was still in effect. The king was unable to change the law. God had not yet delivered them from their enemies. Look back at Esther 8:11—"the right to assemble and to defend their lives, to destroy, to kill and to annihilate the entire army of any people or province which might attack them, including children and women, and to plunder their spoil." God had blessed them by delivering them from Haman, but had not delivered them from the upcoming massacre.

What He had given them was freedom to assemble and the opportunity to fight.

Principle 43: God often blesses us—not with success, but with the opportunity to succeed.

When you are suffering and you need divine help, does God always bless you by solving your entire problem, giving you everything you ask, and making everything just the way you want it to be? Does God give you what you need and then require you to use that blessing in the right way to resolve issues? We do need to remember that our idea of success is not always the same as God's.

God blesses us in more ways than we can ever know. The simple fact we are alive is a blessing. The fact that Jesus Christ paid our debt on the cross, giving us opportunity for salvation, is a blessing. He gives us freedom to choose for Him or against Him. He provides all that we need; yet to share in His blessings, we have to follow His plan. For salvation, it is belief in Jesus Christ. For those who believe in His Son, He does guarantee eternal life (John 3:15; 10:28; 1 John 11-12). He provides numerous guarantees on earth for us as well; we are adopted by God (Romans 8:15; Galatians 4:4-5; Ephesians 1:5), we have access to God (Romans 5:2; Ephesians 2:18), we are recipients of the ministry of the Holy Spirit (Romans 5:5; 1 Corinthians 6:19), and possess every spiritual blessing granted in eternity past (Ephesians 1:3). These are but a few of the things God gives us when we put our faith in His son, Jesus Christ. Yet we still live in the human world, and our volition determines so much of what we encounter. The opportunity God gives us does not guarantee our human success. We have to follow His plan.

Government leaders need to understand this principle. The second sentence of the Unanimous Declaration of the Thirteen United States of America, July 4, 1776, states, "We hold these truths to be self-evident, that all men are created equal, that they are endowed by their creator with certain unalienable rights, that among these are life, liberty, and the pursuit of happiness." The word "rights" does not mean the government is responsible to determine individual success or failure. It does mean the government has the responsibility to *not* prohibit individuals from seeking success or failure. Each individual has the right to succeed or fail on his or her own. The government has no right to try to make people equal in any category, whether it is physical, social, or economic. If God blesses us with freedom and opportunity to succeed or fail, the government should do no less. Any attempt to do otherwise is against God's will.

God blesses with equality of opportunity, not equality of outcome when His plan is not followed. God, through His absolute righteousness, justice, and love, gives every human being the opportunity to believe in His Son, Jesus Christ, and have eternal salvation. He further gives every believer the opportunity to "be transformed by the renewing of your mind" (Romans 12:2) and to "grow in the grace and knowledge of our Lord and Savior Jesus Christ" (2 Peter 3:18). Personal volition that chooses to reject God's plan regarding salvation results in eternity in the lake of fire. Personal volition of believers who choose to reject God's plan after salvation results in spiritual failure on earth and loss of rewards in heaven. Personal volition of believers who choose to follow God's plan after salvation results in a victorious outcome, both on earth and in heaven (1 Corinthians 3:10-15). God does reward those who follow His plan, and He does reject those who reject the saving grace of Jesus Christ.

As stated elsewhere in this book, God's blessings to humanity do not equal prosperity of wealth and health. At times, God does provide financial and health blessings. At other times, He does not. We will have adversity here on earth. We should never associate adversity with failure to follow God, nor should we associate success with spiritual growth.

Human government should follow these guidelines. The government should provide equality of opportunity, not equality of outcome. Human volition will rightfully decide success or failure. This does not mean every person will end up with the same degree of financial or personal success. Remember, we live in a sin-torn world where God allows adversity in order to test us, bless us and sanctify us. As believers we must reach out and be God's hands to help those in need. America has been the greatest nation in the history of the world in providing relief around the world when it is needed. It simply means the government cannot and should not try to make people equal, whether by redistributing wealth or by changing laws to elevate those who are unsuccessful at the expense of penalizing those who are successful.

Remember the second section in the first chapter, Biblical Heroes. Think of heroes such as David, Moses, and Paul, who faced multiple adversities. Each learned to trust and obey God. Each was blessed by God. Each used their blessings to accomplish the works God had planned for them. Although God certainly performed miracles which benefitted each, most of the time, these men had to take what God had given them and then use their human abilities to accomplish God's purpose. Although David died as a king and Moses died after leading the Israelites to the Promised Land, Paul, who was a genius believer who wrote half of the New Testament, died penniless in a Roman prison. All three men fulfilled their purpose in life, yet God presented each with hardship and ultimate death.

Remember in Chapter Three, Context, under principle 1, "when a leader sins and rejects God's authority, all those under the leader's authority are affected" and Chapter Six, Esther Three, under principle 25, "every person has to bear some responsibility in the decisions, policies, and actions of the nation, as well as their consequences." We discussed the Israelites' failure to enter Canaan when God commanded them to do so. God had blessed the Jews with the opportunity to enter the Promised Land, yet they failed to act and follow His plan. I believe the history of the Jews would have been different if all twelve of the spies had trusted God and followed Him as He led them into Canaan.

The Jews were going to have to fight their enemies if they wanted to survive. God was not simply killing them as he did with the Assyrians under Sennacherib when Hezekiah was king. How were the Jews blessed with opportunity?

Principle 44: Freedom to use God's blessings is a great blessing itself.

What we do with that freedom often determines our physical and spiritual success or failure. Remember Esther in Esther 2:8–11. Having been taken from Mordecai and placed in the harem, she used the blessings God had given her (faith, character, beauty) and won the favor of those with whom she came in contact.

With what freedoms does God bless us in this country? Freedom to worship, live where one desires, work at the job one chooses, and marry and raise a family are just a few. What would life be like without those freedoms? Most of these things we often take for granted. Do you thank God for them? Do you use them in the way He desires?

Sometimes we are not aware of the blessings God has given us. This may be because of ignorance of His Word, living in sin, or simply being so busy in our own personal affairs we do not see the marvelous things God has done for us. A challenge for all believers is to read the first chapter of Ephesians. Here you will see Paul present God's revelation concerning the most incredible blessings guaranteed for those who have put their faith in Jesus Christ.

"Blessed be the God and Father of our Lord Jesus Christ, who has blessed us with every spiritual blessing in the heavenly places in Christ" (Ephesians 1:3).

In the following verses, Paul describes those blessings present for believers on earth and in heaven.

"In each and every province and in each and every city, wherever the king's commandment and his decree arrived, there was gladness and joy for the Jews, a feast and a holiday. And many among the peoples of the land became Jews, for the dread of the Jews had fallen on them" (Esther 8:17).

Jews throughout the empire had feasts and holidays. And many Gentiles became Jews. Why did people want to become Jews? Were they afraid the Jews might rise up against them? Did they understand the miracle of how God was protecting the Jews, and did they want to be a part of things?

I was in the United States Air Force in the late 1980s. Ronald Reagan was president, followed by George Bush. Being in the military was looked upon with approval. I remember wearing my uniform off base and seeing a look of patriotism in the eyes of people I encountered. There was "gladness and joy" for most servicemen and servicewomen. In contrast, I recall the mood of many people and much of the country when service members returned from Vietnam in the early 1970s. A great disservice was done to the men and women of the armed forces with the anti-military protests. What a difference a few years makes.

Principle 45: God often uses suffering and obedience of believers to bring people to Him.

When you are going through suffering, do you ever wonder how it might eventually bless you and others? If your spiritual response is one of thankfulness, humility, and praise toward God, you are following His will. If your outward response is the same, others will notice. Your obedience to God during times of suffering will bring glory to God—and may lead others to Him, as well.

In many of the works God has prepared for us (Ephesians 2:10), overt activities such as ministering to others, giving, teaching the Word, and helping those in need are required. I believe many of the works may also involve our response to periods of adversity. In times of suffering, if we keep our eyes on God and obey Him, we bring glory to Him. Trust and obedience to God in times of adversity are just as important in God's plan as the pastor preaching on Sunday morning.

"For you were formerly darkness, but now you are Light in the Lord; walk as children of Light (for the fruit of the Light consists in all goodness and righteousness and truth)" (Ephesians 5:8–9).

Theme Statement

The empire rejoices in the law to free Jews.

Points to Remember

Theme Statements

Esther 8:1–2—Mordecai is given the king's ring and authority over Haman's house.

Esther 8:3–8—Esther implores the king to save the Jews.

Esther 8:9–14—The law to allow Jews to destroy attackers is spread throughout the empire.

Esther 8:15–17—The empire rejoices in the law to free the Jews.

Principles

42. Personal failure demands the acceptance of responsibility for failure.

43. God often blesses us—not with success, but with the opportunity to succeed.

44. Freedom to use God's blessings is a great blessing itself.

45. God often uses suffering and obedience of believers to bring people to Him.

Chapter Twelve

ESTHER 9–10:
MILITARY VICTORY AND CELEBRATION

Preparation and War

"Now in the twelfth month (that is, the month Adar), on the thirteenth day when the king's command and edict were about to be executed, on the day when the enemies of the Jews hoped to gain the mastery over them, it was turned to the contrary so that the Jews themselves gained the mastery over those who hated them. The Jews assembled in their cities throughout all the provinces of King Ahasuerus to lay hands on those who sought their harm; and no one could stand before them, for the dread of them had fallen on all the peoples. Even all the princes of the provinces, the satraps, the governors and those who were doing the king's business assisted the Jews, because the dread of Mordecai had fallen on them. Indeed, Mordecai was great in the king's house, and his fame spread throughout all the provinces; for the man Mordecai became greater and greater. Thus the Jews struck all their enemies with the sword, killing and destroying; and they did what they pleased to those who hated them. At the citadel in Susa the Jews killed and destroyed five hundred men, and Parshandatha, Dalphon, Aspatha, Poratha, Adalia, Aridatha, Parmashta, Arisai, Aridai and Vaizatha, the ten sons of Haman the son of Hammedatha, the Jews' enemy; but they did not lay their hands on the plunder" (Esther 9:1–10).

257

Where

Cities throughout all the provinces.

When

Chapter 8—474 BC, after the twenty-third day, third month, Sivan (which is June/July).

Chapter 9—474 BC, thirteenth day, twelfth month, Adar (which is February/March).

For the Jew-haters, it probably seemed like Friday the 13th.

X 474 BC—month Nisan—Haman casts lot
  X 474 BC—thirteenth day of Nisan—king's scribes summoned
    X 474 BC—sometime after the 13th day of the first month, Nisan—Mordecai mourns
      X 474 BC—Esther learns of Mordecai's mourning and edict to kill Jews
        X 474 BC—Esther agrees to go to king
          X 474 BC—Esther goes to king after three days of fasting
            X day after Esther went to king, second banquet, Haman exposed, hanged
              X 23rd day of third month, Sivan—Esther implores king to save Jews—
              Edict written to save Jews, sent by couriers
              --------Time period from second edict to 13th day of Adar-------

474 BC, 13th day Adar—when Jews are to be destroyed X

---

*   *   *   *   *   *   *   *   *   *   *   *   *

474

Nisan	Sivan	Av	Tishri	Chislev	Shebat	(Adar II)
(Ma/Ap)	(May/Jun)	(Jul/Aug)	(Sep/Oct)	(Nov/Dec)	(Jan/Feb)	(leap yr)
Iyyar	Tammuz	Elul	Cheshvan	Tebeth	Adar	
(Ap/May)	(Jun/Jul)	(Aug/Sep)	(Oct/Nov)	(Dec/Jan)	(Feb/Mar)	

There are historical events in which we have limited records of what people thought or did during that time. Some of these I look forward to finding out more in heaven by talking to the people who were there. This is one of those times.

What has happened between Esther 8 and 9 in the last eight or nine months? For the Jew-haters, there was preparation to kill Jews. For the Jews, there was preparation to kill Jew-haters. Talk about an anticipated event. Imagine what people were thinking as this day approached. Both edicts were legal and were to be carried out at the same time.

"Now in the twelfth month (that is, the month Adar), on the thirteenth day when the king's command and edict were about to be executed, on the day when the enemies of the Jews hoped to gain the mastery over them, it was turned to the contrary so that the Jews themselves gained the mastery over those who hated them" (Esther 9:1).

The time for war has finally arrived. It is "the twelfth month (that is, the month Adar), on the thirteenth day." Both edicts are to occur on this same day (Esther 3:7, 13; 8:12).

What new information does this verse tell us? We know Haman hated the Jews (Esther 3:8). We now find it written that there was widespread hatred of the Jews—"enemies of the Jews" in Esther 9:1. This is the anti-Semitism we referenced earlier (Chapter Three, Context). Here it says there was hatred.

Which "king's command and edict" is being spoken of? I think it is Haman's, although the author could be talking about Mordecai's as well. What does "Jews themselves gained the mastery over those who hated them" mean? "Mastery," or *shalat* (shaw-lat'), means "to dominate, i.e., govern; by implication, to permit: (bear, have) rule, have dominion, give (have) power." How did the Jews gain mastery over everyone who was against them? The answer is found in the next verse.

"The Jews assembled in their cities throughout all the provinces of King Ahasuerus to lay hands on those who sought their harm; and no one could stand before them, for the dread of them had fallen on all the peoples" (Esther 9:2).

The Jews gathered together. In Esther 8:11, it says the Jews were given this right, and we have discussed its importance. I am sure all the Jews knew the story to date—everything about the king, Haman, Esther, and Mordecai. The first edict said they were going to be slaughtered. The second edict gave them an opportunity to destroy their enemies.

For the context of our study, we started in 900 BC with the reign of Solomon. We went through 300 years of the Jews resisting God and doing their own thing. We saw God put them in exile in Babylon. We saw them change in their relationship to God as well as their desire to trust and obey Him. The Jews in 474 BC came together as one people with faith in God and united against a common enemy. I think the entire nation of Persia saw this unification and feared it. Most Persians did not want to fight against the Jews. I think only those who were filled with anti-Semitic hate continued in their desire to fight.

Hebrew words:

> "Dread"—*pachad* (pakh'-ad), "a (sudden) alarm (properly, the object feared, by implication, the feeling): dread (-ful), fear, (thing) great [fear, -ly feared], terror."

I get the feeling all non-Jews now feared the Jews.

> "Even all the princes of the provinces, the satraps, the governors and those who were doing the king's business assisted the Jews, because the dread of Mordecai had fallen on them" (Esther 9:3).

Some movements begin at the grassroots level and spread throughout a nation. Some begin at levels of leadership and spread to the population. Here I see a little of both. In this case, the grassroots organization is the entire Jewish community. Remember in Esther 4:6 when all the Jews in Susa fasted and prayed? We now have Jews throughout Persia assembling against their enemies.

Mordecai's leadership was all that was needed to advance the Jews to victory. The result is that non-Jews in leadership positions sided with Jews. Mayors, governors, and princes feared the Jews. When it says "the dread of Mordecai had fallen on them," it means non-Jewish leaders in Persia feared Mordecai. Not only was he leading the Jews, he had the signet ring and was second in command only to the king. Anyone who challenged him was challenging the king. The result is that not only did Persian leaders not help the Jew-haters; they assisted the Jews in their preparation to kill the Jew-haters. I do not think they assisted in the actual killing of non-Jews, however. It was not in the edict (Esther 8:11). Esther 9:5 says "thus the Jews struck all their enemies with the sword."

> "Indeed, Mordecai was great in the king's house, and his fame spread throughout all the provinces; for the man Mordecai became greater and greater" (Esther 9:4).

When Mordecai received the king's signet ring and became the second most powerful person in the land, being a Jew took on a whole new meaning. Before, when Haman was number two, being a Jew became a death sentence after the first edict was sent. I think everyone shunned them. Now, with Mordecai as number two, either you wanted to become a Jew or you wanted to help them. As they grew stronger in numbers and in their resolve to kill their enemies, people feared them.

I think in the nine months leading up to this day, Mordecai had shown himself to be wise. He brought honor and stability to the kingdom. Again, compare the "confusion" of Susa in Esther 3:15 and the "gladness and joy" in "each and every province" in Esther 8:17. This pleased Ahasuerus. Do you think Mordecai personally traveled to different parts of the kingdom in support of the Jews? This would also bring fear into the hearts of the Jew-haters. Whatever Mordecai said, people had to follow.

Do you see similarities between Joseph in Egypt and Mordecai in Persia?

Principle 46: God prepares and promotes those in whom He has a work to accomplish.

Esther was promoted to queen to expose Haman and petition the king. Mordecai was promoted to lead the Jews in the defeat of their enemies. Once again, read the following verse:

"For we are His workmanship, created in Christ Jesus for good works, which God prepared beforehand so that we would walk in them" (Ephesians 2:10).

I think this principle is as true for you and me as it was for Esther and Mordecai. Remember Principle 9: "God puts us on the sideline so we will learn to follow His game plan." In Chapter Three—Context, "The Road to Esther," the sideline was presented as a time the Jews had to spend in exile. The result was that the Jews became prepared for the works God had planned for them as a nation.

When God has a designed work for you He prepares you and then promotes you into the position to do His will. Often we do not know what specific works God has designed for us. We can, however, prepare ourselves for when God is ready to use us. We do so by the filling of the Holy Spirit, learning His Word, and prayer. Be ready for wherever and whenever He calls.

I have found that God usually gives us small tasks to mature us. When we are ready, He puts us in more difficult situations. We need to remember that all we do for Him should be for His glory, not ours.

Have you ever thought that God could or should be using you in a different way? Have you ever thought God should be using you to do what you want to do *right now?* Don't fall into that trap. God knows exactly when and where to use you. Rather, ask yourself if you are preparing for those works. Are you learning His Word daily, are you spending time in prayer, is the Holy Spirit directing you, and are you listening? Are you working in the *small* things He has asked you to do?

In 1915, Dwight David Eisenhower graduated from West Point. Twenty-five years later, in 1940, he attained the rank of Colonel; yet was still an obscure Army officer. Four years later, he would be the Supreme Allied Commander, instrumental in the development and execution of the political, diplomatic, and military aspects of winning the war in Europe. How did Eisenhower rise to such a position of authority in such a short time, and what prepared him in those twenty-five years prior? Do you think during this period he ever wondered what he was to become and what affect he would have on history? Would he have been able to do in 1925 what he did in 1944?

If you ever get frustrated in what you are doing and think God is wrong in not using you in some way, stop! Trust Him, obey Him, learn His Word, pray, let the Holy Spirit direct you, and wait on God. Don't let pride tell you that what He has you doing is too *small* for you. No task of service is beneath a believer. Remember, Jesus washed the feet of His disciples (John 13:5). He will use you in His way when you are ready. Until that time, prepare yourself.

"Thus the Jews struck all their enemies with the sword, killing and destroying; and they did what they pleased to those who hated them" (Esther 9:5).

So what do you think of Esther 9:5? Remember what the edict said in Esther 8:11: "In them the king granted the Jews who were in each and every city the right to assemble and to defend their lives, to destroy, to kill and to annihilate the entire army of any people or province which might attack them, including children and women, and to plunder their spoil." Think back a little. God commanded Saul to do something similar with the Amalekites. He did not, and it got him in trouble.

> "Now go and strike Amalek and utterly destroy all that he has, and do not spare him; but put to death both man and woman, child and infant, ox and sheep, camel and donkey" (1 Samuel 15:3).

For the war in Esther, the Jews obeyed the edict—except for one thing, which we will see in Esther 9:10. There were no negotiations. There was no cease-fire. There were no prisoners taken. There was no political correctness. There was no mercy shown. There was only the complete destruction of the enemy. This was not a defensive, "protect the Jews" campaign. It was an offensive operation all the way. This is an example of how you fight your enemies when the goal is military victory. I think the degree to which the Jews slaughtered their enemies shows there had to have been widespread anti-Semitism for years in Persia.

> "At the citadel in Susa the Jews killed and destroyed five hundred men, and Parshandatha, Dalphon, Aspatha, Poratha, Adalia, Aridatha, Parmashta, Arisai, Aridai and Vaizatha, the ten sons of Haman the son of Hammedatha, the Jews' enemy; but they did not lay their hands on the plunder" (Esther 9:6).

When we began Esther, I said the author was a master storyteller. I love the way he emphasizes what the Jews did. It is not enough to just kill the enemy. In both Esther 9:5 and 9:6, he says "killed and destroyed." Five hundred men at the citadel in Susa were killed, as well as the ten sons of Haman. It does not say so, but I would think the ten sons of Haman were part of the Jew-haters. I guess even if they were not a part of their father's plan, they were guilty by association. It says the Jews did not take any of the plunder as it stated they could do so in the edict according to Esther 8:11. It also says this in Esther 9:15–16.

Theme Statement

The Jews kill and destroy their enemies.

How to Prosecute a War

> "On that day the number of those who were killed at the citadel in Susa was reported to the king. The king said to Queen Esther, 'The Jews have killed and destroyed five hundred men and the ten sons of Haman at the citadel in Susa. What then have they done in the rest of the king's provinces! Now what is your petition? It shall even be granted you. And what is your further request? It shall also be done.' Then said Esther, 'If it pleases the king, let tomorrow also be granted to the Jews who are in Susa to do according to the edict of today; and let Haman's ten sons be hanged on the gallows.' So the king commanded that it should be done so; and an edict was issued in Susa, and Haman's ten sons were hanged. The Jews who were in Susa assembled also on the fourteenth day of the month Adar and killed three hundred men in Susa, but they did not lay their hands on the plunder" (Esther 9:11–15).

Where

The citadel in Susa; the city of Susa.

When

474 BC, 13th and 14th days, twelfth month (month of Adar—February/March).

> "On that day the number of those who were killed at the citadel in Susa was reported to the king. The king said to Queen Esther, 'The Jews have killed and destroyed five hundred men and the ten sons of Haman at the citadel in Susa. What then have they done in the rest of the king's provinces! Now what is your petition? It shall even be granted you. And what is your further request? It shall also be done'" (Esther 9:11–12).

We begin on the 13th day. In Esther 9:11, somebody reports to the king the number of people killed. Notice the report is of killing that took place "at the citadel in Susa." It appears there was a significant battle at the palace. There is no comment as to the rest of the city. We find out in Esther 9:12 the Jews have killed and destroyed five hundred men and the ten sons of Haman, similar to Esther 9:6. The king wants to know what has happened in the rest of the kingdom.

In what way do you think the king asked this question? Who and what were important to the king at this time? I think he asks it with gleeful anticipation for the destruction of a national evil. Look again at Esther 9:3–4. Mordecai had brought positive leadership to the king. The nation had rallied around him. The king wanted him to succeed, and he wanted Esther to be happy. The king now says, "Now what is your petition? It shall even be granted you. And what is your further request? It shall also be done."

> "Then said Esther, 'If it pleases the king, let tomorrow also be granted to the Jews who are in Susa to do according to the edict of today; and let Haman's ten sons be hanged on the gallows'" (Esther 9:13).

What is the significance of hanging the ten dead sons of Haman on the gallows? It would be a visual warning or reminder to anyone who might have thoughts of challenging the Jews in the future. It would deter future attempts to destroy the Jews. It is what Haman wanted to do with Mordecai (Esther 5:14) and what the king had done to Haman (Esther 7:10).

In Esther 5, I said Esther had ice water running through her veins. I did not mean it in a critical way—just in a way that meant she knew the problem, the solution, and would coolly and calmly see it through. What do you think of her response in Esther 9:13? What do you think of Esther now? To her, it is not enough to kill most of the Jew-haters. She wants the enemy completely destroyed.

> "So the king commanded that it should be done so; and an edict was issued in Susa, and Haman's ten sons were hanged. The Jews who were in Susa assembled also on the fourteenth day of the month Adar and killed three hundred men in Susa, but they did not lay their hands on the plunder" (Esther 9:14–15).

The king agrees with Esther and issues the edict for the city of Susa. The next day, the Jews kill an additional 300 men in the city of Susa. Notice there is no mention of those wounded in action, and there is no mention of prisoners of war. Notice also that the Jews do not take any of the possessions. It only mentions men being killed. It says nothing of women and children.

Theme Statement

Jews in Susa kill 810 Jew-haters in two days.

Counting the enemy killed

> "Now the rest of the Jews who were in the king's provinces assembled, to defend their lives and rid themselves of their enemies, and kill 75,000 of those who hated them; but they did not lay their hands on the plunder. This was done on the thirteenth day of the month Adar, and on the fourteenth day they rested and made it a day of feasting and rejoicing" (Esther 9:16–17).

Where

The king's provinces.

When

474 BC, 13th and 14th day, twelfth month (month of Adar—February/March).

What type of connector is *now?* It is a temporal connector. The commentary changes to what happened in the rest of the kingdom. The Jews assemble. When it says "to defend their lives," it sounds like they were only trying to protect themselves. When it says "to rid themselves of their enemies," it sounds like an offensive attack. The result is the killing of 75,000 Jew-haters. It does not say "men." It does not say if women and children are included. There was only one day of fighting, the 13th. On the 14th, the Jews rested, feasted, and rejoiced.

Hebrew words:

"Rejoice"—*simchah* (sim-khaw'); "blithesomeness or glee, (religious or festival): exceeding (-ly), gladness, joy (-fulness), mirth, pleasure, rejoice (-ing)."

In Chapter Three—Context, "The Road to Esther," we discussed the history leading up to Esther. Prior to the Exile, the Jews disobeyed God most of the time, and they were disciplined as a result. At times, they did turn to God. Hezekiah turned Judah to God when Sennacherib, the Assyrian, was going to destroy the nation. Remember Principle 4, "God's justice and righteousness work in perfect union with His love, and the three together are in harmony with His divine will and plan" and Principle 5, "God uses nations to punish His chosen people, then judges those nations." A very specific principle is seen with the action of the Jews in Persia.

Principle 47: God authorizes and mandates nations to destroy evil—particularly anti-Semitism.

The action of the Jews lead by Mordecai could be considered a national event. Look back at Esther 9:3. The leadership in Persia assisted. History has shown God's wrath poured out on those nations who practice evil and anti-Semitism. In our recent history, we can look to World War II. Hitler and Germany were definitely evil in their anti-Semitism. I believe God justly brought nations together to defeat the Axis powers.

Is the reverse of this principle also true? Does God bless those nations that support and maintain Israel? Remember what God told Abram:

"Now the Lord said to Abram, 'Go forth from your country, and from your relatives and from your father's house, to the land which I will show you; and I will make you a great nation, and I will bless you, and make your name great; and so you shall be a blessing; and I will bless those who bless you, and the one who curses you I will curse" (Genesis 12:1–3).

Theme statement

The Jews in the nation kill 75,000 Jew-haters, feast, and rejoice.

Reason for Rejoicing

"But the Jews who were in Susa assembled on the thirteenth and the fourteenth of the same month, and they rested on the fifteenth day and made it a day of feasting and rejoicing. Therefore the Jews of the rural areas, who live in the rural towns, make the fourteenth day of the month Adar a holiday for rejoicing and feasting and sending portions of food to one another" (Esther 9:18–19).

Where

Susa and rural areas.

When

13th and 14th day, twelfth month (month of Adar—February/March).

This paragraph explains why the Jews in Susa rejoice on the 15th day, after the killing on the 13th and 14th, and those in rural areas rejoice on the 14th day, after the killing on the 13th.

Theme Statement

Susa Jews rejoice on the 15th; rural Jews rejoice on the 14th.

Requirement to celebrate

The next two paragraphs discuss the Feast of Purim. Remember, the Feast of Purim was not set forth in the Mosaic Law. Do you remember what other feast was established after the Mosaic Law? Hanukkah.

"Then Mordecai recorded these events, and he sent letters to all the Jews who were in all the provinces of King Ahasuerus, both near and far, obliging them to celebrate the fourteenth day of the month Adar, and the fifteenth day of the same month, annually, because on those days the Jews rid themselves of their enemies, and it was a month which was turned for them from sorrow into gladness and from mourning into a holiday; that they should make them days of feasting and rejoicing and sending portions of food to one another and gifts to the poor" (Esther 9:20–22).

Where

All the provinces of King Ahasuerus.

When

474 BC, after the 15th of Adar.

X 474 BC—month Nisan—Haman casts lot

X 474 BC—thirteenth day of Nisan—king's scribes summoned

X 474 BC—sometime after the 13th day of the first month, Nisan—Mordecai mourns

X 474 BC—Esther learns of Mordecai's mourning and edict to kill Jews

X 474 BC—Esther agrees to go to king

X 474 BC—Esther goes to king after three days of fasting

X day after Esther went to king, second banquet, Haman exposed, hanged

X 23rd day of third month, Sivan—Esther implores king to save Jews—Edict written to save Jews, sent by couriers

--------Time period from second edict to 13th day of Adar--------

474 BC—13th day Adar—when Jews are to be destroyed X

After the 15th day of Adar X

*	*	*	*	*	*	*	*	*	*	*	*	*	*

474

Nisan	Sivan	Av	Tishri	Chislev	Shebat	(Adar II)
(Ma/Ap)	(May/Jun)	(Jul/Aug)	(Sep/Oct)	(Nov/Dec)	(Jan/Feb)	(leap yr)

Iyyar	Tammuz	Elul	Cheshvan	Tebeth	Adar
(Ap/May)	(Jun/Jul)	(Aug/Sep)	(Oct/Nov)	(Dec/Jan)	(Feb/Mar)

Mordecai writes down all that has happened with the Jews destroying their enemies. He sends a letter to all the Jews in the provinces. We will see some of the discussion of this second letter in the next paragraph.

Hebrew words:

"Obliging them"—

quwm (koom); "abide, accomplish, confirm, decree"

hayah (haw-yaw); "accomplish, committed"

`*asah* (aw-saw'); "accomplish, appoint, have the charge of"

You get the feeling that Mordecai was giving a command to the Jews for them to annually celebrate the 14th and 15th of Adar. It was more than saying, "if you want to celebrate, do so." It was saying, "you are commanded to do so." Why would they make such a big deal of this? The Jews had "rid themselves of their enemies"—all the Jew-haters who were planning to kill them. It was a time in which "sorrow" was turned "into gladness" and "mourning into a holiday." I do not know if it is possible for us to fully realize the magnitude of emotion these people had at this time. They had gone from certain death to absolute victory.

Let's count back in time the major sequence of events:

- 474 BC, 13th and 14th days, twelfth month of the year, Adar—the Jews had killed their enemies.

- 474 BC, 23rd day, third month of the year, Sivan (which is June/July)—the Jews had been given the edict to assemble and destroy any people who might attack them. This was Mordecai's edict.

- 474 BC, 13th day, first month of the year, Nisan (which is March/April)—the edict had been issued for the destruction of the Jews. This is Haman's edict.

- 479 BC, tenth month of the year, Tebeth (which is December/January)—Esther had become queen.

- 483 BC, 3rd year of reign of King Ahasuerus—our story began.

How many years of anti-Semitic oppression had the Jews endured prior to this? To some extent, since God first talked to Abraham. The Jews in the book of Esther had always been aware of it. Now in 474 BC, they were free from its oppression.

Life magazine was famous for its covers. A cover picture in 1945 titled "The Kiss" was taken on V-J Day in Times Square. It is based on the tremendous elation Americans had knowing the US would not have to invade Japan. The estimates were for a million American lives lost if they had to do so. There was elation in the whole country.

What were the Jews supposed to do? They were to feast, rejoice, send portions of food to one another, and send gifts to the poor. Although this was 2,484 years ago (474 BC to 2010), the Jews still celebrate this event.

Theme Statement

Mordecai commands the Jews to celebrate deliverance.

Reason for Purim

"Thus the Jews undertook what they had started to do, and what Mordecai had written to them. For Haman the son of Hammedatha, the Agagite, the adversary of all the Jews, had schemed against the Jews to destroy them and had cast Pur, that is the lot, to disturb them and destroy them. But when it came to the king's attention, he commanded by letter that his wicked scheme which he had devised against the Jews, should return on his own head and that he and his sons should be hanged on the gallows. Therefore they called these days Purim after the name of Pur. And because of the instructions in this letter, both what they had seen in this regard and what had happened to them, the Jews established and made a custom for themselves and for their descendants and for all those who allied themselves with them, so that they would not fail to celebrate these two days according to their regulation and according to their appointed time annually. So these days were to be remembered and celebrated throughout every generation, every family, every province and every city; and these days of Purim were not to fail from among the Jews, or their memory fade from their descendants" (Esther 9:23–28).

Where

All the provinces of King Ahasuerus.

When

474 BC, after the 15th of Adar.

This paragraph continues the explanation of the feast of Purim. Mordecai summarizes the events which have lead up to the rejoicing.

When we read Esther 9:25, we see that the king did not know what Haman was planning until Esther told him. What do you think of the way the author describes the king's involvement in the ordeal? I think he is being kind to the king. If you had not read up to this point and had read only these two verses, you might think the king came up with the ideas solely on his own to hang Haman and his sons and to allow the Jews to fight the Jew-haters.

The king did say to hang Haman, but he had some encouragement. "Then Harbonah, one of the eunuchs who were before the king said, 'Behold indeed, the gallows standing at Haman's house fifty cubits high, which Haman made for Mordecai who spoke good on behalf of the king!' And the king said, 'Hang him on it'" (Esther 7:9). Concerning the edict to allow the Jews to assemble and fight back, the statement in Esther 9:25 does not specifically address Mordecai's edict, but I think "commanded by letter" implies it. I think this is Mordecai's edict. The author is giving the king credit, when in reality it was Mordecai who wrote the edict. "Now you write to the Jews as you see fit, in the king's name, and seal it with the kin"s signet ring; for a decree which is written in the name of the king and sealed with the king's signet ring may not be revoked" (Esther 8:8).

Regarding who said to hang Haman's sons on the gallows, it was Esther, not the king. "Then said Esther, 'If it pleases the king, let tomorrow also be granted to the Jews who are in Susa to do according to the edict of today; and let Haman's ten sons be hanged on the gallows.' So the king commanded that it should be done so; and an edict was issued in Susa, and Haman's ten sons were hanged" (Esther 9:13–14).

There are two ways to look at this. The easy way is to say the king should take credit for what Esther and Mordecai did. He is the authority over the two and has a certain right to do so. The problem with that is that if he takes credit for what Mordecai wrote in his edict to the Jews, the king should have to take responsibility for what Haman wrote in his edict.

I tend to give a little less credit to the king and say the author is making the king look good. The author is letting the king take credit for things he did not do. The book is written after the king's death, and other than the fact that God chose how the book was written, I am not sure why the human author records things this way.

In Esther 9:26, we see the name "Purim" originating from the name *pur*. We find out Mordecai believed it was critical that clear instructions needed to be given for this feast, both the event itself and the reason behind it (Esther 9:26–28).

What do you think of the words "days were to be remembered and celebrated?" I think it provides both a sobering warning to the people never to forget the persecution of the Jews and a hopeful reminder of God's deliverance that should be celebrated with thankfulness and rejoicing. This time period was not to be forgotten. How do you compare Jews today remembering the feast of Purim and Americans remembering significant historic events in the founding and preservation of our country and freedom?

Theme Statement

Jews remember and celebrate Purim.

Authority of Esther and Mordecai

"Then Queen Esther, daughter of Abihail, with Mordecai the Jew, wrote with full authority to confirm this second letter about Purim. He sent letters to all the Jews, to the 127 provinces of the kingdom of Ahasuerus, namely, words of peace and truth, to establish these days of Purim at their appointed times, just as Mordecai the Jew and Queen Esther had established for them, and just as they had established for themselves and for their descendants with instructions for their times of fasting and their lamentations. The command of Esther established these customs for Purim, and it was written in the book" (Esther 9:29–32).

Where

All the provinces of King Ahasuerus.

When

474 BC, after the 15th of Adar.

In the last two paragraphs, we learned Mordecai commanded the feast of Purim. Here it says Esther confirmed it with her authority. It appears both Esther and Mordecai write a second letter to the Jews. There were "words of peace and truth," it was to "establish days of Purim," with reference to fasting and Lamentations. It concludes with "the command of Esther established these customs for Purim, and it was written in the book."

Some questions for you to think on as we close this chapter: What was Esther's authority? Was it for the Jews or the whole kingdom? Was it backed by the king or her position as a Jew? What do you think of Esther's and Mordecai's promotions to positions of authority? Who was responsible? What do you think of the Jews' deliverance? What was the reason for their victory? What role did humans have in their victory? What role did God play?

Theme Statement

Esther and Mordecai establish Purim.

Honor to Mordecai

"Now King Ahasuerus laid a tribute on the land and on the coastlands of the sea. And all the accomplishments of his authority and strength, and the full account of the greatness of Mordecai to which the king advanced him, are they not written in the Book of the Chronicles of the Kings of Media and Persia? For Mordecai the Jew was second only to King Ahasuerus, and great among the Jews and in favor with his many kinsmen, one who sought the good of his people and one who spoke for the welfare of his whole nation" (Esther 10:1–3).

Where

All the provinces of King Ahasuerus.

When

The remainder of the lives of Ahasuerus and Mordecai.

We find out that Ahasuerus imposed either a monetary tax or forced labor on the people of Persia. "Tribute"—*mac* (mas) is "a tax in the form of forced labor." Why it is included is not known. Is there any relationship between Joseph and the taxes in Egypt (putting grain away for the famine) and Mordecai and the tribute the king is making the people pay?

We find out that the accomplishments of Ahasuerus are recorded in the Book of Chronicles. It also tells us Mordecai did great things and that they are also recorded. It is recorded that Mordecai was a great leader for the Jews and did great things for the whole nation.

Theme Statement

Mordecai's greatness is recorded.

Three final principles as we close this chapter:

Principle 48: God blesses individual and national obedience.

When we obey God, He blesses us. A sign of obedience is humility.

"You younger men, likewise, be subject to your elders; and all of you, clothe yourselves with humility toward one another, for God is opposed to the proud, but gives grace to the humble" (1 Peter 5:5).

As we have said on several occasions in this study, blessing does not always mean prosperity of wealth or health. Even when there is adversity in both areas, however, God does provide spiritual blessings. There are times when He provides logistical blessings—air to breathe, food to eat, a healthy body, clothes to wear, and a place to sleep—and we are able to live. We often take these for granted. There are times when logistical blessings are removed, which may ultimately lead to death. It is important to remember that whether a person is in prosperity or adversity, in health or near death, God's grace is present. He provides for our needs. When we trust and obey, we have a closer walk with our Lord Jesus Christ.

Principle 49: God blesses by association.

"How blessed is the man who does not walk in the counsel of the wicked, nor stand in the path of sinners, nor sit in the seat of scoffers!" (Psalm 1:1). God blesses when there is association with believers who are growing spiritually.

The Jews and the Persian nation were blessed because of the trust and obedience of Jews in 474 BC. Specifically, it was the trust and obedience of Esther, Mordecai, and the Jews in Susa (Esther 4:16). After Mordecai came to power, it appears most or all of the other Jews in the nation followed the edict to kill the Jew-haters. It is important to remember that it does not take 100 percent of the population trusting and obeying for God to bless. We see this many times throughout the history of nations in the Bible.

There will never by a time when 100 percent of people in any family, group, organization, community, church, or nation will be mature believers, in fellowship with God, walking in the works God prepared for them in eternity past, and growing in the grace and knowledge of Jesus Christ. As we have discussed earlier, we all have sinful natures, and we all sin. It is also true that individuals are at different levels of spiritual growth. God blesses those who trust and obey. The blessings we receive are not always what we want them to be. Sometimes our blessing is that God gives us more adversity. His plan is to make us more Christ-like. Our blessing may be a closer relationship with Jesus Christ (both here on earth and in heaven).

God blesses families, groups, organizations, communities, churches, and nations when individuals in the group are growing spiritually. It does not take everyone in the group trusting and obeying for God to bless the organization. God blesses by association. Personally, I know I have been blessed throughout my life because of my mother's close walk with Christ. The challenge for every church body is to realize that God may be looking at individuals in your church as He looked at Esther, Mordecai, and the Jews of Susa. The result of your trust, obedience, and spiritual growth may be the restoration of your church, town or city, state, or nation.

Is the United States of America being blessed by God? Are we doing everything He commands of us? Are there enough mature believers in our nation so there is blessing by association? Our trust and obedience to God, spiritual growth, prayer life, and fruit of the Spirit will make a difference in the future of our country.

Principle 50: God's divine plan works all things for good, both for His ultimate glory as well as for those who choose to follow Him.

"And we know that God causes all things to work together for good to those who love God, to those who are called according to His purpose" (Romans 8:28).

We have spent a great deal of time looking at and discussing God's sovereignty in relation to man's free will. Many principles have been developed from Esther defining the roles, responsibilities, results, blessings, and adversities of following or rejecting God's sovereignty. Application has been made to individuals as well as those in leadership and authority positions.

An area of emphasis regarding sovereignty and free will is that God does not make everyone equal. Circumstances for every human being are different. Genetic makeup determining physical and mental capabilities, family, financial resources, education, government, health, blessings or adversities, and opportunities are areas in which there is wide individual variance. No one has control over how or in what setting they are brought into this world, and often times there are limitations that prevent escape from an adverse environment. Does this mean God is unfair? Does this violate Romans 8:28 above?

The fact we are brought into this world in different environments and with different human opportunities does not mean God is unfair. God is completely fair. The problem is that we live in a sin-torn world whose ruler tries to undo everything good that comes from God. Sin—and its father, Satan—is the source of all things evil and bad. Lucifer's revolt against God, Adam's sin in the Garden, and humankind's continued personal sin has corrupted every aspect of the world. The facts that life is unfair, there is pain and suffering in the world, and there is death are due to Satan, not God. God gives life, not death.

Is it fair to say, "God, you are not fair, because you put me in a sin-torn world? I would be happy, live a perfect life, and love you completely if I lived in a perfect environment." I think most of us have had some type of thoughts like this. The fact is that Adam and Eve had such an environment of perfection and failed. If we are honest, we need to admit that if put in the same situation, we would also fail.

God's solution is not to make the environment perfect for every human being. To do so would not tackle the real issue, which is sin. We would still be left separate from Him. God has indeed offered a solution to the issue of sin—His Son, Jesus Christ, our Savior. Accepting Jesus Christ as our Savior puts us into a right relationship with God. This relationship begins at the moment of acceptance (salvation) and continues throughout eternity.

This relationship does not make everything perfect on earth in regard to our environment. We live in a sin-torn world. Even more so, God tells us we will have trials and tribulations as believers.

"Consider it all joy, my brethren, when you encounter various trials, knowing that the testing of your faith produces endurance. And let endurance have its perfect result, so that you may be perfect and complete, lacking in nothing" (James 1:2–4).

"Beloved, do not be surprised at the fiery ordeal among you, which comes upon you for your testing, as though some strange thing were happening to you; but to the degree that you share the sufferings of Christ, keep on rejoicing, so that also at the revelation of His glory you may rejoice with exultation" (1 Peter 4:12–13).

I believe it is the desire of most people for all people to have physical and financial prosperity. As stated elsewhere, it is God's desire for all to believe in Jesus Christ and spend eternity in heaven. The reality is that neither of these desires will occur. Human volition willfully chooses otherwise in many cases, both regarding human viewpoint and divine viewpoint. As a physician, I see many patients who would probably like to be healthy; however, they do not want to assume any responsibility for their health. Tobacco use, excessive alcohol, poor nutrition, no exercise, risky sexual behavior, and refusal to take recommended medications are choices made by some that lead to poor health. I can—and do—make recommendations for what they should and should not do, as well as tell the truth of the consequences of their choices, should they continue down the self-destructive road they are following. Ultimately, it is the responsibility of the individual to accept the outcome of their choices.

As a believer in Jesus Christ, I have a desire for all to put their faith in Jesus Christ. Living in a sin-torn world, I know that such will never happen. As a believer, it is my responsibility to follow the command of Jesus:

"Go therefore and make disciples of all the nations, baptizing them in the name of the Father and the Son and the Holy Spirit, teaching them to observe all that I commanded you; and lo, I am with you always, even to the end of the age" (Matthew 28:19–20).

It is up to God to do the rest, and it is up to the individual to respond to or reject the Gospel. As much as I want all to believe and spend eternity in heaven, I know many will choose to not believe.

Much of Esther deals with leadership and legal authority. Many of the principles developed in our study have application in this area. In relationship to the comments made above regarding principle 50, I would like to make application to governmental leadership. If we live in an unfair, sin-marred world, and if God does not make everyone equal from birth to death, does government have the right to try to make everyone equal? If God is sovereign, and yet allows people to freely choose whether or not to believe in Jesus Christ and then decide whether or not to follow His plan, is it right for the government—which is not sovereign—to take away the freedom of people to choose whether or not they will succeed or fail? I believe the government has no such right. "We know that God causes all things to work together for good." We should know that the government has no such right or ability.

This does not mean believers are not to help those in need—whether believers or unbelievers—nor does it mean that the government is not to help in times of need. It does mean there is no biblical support for individuals or nations to try to make the personal environment equal for everyone. There is a great deal of biblical doctrine that addresses roles and responsibilities of believers in relation to work, saving, giving, and caring for those less fortunate and responsibility for the same. This is beyond the scope of this book.

Points to Remember

Theme Statements

Esther 9:1–10—The Jews kill and destroy their enemies.

Esther 9:11–15—Jews in Susa kill 810 Jew-haters in two days.

Esther 9:16–17—The Jews in the nation kill 75,000 Jew-haters, feast, and rejoice.

Esther 9:18–19—Susa Jews rejoice on 15th; rural Jews rejoice on the 14th.

Esther 9:20–22—Mordecai commands the Jews to celebrate deliverance.

Esther 9:23–28—Jews remember and celebrate Purim.

Esther 9:29–32—Esther and Mordecai establish Purim.

Esther 10:1–3—Mordecai's greatness is recorded.

Principles

46. God prepares and promotes those in whom He has a work to accomplish.

47. God authorizes and mandates nations to destroy evil—particularly anti-Semitism.

48. God blesses individual and national obedience.

49. God blesses by association.

50. God's divine plan works all things for good, both for His ultimate glory as well as for those who choose to follow Him.

Chapter Thirteen

SYNTHETIC CHART

So what do you think of the paragraph analysis? There is quite a bit of information for a book that has only nine chapters plus three verses. Have you ever worked on a project for a long time and gotten close to completing it? You are just waiting to put the final pieces together. That is how I felt when I first arrived at this point in the study of Esther.

We have studied the entire book, paragraph-by-paragraph. Along the way, we noted theme statements for each paragraph. We now want to put them together to make a structural outline of the book. In looking at the theme statements chronologically, I was able to divide the book into three sections.

Section 1 (Esther 1:1–3:15): Conflicts defined

Esther 1:1–4—Ahasuerus gives banquets; obtains military and political support for war.

Esther 1:5–9—King gives banquet, shows wealth and thanks supporters.

Esther 1:10–12—Ahasuerus becomes drunk and summons Vashti, who refuses to appear.

Esther 1:13–20—Wise men exaggerate queen's disobedience and recommend her dismissal.

Esther 1:21–22—Queen is dismissed; men remain masters at home.

Esther 2:1–4—King's remembrance leads to planned, enforced slavery of virgins.

Esther 2:5–7—Mordecai, a Jew, acts as father to his beautiful cousin, Esther.

Esther 2:8–11—Esther finds favor in harem and is rewarded.

Esther 2:12–14—Virgins are purified, have sex with king, become concubines.

Esther 2:15–16—Esther goes to the king with poise and grace.

Esther 2:17–20—God and the king show favor on Esther, and she is made queen.

Esther 2:21–23—Mordecai discovers plot to assassinate king; plot is thwarted.

Esther 3:1–6—Mordecai disrespects Haman, who then plans to exterminate the Jewish race.

Esther 3:7–11—Haman gains the king's approval to have a certain people destroyed.

Esther 3:12–15—Law to have Jews destroyed is spread throughout empire.

Section 2 (Esther 4:1–6:14): Trust and obey

Esther 4:1–3—Mordecai and Jews mourn impending destruction.

Esther 4:4–8—Mordecai confides in Hathach and instructs him to inform Esther of problem and solution.

Esther 4:9–12—Esther tells Mordecai she may perish if she goes to the king.

Esther 4:13–17—Esther trusts and obeys God and agrees to go to the king. "Victory is snatched from the jaws of defeat."

Esther 5:1–4—Esther obtains the king's favor and invites him and Haman to a banquet.

Esther 5:5–8—Esther impresses the king and plans another banquet.

Esther 5:9–14—Haman's pride leads him to plan Mordecai's murder.

Esther 6:1–9—The king plans to honor Mordecai; Haman lusts for acknowledgement.

Esther 6:10–11—The king honors Mordecai instead of Haman.

Esther 6:12–13—Haman mourns his demise.

Esther 6:14—Haman is brought to the second banquet.

Section 3 (Esther 7:1–10:3): Conflicts resolved

Esther 7:1–6—Esther tells the king Haman plans to kill her and Jews.

Esther 7:7–10—Haman is hanged on the gallows.

Esther 8:1–2—Mordecai is given the king's ring and authority over Haman's house.

Esther 8:3–8—Esther implores the king to save the Jews.

Esther 8:9–14—The law to allow Jews to destroy attackers is spread throughout the empire.

Esther 8:15–17—The empire rejoices in the law to free the Jews.

Esther 9:1–10—The Jews kill and destroy their enemies.

Esther 9:11–15—Jews in Susa kill 810 Jew-haters in two days.

Esther 9:16–17—The Jews in the nation kill 75,000 Jew-haters, feast, and rejoice.

Esther 9:18–19—Susa Jews rejoice on 15th; rural Jews rejoice on the 14th.

Esther 9:20–22—Mordecai commands the Jews to celebrate deliverance.

Esther 9:23–28—Jews remember and celebrate Purim.

Esther 9:29–32—Esther and Mordecai establish Purim.

Esther 10:1–3—Mordecai's greatness is recorded.

From this structural outline and our study, several things become apparent which we want to be record. We can define an overall theme for the book, write a title, identify a key verse that helps define our theme, and record those key words we saw throughout the book. This is what I listed under the following headings:

> Theme (Summary Statement): Divine Providence delivers Jews from annihilation.

> Title: Jesus Christ controls history.

> Key verse: "For if you remain silent at this time, relief and deliverance will arise for the Jews from another place and you and your father's house will perish. And who knows whether you have not attained royalty for such a time as this?" (Esther 4:14)

Key words: Banquet, pleases the king, edict, show favor, wine, fast and pray, kill and destroy, rejoice, Feast of Purim.

Finally, we put together a visual aid referred to as a Synthetic Chart (following page). At the top is the Theme or Summary Statement. Underneath is the Key verse. The Title is in the center. There are three divisions with a key verse for each. Key words are in the upper left corner. Miscellaneous information is in the bottom right corner.

We have identified that Esther is a historical narrative. As such, the characters and plot are essential components to the story. Divine providence is the main theme, and we want to include it in the chart. The three columns represent the three sections, which were defined by the theme statements. The three rows represent the four main characters and their personalities, the action and plot being developed, and divine providence as it progresses throughout the book. In the chart, it is easy to see the progression from Esther 1 to 10. With this simple chart, you could probably tell the whole story as well as include many of the principles we have discussed. Try your hand at making your own chart.

Esther: Divine Providence Delivers Jews From Annihilation

Key verse: 4:14 For if you remain silent at this time, relief and deliverance will arise for the Jews from another place and you and your father's house will perish. And who knows whether you have not attained royalty for such a time as this?

Jesus Christ Controls History

Key Words: Banquet, Pleases the king, Edict, Show favor, wine, Fast and pray, kill and destroy, Rejoice, Feast of Purim

Conflicts Defined (1:1 – 3:15) 3:13	Trust and obey (4:1 – 6:14) 4:16	Conflicts Resolved (7:1 – 10:3) 9:5
Ahasuerus impulsive, dependant on others	Just	Impulsive, content
Esther innocent, obedient	Fearful; faithful, trust, obedience	Esther integrity, leadership, resolve
Mordecai honorable, prideful	Humble, mournful, resolute	Leadership, determination
Haman evil	Prideful, arrogant, fearful	Fearful, dead
(A) Dismisses Vashti, gives Haman power	Desires to honor Mordecai, please Esther	Supports Esther and Mordecai
(E) Obtains favor, made queen	Goes before king, plans banquets	Traps Haman, leads Jews
(M) Saves king, disrespects Haman	Implores Esther to act	Leads Jews and Nation
(H) Plans to annihilate Jews	Plans to be honored, hang Mordecai	Pleads for life, hanged
(A) Defeated by Greeks, led to select Esther	Led to receive Esther, honor Mordecai	Led to place Mordecai in charge
(E) Blessed with beauty, protected by God	Blessed with courage, grace, protection	Blessed with strength, wisdom, resolve
(M) Blessed with position, discovers plot	Blessed with wisdom to encourage Esther	Blessed with leadership
(H) Allowed to initiate annihilation plot	Allowed hatred and pride to destroy him	Justly destroyed

Unknown author and date of writing, explain Jewish deliverance and Feast of Purim

Chapter Fourteen

DIVINE PROVIDENCE

In Chapter One, we introduced the concept of divine providence in the relationship between God's sovereignty and human free will. In our paragraph analysis, we have seen the progression of the story through the lives and events of the characters over many years. At times, seemingly meaningless events are recorded, only later determined to be of critical significance. In this chapter, we will look at previously recorded events from the context through the book of Esther as they relate to divine providence.

In Chapter Three, we saw the context leading up to the book of Esther. The very existence of the Jewish race from Solomon to the time of Esther supports divine providence. If it were not for God's superseding grace, both the northern and southern kingdoms would have been wiped off the face of the earth. God protected the Jews, even though He disciplined them greatly. When it came time for the people to return to Judah, God provided King Cyrus of Persia as the directing authority.

What about the wars between Persia and Greece? Because of the defeat of King Darius at the hands of the Athenians at the battle of Marathon, Ahasuerus decides to wage war against Greece. Esther 1 discusses these preparations. If it had not been for the banquets, Vashti may not have been dismissed, and Esther may not have become queen. What about the battle of Salamis? If Ahasuerus had not been defeated by Themistocles would he have gone back to Persia and chosen Esther queen?

If Esther is to be the person to overthrow Haman and implore the king to change his mind about the edict to have the Jews killed, she has to become queen. The primary event which sets the stage for this is the removal of Vashti from her position as queen. Reread the events leading up to this: the 180-day banquet (Esther 1:4), the seven-day banquet (Esther 1:5), the king becoming drunk (Esther 1:10), the king ordering Vashti to appear before him (Esther 1:11), the queen's refusal (Esther 1:12), the wise men convincing the king to have the queen removed (Esther 1:13–20), and king dismissing her (Esther 1:21–22). Was God simply allowing a drunken, pagan king to act foolishly in dismissing his queen? Would Esther have become queen without Vashti's refusal to appear before the king?

In Esther 2, the king remembers Vashti (Esther 2:1). Did God cause this? Did the king's attendants come up with the idea of gathering the virgins, including Esther, or was God directing their actions? When we look at how Esther grew up under the care of Mordecai, we cannot help but see God's presence. Esther was physically beautiful, and her character was full of grace.

Certainly Esther's character was a big factor in her finding favor with Hegai; however, I am sure God was directing her path as well as those in her path. The same was true when "the king loved Esther more than all the women, and she found favor and kindness with him more than all the virgins" (Esther 2:17). God determined Esther was to be queen, and nothing was going to stop that.

At the close of Esther 2, we see God directing the discovery of an assassination plot. Both the fact that Mordecai was responsible for saving the king and the fact that he was not honored at that time play critical roles later in the story.

In Esther 3, one can almost see Satan directing the advancement of Haman. Whether he was demon-possessed or not, Haman's actions are focused on the destruction of the Jews. It is interesting to watch how God allows the evil plot to develop.

The words Mordecai speaks in Esther 4:13–14 are so perfect in their truth, clarity, and divine focus, I believe they were provided by God. Esther's response is so full of strength and resolve I believe she is being led by God.

In Esther 5, Esther begins to unfold her plan to expose Haman and petition the king. Esther speaks when she should speak and is quiet when she needs to be. She waits when necessary and acts when it is time. It is so perfect in design and execution I can only believe God was directing her. At the end of Esther 5, we see Haman's evil plot directed at Mordecai.

God not only allows this; He uses Haman's desire to hang Mordecai as a catalyst to expose Haman.

Don't you just love how Ahasuerus found out it was Mordecai who saved his life? God caused the king to be unable to sleep, He caused the king to have certain records read to him, and He put in the king's mind the need to honor Mordecai. I believe God also caused Haman to approach the king at the exact time he did.

If Esther 5 and 6 were perfect in setting up Haman, Esther 7 is perfect in the execution of his exposure. I believe God was leading Esther in her words and actions. We have previously discussed Haman's "falling on the couch where Esther was" (Esther 7:8). I believe God has a sense of humor.

In Esther 8, the king gives Mordecai the same power he had given Haman. Even though the king was impulsive, this was an unusual honor he bestowed upon Mordecai. I believe it was directed by God. In writing the second edict, the Jews were allowed to assemble. This would have been unusual in that time period. I believe God directed this action as well.

In Esther 9, the Jews slaughter their enemies. This is reminiscent of battles the Jews fought under kings when they were following God. I believe God's wrath was being unleashed against those who were trying to destroy His people. I also believe God was telling the people to remember the event with the feast of Purim.

Do you find any other evidence of divine providence in the book? I wonder if Esther and Mordecai looked back at their lives and saw all the places where God was working to ensure His people would survive. Do you think they thanked Him?

Do you look back on your life and see where God has led you? During difficult times, it may seem you are all alone; yet when you reflect back, you are aware God was not only always present, He was directing your path. When we acknowledge, thank and worship Him, we glorify Him.

Conclusion

So, what do you think of the study? Was the effort worthwhile? Let's look back to our objectives and see if we accomplished what we set out to do.

Our first objective was to "gain an in-depth understanding of the contextual relationships leading up to and including the events in Esther. Include historical background, grammatical context, cultural context, and literary form." Remember all the time we spent in Chapter Three? We went through quite a lot of Old Testament history to develop an understanding of the context of Esther. We started in 970 BC and discussed people, beliefs, obedience and disobedience, God's authority, discipline, and the Exile. Hopefully we also came away with knowledge that will help in future studies of other Old Testament books. That is the way contextual research works. The work you put in today will benefit you down the road in additional studies.

Our second objective was to "gain an in-depth understanding of the narrative of Esther. Include God's purpose in presenting this book in the canon of Scripture as well as a paragraph-by-paragraph interpretation of the book." We said we would look at the forest, the trees, and occasionally the leaves on the trees. I think there were a few times we looked at the process of photosynthesis inside the leaves. In doing this paragraph-by-paragraph analysis, we critically evaluated the entire story. It was definitely a lot of work, but well worth it.

Our third objective was to "gain an initial understanding of the principles of hermeneutics. Include methods on how to methodically interpret Scripture, which will make future studies more profitable." This discipline is one that will become easier the more it is used. Are you a better fisherman or fisherwoman than when we started? You can catch, cook, and eat your own Spiritual food; but don't forget, it is the Holy Spirit who teaches.

Our fourth objective was to "gain an understanding of godly principles as they relate to Esther. Include contemporary illustrations for our lives." What did you think of the principles that were presented? Did you agree or disagree? Are there any you can apply to your life? Are there others you can think of?

What did you think of the Synthetic Chart? Are there things you would add or subtract from it? Would you be able to tell the story and include the important themes by using the chart?

Finally, my prayer is that you have put your faith in Jesus Christ and that this book has given you a deeper understanding of God's sovereignty and man's free will, and how the two coexist together. When we get to heaven it will be great to hear Esther and Mordecai give their personal accounts.

PREPARATION FOR BIBLE STUDY

Studying a book of the Bible is work, pure and simple. However, it is something that God commands us to do. Study is defined as "application of the mental faculties to the acquisition of knowledge." [1]

> "Be diligent [study] to present yourself approved to God as a workman who does not need to be ashamed, accurately handling the word of truth" (2 Timothy 2:15).

Σπούδασον ("Be diligent, study") is an imperative command Paul gave to Timothy. The lexical form is σπουδάζω (spoudazo). As used in this verse, it means "to be especially conscientious in discharging an obligation, be zealous/eager, take pains, make every effort, be conscientious." [2] The emphasis is on making every effort to try. Regarding His Word, God gives this very specific command to each of us.

Before we can *handle* the Word of truth, we must know it and understand it. This requires work. The rewards, however, are so wonderful, the benefits far outweigh the mental and spiritual effort expended. When learning something new, the tendency is to let a teacher or an author spoon-feed you information. The truth is, you learn much more when you become an active participant in the learning process.

---

1   Merriam-Webster, Inc. 2003. *Merriam-Webster's Collegiate Dictionary, Eleventh ed.* Springfield, Mass.: Merriam-Webster, Inc.

2   Bauer, W., F. W. Danker, W. F. Arndt, and F. W. Gingrich. 2000. *A Greek-English Lexicon, Third ed.* Chicago: The University of Chicago Press, 939.

I encourage each and every one of you to participate in the work of studying this book. There will be some spoon-feeding, but everyone will need their own knives and forks. Esther is a short book, and it may seem like a tasty snack. When it is studied, it becomes a rich, full, seven-course meal.

Have you ever worked hard on something, and then after you have completed the task, looked back and felt good about what you accomplished? I think you will feel this way when we complete the study. I surely did.

Can everyone understand God's Word? Does communication of God's Word have to be complicated? God gave us His infallible Word so that we could know it, understand it, and apply it.

> "For to us God revealed them through the Spirit; for the Spirit searches all things, even the depths of God. For who among men knows the thoughts of a man except the spirit of the man which is in him? Even so the thoughts of God no one knows except the Spirit of God. Now we have received, not the spirit of the world, but the Spirit who is from God, so that we may know the things freely given to us by God, which things we also speak, not in words taught by human wisdom, but in those taught by the Spirit, combining spiritual thoughts with spiritual words. But a natural man does not accept the things of the Spirit of God, for they are foolishness to him; and he cannot understand them, because they are spiritually appraised. But he who is spiritual appraises all things, yet he himself is appraised by no one. For who has known the mind of the Lord, that He will instruct him? But we have the mind of Christ" (1 Corinthians 2:10–16).

Even though not complete as the canon of Scripture, the *mind of Christ* Paul speaks of is the Bible.

> "For the word of God is living and active and sharper than any two-edged sword, and piercing as far as the division of soul and spirit, of both joints and marrow, and able to judge the thoughts and intentions of the heart" (Hebrews 4:12).

> "All Scripture is inspired by God and profitable for teaching, for reproof, for correction, for training in righteousness; so that the man of God may be adequate, equipped for every good work" (2 Timothy 3:16–17).

Understanding God's Word does not require genius mentality, nor does it require Bible college or seminary training. It does, however, require a methodical, systematic, and disciplined approach to study. We will discuss and apply principles of the hermeneutic process in our study of Esther. Lest one think that understanding God's Word is simply a human endeavor, we should always remember that it is the Holy Spirit who teaches and enables us to understand the *mind of Christ*.

> "But the Helper, the Holy Spirit, whom the Father will send in My name, He will teach you all things, and bring to your remembrance all that I said to you" (John 14:26).

> "But when He, the Spirit of truth, comes, He will guide you into all the truth; for He will not speak on His own initiative, but whatever He hears, He will speak; and He will disclose to you what is to come. He will glorify Me, for He will take of Mine and will disclose it to you. All things that the Father has are Mine; therefore I said that He takes of Mine and will disclose it to you" (John 16:13–15).

If we are to understand God's Word, there must first be belief in Jesus Christ as personal savior.

> "He who believes in the Son has eternal life; but he who does not obey the Son will not see life, but the wrath of God abides on him." (John 3:36).

Second, there must be the filling of the Holy Spirit, of which we are commanded. As previously stated, it is the Holy Spirit who teaches us.

> "And do not get drunk with wine, for that is dissipation, but be filled with the Spirit" (Ephesians 5:18).

God has given us the Holy Spirit to learn and understand His Word of truth.

> "God is spirit, and those who worship Him must worship in spirit and truth" (John 4:24).

A right relationship with God is necessary to learn His Word. Sin disrupts that relationship. If sin is present, confession is mandatory for restoration of the right relationship.

"If we confess our sins, He is faithful and righteous to forgive us our sins and to cleanse us from all unrighteousness" (1 John 1:9).

Take great joy in your Bible study! God has truly blessed us with revelation in His Word

Appendix B

HERMENEUTICAL PRINCIPLES

Other terms and definitions of different processes in Bible study and communication include:

Exegesis: "the determination of the meaning of the biblical text in its historical context."[1]

Exposition: "the communication of the meaning of the text along with its relevance to present-day hearers."[2]

Homiletics: "the science [principles] and art [task] by which the meaning and relevance of the biblical text are communicated in a preaching situation."[3]

Pedagogy: "the science [principles] and art [task] by which the meaning and relevance of the biblical text are communicated in a teaching situation."[4]

Theology [systematic]: "the science [principles] and art [task] by which the meanings of all biblical texts are systematized into a harmonious whole structured around the dominant

---

1   Zuck, Roy B. 1991. *Basic Bible Interpretation*. Colorado Springs: Cook Communications Ministries, 20.

2   Ibid.

3   Ibid.

4   Ibid.

themes of Scripture [God; Jesus Christ, the Son; the Holy Spirit; humanity; angels; sin; salvation; etc.]."[5]

Edification: "the explanation and application of Scripture to the life of believers so as to produce growth into Christ-likeness (John 17:17)."[6]

Howard G. Hendricks and William D. Hendricks, co-authors of *Living by the Book*, have presented ten strategies that will help you in the observation process when you read the Bible. They are to read "thoughtfully, repeatedly, patiently, selectively, prayerfully, imaginatively, meditatively, purposefully, acquisitively, and telescopically".[7]

In this process, there are four things that need to be observed. The first is to identify *terms*. "A term is a given word as it is used in a given context."[8] We identify, define, and record words that we want to know more about. Specifically, we look at recurring or repeating words, rare or unusual words, verbs, nouns, and figures of speech. Dr. Zuck has an excellent section in *Basic Bible Interpretation* on forms and functions of words that help explain the concept of terms.[9]

The next thing we want to observe is *structure*. "Structure involves all of the relations and interrelations which bind terms into a literary unit, from the minutest to the broadest, from the least significant to the most significant."[10] From the smallest unit to the largest, it includes "phrase, clause, sentence, paragraph, segment, subsection, section, division, and book."[11] In Bible study, the focus is primarily on the paragraph.

In observing structure, we also look at *structural progression,* which shows how the author develops or builds his or her thoughts. Five types include biographical, which emphasizes *who;* historical, which emphasizes *what;* chronological, which emphasizes *when;* geographical, which emphasizes *where;* and logical or ideological, which emphasizes *why.*[12]

5   Hanna, Ken. 2007. BE101 class notes, Dallas Theological Seminary, 42.

6   Ibid.

7   Hendricks, Howard G. and William D. Hendricks. 2007. *Living by the Book.* Chicago: Moody Publishers, 77.

8   Traina, Robert A. 1980. *Methodical Bible Study.* Grand Rapids: Zondervan, 34

9   Ibid., Zuck, 112-117.

10   Ibid., Traina, 36.

11   Ibid., 36-37.

12   Ibid., Hanna, 10.

In observing structure, we also look at *structural relationship,* which shows how thoughts are held together. *Words of connection* move the reader from one idea to another. They include:[13]

Temporal connectors such as *after, as, before, now, then, until, when, (in)*

Emphatic connectors such as *indeed, only*

Local connectors such as *where*

Logical connectors of reason such as *because, for, since*

Logical connectors of result such as *so, then, therefore, thus*

Logical connectors of purpose such as *in order that, so that*

Logical connectors of contrast such as *although, but, much more, nevertheless, otherwise*

Logical connectors of comparison such as *also, as, as-so, just as-so, likewise, so als*o

Logical connectors of series of facts such as *and, first of all, last of all, or*

Logical connectors of condition such as *if*

Finally, in observing structure, "we now move to those broader structural elements, which are more literary than purely grammatical."[14] Up to this point, structure has been defined inside the paragraph. Structure also exists within those increasingly larger elements such as segment, subsection, section, division, and book. Traina gives a "list of the main literary relations which operate to make possible the framework of Biblical books."[15] They are often referred to as literary laws, and include "comparison, contrast, repetition, continuity, continuation, climax, cruciality, interchange, particularization and generalization, causation and substantiation, instrumentation, explanation or analysis, preparation or introduction, summarization, interrogation and harmony."[16] Dr. Hanna adds a seventeenth law, *proportion.*[17] We will not spend much time on literary laws in this study, however, when applicable, a law will be

13   Ibid., Traina, 42-43.
14   Ibid., Traina, 50.
15   Ibid.
16   Ibid., 50-51.
17   Ibid., Hanna, 19.

identified. They are presented here so that you are aware of their presence in the observational process.

Following *terms* and *structure,* the third area of observation is *literary form.* Traina states, "This element is distinct from both those of terms and structure, for the same terms and the same structural relations effected by the same materials may be utilized to compose different kinds of literature. Therefore, to note terms and structural connections is not sufficient for thorough observation; one must also see the general type of literature used by an author."[18] The five types of literary forms include "narrative, epistles, parables, poetry, and visionary."[19] Each includes specific characteristics, which when recognized will help the reader understand what the writer is trying to say.

Esther is an historical narrative. As such, we will want to look for and understand those things that must be present in narratives. Specifically, we will look to see what makes up the setting of the story, the "background, atmosphere, characters, and themes."[20] In looking at the characters, we will want to know the protagonist, the antagonist, and the other agents involved. We will want to know how the characters are developed in the story and how God reveals them through the author's words. Finally, the plot will be explored. Setting, characters and plot are usually interrelated, and we will see this in depth in Esther.

The fourth and final area of observation is *atmosphere* or *context.* In Chapter One, I stated our first objective was to "gain an in-depth understanding of the contextual relationships leading up to and including the events in Esther. Included is the historical background, the grammatical context, the cultural context, and the literary form." We simply cannot understand what the writer is saying if we do not understand the atmosphere or context in which it was written.

To understand the *historical background,* we want to know as much as we can about the author, date, and audience.[21]

> **Author**—family heritage, educational background, occupational skills, occasion and circumstance of writing, religious experience.

---

18   Ibid., Traina, 68.

19   Ibid., Hanna, 59-76.

20   Ibid., 60.

21   Ibid., 46-49.

Date—when the book was written, whether the author dates their writing, whether it is early or late in Old Testament or New Testament.

Audience, including:

People—Old Testament or New Testament, Jew or Gentile, believers or unbelievers, familiar or unfamiliar

Place—what country or city, what is known about the place, how the author relates to the place, how the place relates to the events of the book

Problems—social or spiritual

Purpose—why the book was written

Occasion and Circumstances surrounding the writing of the book

To understand the *cultural context,* we want to know what people thought, did, said, and made. Zuck defines eleven categories of culture that are important: "political, religious, economic, legal, agricultural, architectural, clothing, domestic, geographical, military, and social."[22]

Since we communicate with words, understanding *grammatical context* is critical in understanding what God is revealing in His Word. Zuck states, "When we speak of interpreting the Bible grammatically, we are referring to the process of seeking to determine its meaning by ascertaining four things: (a) the meaning of words (lexicology), (b) the form of words (morphology), (c) the function of words (parts of speech), and (d) the relationships of words (syntax)."[23]

Content Analysis

In observing and analyzing the content of each paragraph, we want to record *terms, structure, literary form,* and *context*. Look for progression or flow within each paragraph and between paragraphs. Ask the following six questions when studying each paragraph: who, what, when, where, why, and how. In analyzing your observations, identify the central thought of each paragraph. Write a theme statement for each paragraph. I have

---

22   Ibid., Zuck, 80.

23   Ibid., 100.

included a template worksheet at the end of this chapter that may help you when doing the paragraph analysis.

After analyzing each and every paragraph, we compile our data into a book synthesis. Synthesis is defined as "the composition or combination of parts or elements so as to form a whole."[24] Theme statements of each paragraph are grouped into larger segments. As this is done, a structure or outline of the book is developed, and a general theme—or central idea—of the book becomes apparent.

It is important to identify specific details of the study. Theme, including summary statement and title, key verse, type of literature, key words, recurring features, structure, and literary composition, should be recorded. A chart is used to visually present the information. "A chart is to the Bible student what a map is to a mariner. It aids him or her in navigating an ocean of words, pages, books, ideas, characters, events, and other information."[25]

At the conclusion of our study of Esther, we will prepare a synthetic chart which "allows for the display of a large amount of information in a format that is clear and self-explanatory."[26] The synthetic chart is required as part of the curriculum by the Bible Department of Dallas Theological Seminary when books of the Bible are studied in class.

Context Research

It is important to do the content analysis of Scripture before external sources are used in research. Give yourself an opportunity to observe before you read what others have to say about the passage. Researching the context requires "the use of research tools such as introductions, language, commentaries, and background studies."[27] Use reputable sources. Old and New Testament introductions, Bible encyclopedias, and commentaries are good places to begin. Although context research is done after content analysis, the information discovered will be used in the chart synthesis.

---

24   Ibid., Merriam-Webster, Inc.

25   Ibid., Hendricks, 185.

26   Ibid., Hanna, 26.

27   Ibid., 33.

Synthesis of Content and Context

Following content analysis and context research, the next step is to synthesize the two. The final step is the "assimilation of all the data and the preparation of a synthesis of the book that includes contextual information, a description of the literary content, synthetic chart, and the author's argument."[28] This study is presented as a synthesis of the content and context of the book of Esther.

Paragraph Template

Terms, words, phrases

Non-routine

Key

Main nouns

Verbs

Repetition

Structure

Connectors

Structural progression

Literary laws

---

28   Ibid., 35.

Content Analysis

Compare/contrast

_____

Paragraph progression

_____

Relationship of connectors

_____

Detail Analysis

Who

_____

What

_____

Where

_____

When

_____

Why

_____

How

_____

Theme Statement

_____

Outline of Paragraph

_____

_____

PRINCIPLES FROM THE BOOK OF ESTHER

The following is a list of principles from the book of Esther. The number and location of each correlate to when they were presented in the study. Each falls under one of three divisions, based on relationship to God, individuals or leaders. In many cases, a principle may relate to more than one category, although only one is listed here.

God in relation to man

2. God uses unbelievers and believers who are out of fellowship to discipline believers who are in sin and are rejecting Him. (Chapter Three, Context)

4. God's righteousness and justice work in perfect union with His love, and the three together are in harmony with His divine will and plan. (Chapter Three, Context)

5. God uses nations to punish His chosen people—and then judges those nations. (Chapter Three, Context)

9. God puts us on the sideline so we will learn to follow His game plan. (Chapter Three, Context)

17. God commands the believer to trust, obey and rejoice, even when circumstances seem unfair. (Chapter Five, Esther 2)

20. God shows favor based on His perfect character. (Chapter Five, Esther 2)

22. God in His sovereignty is always in control of the circumstances in our lives. (Chapter Five, Esther 2)

36. Jesus Christ controls history. (Chapter Nine, Esther 6)

37. God's timing is perfect. (Chapter Nine, Esther 6)

43. God often blesses us—not with success, but with the opportunity to succeed. (Chapter Eleven, Esther 8)

45. God often uses suffering and obedience of believers to bring people to Him. (Chapter Eleven, Esther 8)

46. God prepares and promotes those in whom He has a work to accomplish. (Chapter Twelve, Esther 9 and 10)

47. God authorizes and mandates nations to destroy evil—particularly anti-Semitism. (Chapter Twelve, Esther 9 and 10)

48. God blesses individual and national obedience. (Chapter Twelve, Esther 9 and 10)

49. God blesses by association. (Chapter Twelve, Esther 9 and 10)

50. God's divine plan works all things for good, both for His ultimate glory as well as for those who choose to follow Him. (Chapter Twelve, Esther 9 and 10)

Man in relation to God, himself and others

3. Man's sinful nature leads him to disobey and reject God. (Chapter Three, Context)

6. Your spiritual life and your relationship with God are determined by *your* decision to trust and obey God, not by your parents. (Chapter Three, Context)

7. God blesses through adversity. He uses hardship for believers to improve their relationship with Him. Obedience to God is required for blessing. Obedience to God's discipline results in blessing for the believer. (Chapter Three, Context)

8. Disobedience to God in times of discipline leads to further discipline. (Chapter Three, Context)

10. Making decisions when you are not in fellowship with God often leads to actions that are not in line with His plan. (Chapter Four, Esther 1)

11. Mental sins lead to bad decisions which result in destructive behavior. (Chapter Four, Esther 1)

12. Respond with truth, honesty, and integrity in your relationships. (Chapter Four, Esther 1)

14. Listening to false praise can lead to ungodly decisions. (Chapter Four, Esther 1)

15. The solution to error is to admit, apologize, accept consequences, make restitution if possible, alter behavior, and move on. (Chapter Five, Esther 2)

16. Making godly decisions and advising those who lead requires putting the interest of others over your own. (Chapter Five, Esther 2)

18. Maximum knowledge of Bible doctrine, filling of the Holy Spirit, and prayer are critical in making right decisions in your life. (Chapter Five, Esther 2)

19. Godly character and integrity result in blessing. (Chapter Five, Esther 2)

21. Worldly things can influence and change your relationship with God. (Chapter Five, Esther 2)

23. God expects us to follow the legal authority over us when it does not violate His commands. (Chapter Six, Esther 3)

24. Replacing trust in and obedience to God with human arrogance, stubbornness, and pride leads to conflict for you and those around you. (Chapter Six, Esther 3)

25. Every person has to bear some responsibility in the decisions, policies, and actions of the nation, as well as their consequences. (Chapter Six, Esther 3)

26. Life is not fair. In our fallen world bad things will happen to you, whether you deserve them or not. (Chapter Seven, Esther 4)

28. Fear comes from a failure to trust God. When facing adversity, trust and obey God. (Chapter Seven, Esther 4)

29. You cannot make right decisions while under stress unless you look to God for the solution and you trust and obey Him. (Chapter Seven, Esther 4)

30. We should pray for our leaders, whether we agree or disagree with them. (Chapter Seven, Esther 4)

31. It is not necessary to know the outcome when you walk in the works God has prepared for you. (Chapter Seven, Esther 4)

32. Be patient as God leads you. (Chapter Eight, Esther 5)

34. Pride and arrogance will destroy you. (Chapter Eight, Esther 5)

35. When you are full of pride and arrogance, you are vulnerable to ungodly influence, following bad advice, and making wrong decisions. (Chapter Eight Esther 5)

38. Lust for personal acknowledgment and praise is destructive. (Chapter Nine, Esther 6)

39. Everyone is responsible for their own actions, even when advice has been taken from others. (Chapter Nine, Esther 6)

40. When God calls you to act, do not hesitate. (Chapter Ten, Esther 7)

41. When you plan evil for others, God may allow that evil to be turned on you. (Chapter Ten, Esther 7)

44. Freedom to use God's blessings is a great blessing itself. (Chapter Eleven, Esther 8)

Authority or leadership

1. When a leader sins and rejects God's authority, all those under the leader's authority are affected. (Chapter Three, Context)

13. When governmental leadership puts self-interest before law and freedom, there is national decay. (Chapter Four, Esther 1)

27. Good leaders do what they tell others to do and do not do what they tell others not to do. (Chapter Seven, Esther 4)

33. Grace and humility are effective tools in leadership and communication. (Chapter Eight, Esther 5)

42. Personal failure demands the acceptance of responsibility for failure. (Chapter Eleven, Esther 8)

Scripture Index

311

313

318

Word Index

Breinigsville, PA USA
03 December 2010
250627BV00001B/5/P